THE WORK OF OUR HANDS

The Life and Death of the Small Family Farm

FRED GONNERMAN

Kirk House Publishers
Minneapolis, Minnesota

THE WORK OF OUR HANDS

The Life and Death of the Small Family Farm

By Fred Gonnerman

ISBN 978-1-933794-85-3

Kirk House Publishers, PO Box 390759, Minneapolis, MN 55431
www.kirkhouse.com
Printed in the United States of America

DEDICATION

It's the only possible choice.
This book is dedicated to the memory
of my mom and dad.

TABLE OF CONTENTS

Prologue 7

Dad 11

Mom 29

Life on the Farm 47

Tale of Two Houses 65

Growing Up 123

Ritual and Revolution 179

Historical Context 225

The Ethnic Divide 273

Appendix One: The Gonnerman Genealogy 294

Appendix Two: Bibliography 313

PROLOGUE

The longer I worked on this memoir, the more I realized that memoirs are more than the dates and places of births, deaths, and marriages. Memoirs are also more than the interactions of spouses, siblings, aunts, uncles, and cousins. Remembrances of ancestors uncovers the poverty of subsistence existence in the "old country," the dreams of a better life in another place, reasons for their immigration, the courage to move to a different location even when it's an unknown prairie across an ocean, difficulties of assimilation, ethnic eccentricities, the roots of multiple prejudices, attitudes regarding education, the speed or slowness of adaptation to mechanical and electronic revolutions.

Memoirs are about the local, national, and international events that happen in peoples' lives, how the people relate to those events, and how different events shape the lives of those who live in them and experience the bright mountaintops of joy, the dark valleys of sadness, the unsettledness of disruptions, and the satisfaction of events that develop and conclude the way you wished them to.

That's why the longest chapters of this memoir pay homage to the "revolutions" that shaped the thoughts and lives of not only Mom and Dad but also their children and grandchildren during the rush of monumental history through the twentieth century. Mom and Dad didn't know it, and those who have come after them were equally ignorant while they and we lived through these "revolutions," but the last century – with its farming phenomenon and the social, cultural, political, and technological divides – was a rush of change, turmoil, wonderment unlike any ten decades before it.

Many times as I was working on this memoir I have wished that I would have had conversations with Mom and Dad, together or individually, that plumbed the events and issues that made headlines in our lives year after year. Perhaps we did have such conversations, but if we did, I have little memory of them. Throughout this memoir I have been forced to extrapolate from the haziest of memories what I think Mom and Dad would have thought and how passionately they would have thought it. Part of that deficiency is my fault.

I did not know the questions to ask which might have brought out Mom's and Dad's thinking about the things that were happening to them and around them. I didn't even ask the simple questions: How did you meet? Why did you farm? How did you and your children survive during the Great Depression? What did you learn, Dad, when you studied radio and television in Chicago? Why didn't you pursue that line of work? How did you learn to play the violin well enough to perform in an orchestra? Mom, why did you become a nurse? How important was nursing in your and Dad's life? Why did you settle on the farm that bordered Nachusa? Mom and Dad, what did you really think about World War II, the United Nations, the civil rights movement, the Vietnam War, a man on the moon?

I can assume Dad's and Mom's answers to some of those questions. In fact, I did. But for many of those questions the answers are simply too far out of reach for me. I thank my siblings, Donna, Paul, and Mary Ann, for providing data and clues that helped fill in more gaps than I can count.

I am envious of authors of memoirs who talk about their relationships with parents or other adult relatives and claim to be able to reconstruct conversations about race relations, political dilemmas, international quandaries, the prejudicial motivations of dictators, appropriate uses of technology, the development of social structures. If that happened to Mom and Dad and me, I have no recollections of such talk. Perhaps I'm looking here at the difference between rural and urban living. We really didn't have a whole lot of extra time on the farm to sit around and talk. I imagine that some urban families, living what I think was a more structured life day-to-day, might have found it more easy and natural to have more substantive conversations with their their children.

One rather scary possibility has occurred to me. Perhaps my somewhat conservative religious training set up a barrier that I could not remove. The fourth commandment, "Honor your father and mother," and Martin Luther's explanation, "We are to fear and love God, so that we neither despise nor anger our parents and others in authority, but instead honor, serve, obey, love, and respect them," stretches deeply into my relationships with Mom and Dad.

They were both people of strong convictions. Their opinions were generally fortified by the same kinds of thinking throughout both the patriarchal and matriarchal branches of their extended families. Perhaps I did not initiate many conversations on what might be controversial subjects because I thought I knew what their responses might be, I might disagree with their points of view, and I did not want to "dishonor" them with an argument I feared the discussion might start.

I hope this memoir honors the memories of Mom and Dad, showing a blemish or two along the way, but thanking them for being the concerned and protective parents they were, proud of our achievements and encouraging us to stretch our wings as we fluttered into parenthood ourselves, beyond the farm that formed us and gave us the stability and skills to become who and what we are.

Other people need to be thanked. My wife Ruth was patient with the time I spent on the keyboard and my frustrations at not being able to find materials when I wanted them. She also shared my joy when I thought I had made a breakthrough.

My editor, Karen Walhof, offered sage editing advice. I thank her for the title, *The Work of Our Hands*, from Psalm 90:17.

The men behind the counter of the John Deere franchise in Northfield, Minnesota, helped me catch up on advancements in farm machinery.

Jennifer Hamilton of Kenzley Title Group in Dixon, Illinois, searched records documenting sales of the land that was the "small family farm" Grandpa and Grandma Gonnerman established and Dad and Mom nurtured until they retired, knowing none of their children wanted it.

My son, David, put his photographic creativity to use producing a portfolio of great photos of my hands.

Thanks to everyone.

Fred Gonnerman

DAD

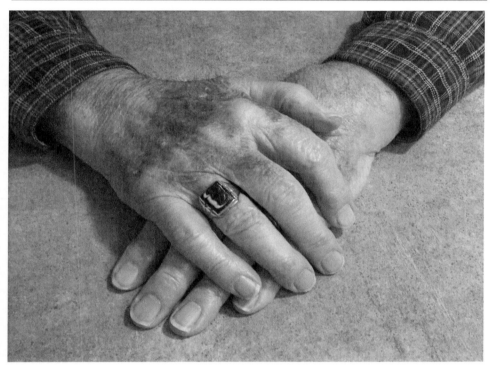

His hands are what I remember first about my Dad.
The geography of our hands is the same.
And then the scars.
All those wounds were part of the chronicle
that was written by Dad's life as a mostly dairy farmer
on 160 acres of fertile land in northern Illinois.

DAD

His hands are what I remember first about my dad. He wore size "large" gloves. I wear "medium." But when I look at my hands, I see his.

The geography of our hands is the same. The protruding dark blue veins, crisscrossing over the tendons that flex with the slightest movement of the fingers. The short, thin, scraggly hair. The small wrinkles that start at the wrist and move to the knuckles across the backs of our hands, perpendicular to the veins and tendons, like repeating eddies on an almost still lake. The purplish splotches where blood pooled under the skin in places inadvertently hit or bumped a few days before. If you asked him, Dad would not remember when those bumps happened or what was involved. I would not either, if you asked me now about mine.

All those things are on or in my hands today, just as they were in Dad's.

And then the scars. Almost black lines from scratches that bled a little but not much only a day or two ago. Lighter lines that tell stories of getting too close to the barbs on a barbed wire fence. Irregular bumps where small cuts were caused by a protruding shard of steel on a manure spreader, a rough burr on a bolt, an undetected sliver on old lumber. Dad usually just ignored it when his hands bled a little from those frequent invasions by foreign materials, but sometimes he wiped them on his bib overalls or his carpenter pants.

When I turn my hands palms up I have a few scars that Dad never had. They are reminders on both wrists of two carpal tunnel surgeries. The problems started with a manual typewriter, then a Smith-Corona portable that was my friend all the way through college and seminary, then a variety of electric typewriters in the parish in Painesville, Ohio; in the offices of The American Lutheran Church in Minneapolis; and when I came to St. Olaf College in Northfield,

Minnesota. Then the ultimate, as every writing aid morphed into computers. I've done a lot of writing – academic work, news stories, magazine features, editorials, letters to the editor, memos suggesting new programs or other ways of dealing with problems, radio scripts, photo essays, film scripts for church conventions, texts for sermons and other public presentations, outlines for workshops, a nontraditional Christmas service, two books. Carpal tunnel syndrome came with the territory.

Dad's fingernails tell more of his story. Black marks that appeared when the head of a hammer found the wrong target or a wrench slipped or a door closed faster than expected. The ugly blemishes started near the cuticle and pushed out toward the tip as the nails continued to grow during the next month or two.

Many farmers hands have knuckles that wouldn't straighten after a forgotten strain or accident. Dad had one. I have one. Fourth finger, right hand.

Most of the incidents that caused these malformations were not remembered much past the time of the beginning of the healing that made a person forget them. But they were incidents that happened regularly in the life of a farmer – or of any man who works with his hands. It's one of the costs of the oftentimes mundane and the sometimes creative work in agronomy, or conservation, or animal husbandry, or mechanics, or carpentry, or plumbing, or electrical work, or the multitude of tasks farmers face and solve every day. Talk about multi-tasking. Farmers used to do it all day long. Many still do.

Dad in 1903.

All those wounds were part of the chronicle that was written by Dad's life as a mostly dairy farmer on 160 acres of fertile land in northern Illinois where he also planned the crop rotations, grew or purchased the seed, and plowed, planted, cultivated, and harvested corn, oats, soybeans, clover, timothy, and alfalfa.

Dad was a cautiously religious man and a member of the Lutheran Church for all of his life. I never heard him use an obscenity, and the few times he swore mildly his oaths were directed exclusively at livestock that didn't go where he wanted it to go or went where he didn't want it to go by trampling a weak spot in a fence between pasture and crops. His swearing was almost always triggered by the hog that wouldn't go through the gate to the pen, or the cow that decided it wanted the almost ripe oats on the opposite side of the fence from its pasture.

The Reverend Carl Wagner, pastor of Immanuel Lutheran Church in Dixon, Illinois, gave me a perspective on swearing. When teaching a catechetical class on the second commandment, "Thou shalt not take the name of the Lord your God in vain," he said, "When you swear in public it lets people around you know that you don't have enough legitimate vocabulary to avoid using that kind of language." That idea has been imbedded in my mind for my entire life.

I remember standing beside Dad in church every week and seeing him put his palms on the pew in front of him and letting his thumb and fingers dangle down the front of the pew whenever we stood during the service. When we prayed, his head was bowed and his hands were always about a foot and a half apart on the pew. Always.

I inherited the pattern and have done the same thing as long as I can remember. And now, when I look at my hands on the pew in front of me in church, I see Dad's.

Dad's Ring

Then there is the ring. Mom bought Dad the ring in 1929. It was beautifully made of four different kinds of gold. The setting was a striated black and white onyx stone carved to portray the heads in profile of two Spartan warriors. The Spartan on top is black onyx. The bottom one is white on a black background. The elegant detail of two maple leaves in a rose-colored gold wore away through the 43 years Dad had it on his finger.

Dad looking dapper in 1931.

The ring had taken a beating throughout Dad's life, both from ordinary wear and from accidents. He wore it as a wedding ring on the ring finger of his left hand where, since he was right handed, it was always susceptible to being hit inadvertently by a wayward hammer, or a wrench that slipped, or some other unintended mechanical mischief. The nose of the white Spartan had been knocked off by one of those incidents; the bottom layer of black onyx had been cracked within the setting and a small corner of the setting had disappeared. That blow might have saved Dad a broken finger.

After Dad died, Mom surprised me, the oldest male of their four children, by giving me his ring. When I first tried it on it was emotionally heavy as it hung on my finger. It was also huge. The first time I had it cut down by two sizes. Then it had be cut down again by another size so the ring was now small enough to fit my right hand ring finger comfortably enough that I wasn't scared it might fall off and be lost. The last time it was cut down I had the damage in the lower layer of onyx repaired. I've worn that ring proudly ever since. It replaced my Wartburg College ring.

Mom paid $29.00 for Dad's ring when she gave it to him in 1929. When sizing and repair work were done for me more than forty years ago, the jeweler appraised that ring at between $400.00 and $600.00. But its value to me is priceless, and it will be passed on to one of my sons when I die.

Learning from Dad

But Dad's hands had a beauty created by work that had made them muddy from messing at the base of a stock tank while trying to find the reason for the overflow, or greasy from taking apart and repairing a tractor carburetor, or milky from cleaning the pipeline system that carried the milk of his cows from the milking machines to the refrigerated holding tank, or bloody from helping a cow deliver her

Dad enjoys watching me splash in the shallow end of the lily pool in Grandma Gonnerman's grand garden in 1934.

calf. His fingernails often displayed what kind of messes he had been working in most recently.

When the situation called for it, Dad was whatever he needed to be to fix the problem or improve the situation – mechanic, carpenter, plumber, electrician, veterinarian. Whatever needed doing, he did. And he was pretty good in every role. Almost from the time I could walk I watched Dad do all of these kinds of things. But even after I was a teenager he seldom asked me to help him. He thought, maybe correctly, I would just get in the way and slow down what he was doing.

After my own experience of fatherhood I have a better idea of what was going on. With "too much to do" always at the base of the daily schedule, he (and later, I) could not see the gleam of expectation in our children's eyes, could not fathom their wish to help and to learn. I and my siblings (and later my own progeny) looked past the expectation to see only the timetable that insisted that everything be done as quickly as possible without interruption. It was (and is) a terrible misreading of that urgency.

Even so, Dad expected me to watch him work and to learn from the watching. And as I grew older he did teach me many things when he thought about it, sometimes because he decided I was big enough to know and sometimes so I would do things right and be a more productive assistant. When I think about it, the list of things I learned from Dad is impressive:

- He taught me how to plow a straight furrow and leave the ground behind the plow clean and black and free of refuse.
- He taught me how to make a straight fence –woven wire, or three-strand barbed wire, or electric – that would keep livestock where it belonged at the same time it looked good to the neighbors passing by. (That was always important.)
- He also taught me how to dig a posthole with either of two kinds of diggers. On our farm we never hit a rock and we seldom even hit clay. The black dirt went too deep. He taught me how to set fence posts in those holes that were perpendicular to flat ground even when the posts stood on sloping terrain.
- He taught me how to milk cows by hand.

- He taught me how to castrate small boars weighing 40 or 50 pounds with a sharp pocket knife so that they would grow up to be market hogs rather than breeding boars. The knife was sterilized by dipping it in rubbing alcohol between every castration.
- He taught me how to organize tools and how to always put a tool – whether it was a spade or a pliers or anything in between – back where it belonged at the end of the day so that I or anyone else could find it the next day or the next week.
- He taught me that every tool used to work in dirt or grease or paint should be cleaned off before it was put away so that it was ready for whatever work the next person who used it might do. If that tool was not expected to be used again right away after it was clean, a couple of drops of oil should be squirted on from the oil can that was always on the work bench, and that oil should be spread over the surface of the spade with a cloth that was also always on the bench.
- He taught me to always point the tines of a rake or a hay or manure fork into the ground so that someone would not be seriously injured by stepping on them accidently.
- He taught me how to dig with any kind of spade by standing it upright, driving straight down on the back edge with my foot, moving the handle back to loosen the soil before lifting it and depositing the dirt in a neat pile far enough from the hole so that it would not sift back in and close enough so it could be easily reached.
- He taught me how to set a ladder up close enough to a building so that a person climbing it would not be putting too much weight on its vertical structure, but far enough away from the building so that you would not pull it backwards away from the building when you climbed it. That's tricky geometry.
- He taught me to always take ladders down from buildings at the end of the day so that children would not be able to climb them when you weren't around.
- He taught me how to swing a hammer by holding it at the end of the handle and driving the nail with full force.
- He taught me the difference between construction and finishing nails and how to choose the nail just big enough for the job and not so big that it split the lumber.

- He taught me how to wire and install an electrical outlet or a wall switch (turn off the power source first, black wire always went to black wire and white wire always went to white).
- He taught me how a wrench was constructed and how to use it by placing it on the nut in a way that provided the most torque with the smallest possibility that it might slip off and make you skin your knuckles.
- He taught me how to drink soda out of a bottle without getting an air lock either on my lips or in the bottle.

One thing he did not teach me was how to use blasting powder. I learned that when I was about ten by simply watching him with fascination. When he first started farming, a few small pieces of land were covered with trees. Dad wanted to get rid of them so he would have more land to plow and plant. He would pick a tree at the edge of a grove, cut it and burn the trunk and branches. Then he would dig around the stump going down a couple of feet or until the roots got too thick for easy digging.

He was moving to the exciting part. Dad would use a hand drill to make one or more two-inch diameter holes about eight to 12 inches deep in the trunk down around where it had grown out of the ground. He would fill those holes with about six inches of black blasting powder, tamp it in, add a fuse that had been cut to be about three feet long, and tap in a hand-carved plug. If I were around, he would make sure I was at least 50 feet away. Then he would light the fuse and walk quickly over to join me. The blasts usually split the stump into several sections and loosened the dirt around the roots.

Dad holds my sister Donna while I stand, getting acquainted with a new puppy, probably named Rex.

Now he could throw a chain around one chunk at a time, hook the chain to the tractor, and pull it out. Dad would drag the chunk of stump over to the bonfire of the cut tree that was still burning and add it to the fire. After the other pieces of stump had been removed, he would throw the dirt back into the hole. He had created another 50 square feet of land to add to his arable acres.

One day I found the bucket Dad kept the blasting powder in. The fuse cord was with it. I decided I would experiment. I poured about a quarter cup of blasting powder on the ground in the middle of the farm yard, laid the tip of a two-foot fuse on top of it, and covered it with a tin can that I pressed into the ground around the pile of powder. I lit the fuse and ran about 40 feet, turned around, and watched to see what would happen. I could see the fuse burn itself right under the can. A loud "pop" blew the can high in the air.

I thought that was quite a bit of fun. I tried it again, using a little more powder and a new can. This time the can went even higher in the air. My sister Donna, then about six, and my brother Paul, then about two, found me and wanted to know what was going on. I tried my experiment one more time, making sure that Donna and Paul were far enough away. They were impressed with the explosion and the flight of the can. I decided not to press my luck and called it a day.

Dad was not pleased when he found out what I had been doing, but he was interested in my experiment. So we "played" with that blasting powder together to see how high we could make the can go. It probably wasn't the smartest thing to do, but it was fun.

Dad was a progressive farmer, but he was not always open to new ideas, particularly when they came from his children.

I was a freshman in high school when I already had a sizable herd of hogs and a growing flock of sheep, both established through my 4-H and Future Farmers of America projects. Both were pastured in sizable plots next to each other and fresh water and feed had to be hauled to them every day. That always involved getting to the gate, getting off the tractor and opening the gate, getting back on the tractor to drive through the gate, getting back off the tractor to close the gate, driving any animals back into the pen that had gotten out when I was driving the tractor through the opening, getting back on the tractor to drive to the waterer and feeder in the pen. Then, after watering and feeding the animals and checking to see if any problems were evident with any of the animals, I got back on the tractor to go through the whole gate opening and closing ritual one more time. It was a tiring and not very efficient procedure.

There had to be a better way. I had to be able to supply water and feed without opening and closing those gates so many times. The feeding was easy. I purchased self-feeders that would hold several days' worth of feed.

The watering problem was a little harder to solve, but I finally decided I could use the law of gravity to my advantage. Dad was not particularly enchanted with my idea, but he didn't tell me I couldn't try it. First, I found a 50-gallon wooden barrel. We already had one that wasn't being used, so I co-opted it. Now I needed a sled. We had lots of old lumber lying around, and I soon found two eight feet long two by sixes which would work just fine. I connected and braced them about four feet apart with two by fours. I built a tower about four feet high on top of the sled out of similar lumber and fastened the wooden barrel on top of the tower. Finally, I tapped the barrel about an inch from the bottom and rigged six feet of old garden hose by screwing it unto the faucet that had been screwed into the tap hole and hooking the end of the hose to the top of the barrel with a wire hook.

Then I filled the barrel with cold water, hooked my creation to the tractor with a chain, and pulled it to the hog pen, parking it close to, but outside, the fence. I reached up and unhooked the hose from the barrel and put the end in the waterer on the other side of the fence in the pen. Gravity pulled the water from the barrel to the waterer. When the waterer was full, I hooked the hose back to the top of the barrel. Then I unhooked the barrel-sled from the tractor and left it outside the fence until the next day when I could simply walk out, take down the hose, and fill the waterer again. And I never had to open and close the gate.

Dad was finally impressed, particularly when my invention won a 4-H award for inventiveness and ingenuity. In fact, I think Dad even used my water carrier himself when I went to college a few years later.

Dad and Mom had been married in 1932 during the Great Depression. No farmer then had the money to pay someone else for something he could figure out how to do himself. If he couldn't fix it, it most likely was not going to get fixed unless a neighbor could do it for free. And if the problem involved something that was absolutely necessary, Dad or that neighbor would find a way to fix it.

Sometimes the work was a little less than professional, but it solved the problem while saving precious dollars.

That frugality is something else that has stayed with me through the years, even after it wasn't always necessary.

Not All Work

I was surprised about two decades after Dad's death when I learned that he also used those hands to play the violin. I had seen the violin in a closet when I was a few years old, but I have no memory of ever having heard him play it. Neither do my siblings.

Then one day, at a dinner with my extended family, my sister-in-law Karen brought out an amazing exhibit. It was the printed program for a concert by the community orchestra in Dixon, Illinois, and Dad's name was included as one of the violinists. Her dad was also listed as a member of the violin section. The concert had been a year of two before Mom and Dad were married.

He already had died when I saw that program. I never had the chance to ask him about that part of his life, and it was plain for reasons Mom never explained that she did not want to talk about it. Mary Ann, my youngest sister, has Dad's violin now. She doesn't play it anymore either. She thinks Dad stopped playing the violin because his autocratic father didn't want him spending time on such frivolity. She might be right.

Even though we never heard the strains of Dad's violin, music was not foreign to our house. We had a piano, but music seldom received more than moderate emphasis.

Dad's and Mom's singing was limited almost exclusively to the hymns and liturgy in church. Dad, having been a violinist, sang quietly but well. Mom, on the other hand, was an enthusiastic but somewhat out-of-control soprano. But she loved to sing the hymns and sang them lustily. Even when the children's voices were added in, the Trapp Family Singers we were not.

Singing was, of course, a major part of each program given by the children in church on each Christmas Eve. I had a decent voice (at least it was loud), so after about the age of nine I was always one of the three Wise Men in the church Christmas program. Each year was the same. Dressed in adult bathrobes with scarves wound around our heads like turbans and cardboard circles that were supposed to resemble crowns, three of us marched individually down the center aisle of the church, lustily singing one or more verses of "We Three Kings of Orient Are." It was some of the best church drama we could get back in the decade of the '40s.

Difficulties Come

When I see Dad's hands as I look at mine, I'm reminded occasionally that Dad's hands, like the hands of most people, also got him into trouble. Two vivid memories come easily to mind.

Fencerows used to be important when livestock was raised on every farm. Fences kept livestock where farmers wanted it to be — most of the time. Fencerow vegetation also gave year-round shelter to a variety of wildlife — rabbits, pheasants, quail, foxes, skunks, groundhogs, and a variety of songbirds on our farm.

But the brush and dead weeds and grass were unsightly when winter's snows had melted. The vegetation renewed itself every year, but could easily get out of hand if not controlled. So Dad would clean up the fencerows every spring in the easiest way possible. He would wait until the refuse was dry and then burn it, making sure that wooden fence posts (usually only at the corners of a field) did not catch fire.

One spring when I was about 16 and attending school Dad decided that, since the breeze was not too strong, it was a good time to burn a fencerow. But he forgot that the fencerow he was about to burn had been infested for years with poison ivy. The dry fencerow burnt well, and most of the time the breeze blew the smoke away. Unfortunately, the breeze occasionally died down and the smoke then swirled around Dad rather than blowing away from him.

That night he began to itch. The next morning, his face, his torso, his arms, and his legs were so swollen he was barely recognizable. The smoke from the poison ivy was infused with the plant's poisonous oil, and Dad, unknowingly, had been repeatedly coated with its terrible deposit whenever he was in that smoke.

The fact that Mom was a nurse was a major blessing. She knew what to do to ease Dad's horrible discomfort. But she could not erase it. He didn't even complain about staying in bed, and I and my siblings were warned not to get too close to him. (We also picked up the slack to milk the cows and do the other chores.) The swelling began to subside in about three days, and by the end of the week Dad had recovered.

The second time Dad's hands got him into trouble was much more serious.

Mom had gone to town to do the grocery shopping. Dad stayed home to work on their second car which hadn't been running well.

He thought the carburetor needed adjustment. He had successfully adjusted many carburetors on cars and tractors before. It was another spring. It had been raining and the ground was much too muddy to work in the fields. The car was in the corncrib pointed west. A bit of a cold breeze was blowing through the large double doors, so Dad closed them.

It's hard to know exactly what happened, but it looked like Dad thought he was finished with the repair and wanted to test it. We assumed that he reached through the driver's side window and turned on the ignition key so that he could start the engine from under the hood and watch how it performed. Apparently, when he turned on the ignition, his sleeve caught on the gearshift lever and pushed it into Drive. (Back in the '60s and '70s the gear shift lever was mounted on the

Dad and Mom on the farm in 1967.

right side of the steering column just above the key that turned on the ignition.) Unaware of what he had done, he went around to the front of the car, leaned over the radiator and started the engine.

I imagine it responded with a roar, the car jumped forward, pushing Dad through those large doors and continuing between the hog house and the machine shed into a plowed field. The field was black mud. That mire dragged Dad under the car which continued on for another 50 yards before it got stuck and the engine died. That was the decision at the inquest.

Perhaps thirty minutes later, Mom returned home and was forced through the trauma of finding Dad in a misshapen heap in the mud. It was a deadly spring. Marcus Frederick Gonnerman died in that muddy field on April 10, 1972. My Dad was dead at the age of 68.

He is buried at Chapel Hill Memorial Park in Dixon, Illinois. Those large, scarred, talented hands had become his undoing. I'm reminded of that every time I see his hands – and his ring – while looking at mine.

Aspirations for Another Career?

He had been born on August 22, 1903, in Ashton, Illinois, only about 25 miles east of where he is buried. He was the son of Alfred (Fred) H. and Anna Schafer Gonnerman.

A colorful certificate, printed in German and made out by H. Stauffenberg, pastor of St. John's Evangelical Lutheran Church in Ashton, lists Dad's name in the German vernacular of Markus Friedrich Gonnermann in the record of his baptism on October 18, 1903. Another document uses the same German form of Dad's name when it records his confirmation in the same church on April 16, 1916. It is signed by Pastor G. Mack.

That same month Dad received a diploma from Common Schools, Lee County, certifying that Marcus F. Gonnerman has "honorably completed the Course of Study in the Common Branches required by law to be taught in the Public Schools of the State of Illinois and by intellectual attainments and correct deportment merits this Diploma." Dated April 28, 1916, the Diploma was signed by Ada Vogel, teacher, and L.W. Miller, County Superintendent of Schools, and stamped with the embossed seal of the County Superintendent of Schools.

Dad had been a member of Immanuel Lutheran Church in Dixon for all of his adult life and had served on the church council. He had been a leader of the Nachusa Nighthawks 4-H Club for 20 years and also served as a Boy Scout leader for the troop that was formed at the Nachusa Children's Home (then known as an orphanage). He had also been elected to the Nachusa Public School Board for several terms.

He and Mom, after retirement from active farming, had also served for nearly a year as house parents for missionary children in the mission field of Papua New Guinea.

Perhaps the most ironic thing about his life is that he probably had never wanted to be a farmer.

He had earned a diploma dated June 13, 1931, from the Radio Division of Coyne Electrical School in Chicago. The diploma states that he had "completed the full course of practical instruction in Radio-Television-Sound Reproduction."

He even had a "Life Scholarship" to Coyne,

> 1. To furnish him with the Complete Radio Training Course taught at the School; 2. To allow him to remain at School as long as necessary; 3. To furnish him additional instruction after graduation, whenever, and as often as he demands same; 4. To furnish Technical Advisory Service at any time; 5. To furnish Employment Service at any time and as often as desired, as long as he is in good standing.

Coyne Electrical School was established in Chicago in 1899 as a branch of Coyne Electrical School in Boston. It became Coyne American Institute when it merged with American Institute of Engineering in the 1960s. Promotional materials claim that "Coyne American Institute and its predecessor schools have trained and placed thousands of students in professional careers." It is now a part of Coyne College, still in Chicago.

I never talked to Dad about his experiences at Coyne. I never even knew he had studied there before my sister, Mary Ann, gave me a copy of his diploma, and that was some 30 years after he died. What had it been like for a young man who knew only the life of living and working on a farm in northern Illinois to move to a metropolis like Chicago to study electronics, a field that was in its infancy?

How did Dad respond to the big city? Did it frighten him, or did he embrace his new environment? What influences did it have on his life then and his life after that when he returned to the farm? I wish I had been given just an inkling of this part of his life when he was still alive. I still want to have been able to talk to him about his study and probe the reasons he had gone to Coyne and the reasons he abandoned what he had learned to return to a life of farming he didn't really want. It's too big a chunk of his life to just lie in the shadows, swallowed by the unknown.

Dad never escaped from farming to go out on his own to use any of the knowledge and talent that his diploma in radio-television-sound reproduction certified he had. Maybe Dad's whole life was one of ambivalence, not wanting to leave his father and mother alone to work the farm, but not wanting to work there, either. But he simply could not break away from the binding tradition that the son follows the father, wherever it leads. Dad's father was autocratic in the extreme. Dad was probably trapped on his father's farm by a father who insisted that he needed Dad there.

I sometimes wonder what life would have been like for my siblings and me if my dad had been able to break away from his dad and pursue the career in radio and television for which he had been prepared, a field then in its infancy, but destined to grow quickly into one of the most influential communications sources in the world.

One thing is sure. My siblings and I would never have had the enjoyment of the life on the farm that gave us the experiences of watching plants and animals grow; gaining an understanding, a respect, and a reverence for the cycles of birth or germination, growth, and death; learning acceptance and tolerance for hardships and frugal living; experiencing the joys of creating efficient and economical solutions for the day-to-day difficulties that challenge anyone who takes life on a farm seriously; and being infused with a work ethic that saw every task as an opportunity that needed to be completed.

The fact that none of my siblings nor I stayed on the farm to carry on some family tradition has nothing to do with our enjoyment of our childhood in an environment that was one big learning experience after another. In fact, those learning experiences provided a foundation for my own, seemingly unconnected career, a ministry of specialized communication in the Evangelical Lutheran Church in America and its institutions.

More than once, in the seminary and later on through my life, I have been able to add a farmer's experience and perspective to the discussions of the many parables of Jesus that deal with the planting and harvesting of seeds and the raising and caring for sheep.

My experiences in 4-H and Future Farmers of America (FFA) and four years of high school classes in vocational agriculture laid a foundation of leadership skills and concerns for the less fortunate, the less well, and the less socially adjusted than I can imagine would have been possible in any other setting.

MOM

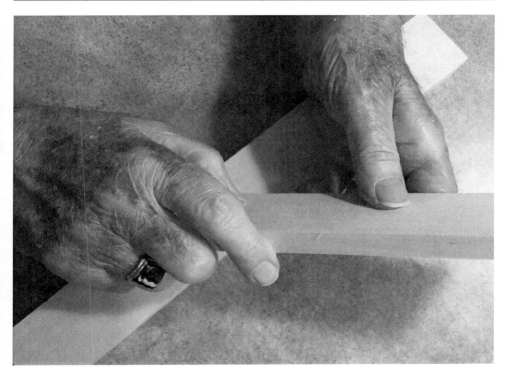

Mom wrote, "My baptism was more important to me than my birthday, as that's when I became at child of God."

MOM

Emotionally, Dad was a stoic. Mom made up for that. She over-flowed with emotion. She could, and sometimes did, turn her face into a fountain of tears — sometimes of fathomless joy, some-times of great grief and sadness. The tears could be turned on by anything from a visit by a distant relative that she had not seen for months, to the good news that a friend had been blessed with a great gift, to the grievous news of the death of a dear friend or neighbor.

My siblings and I all caught some of that from her.

She was also excitable. Her thought processes often ran faster than her ability to voice what she was thinking. Whenever that hap-pened she would slip into a stammering mode until she or someone else changed the subject. The stammer could be particularly notice-able when she was trying to call one of her children to get them to either do or stop doing something.

The order would come out something like, "Frederick! Donna! Paul! Mary Ann!" A pause as Mom collected her thoughts and her voice and decided which or her children she really wanted to address. Then: "Frederick! Stop that right now!" We knew the routine. We also knew that it was not a time to laugh. (Mom always called me Frederick. She never used Fred, the name I prefer and the name that was used by almost all of my oth-er relatives as well as my friends.)

Child of God

Marie Antonietta was born near Char-lotte, Illinois, on November 18, 1905, the first child of Henry and Gesena Hoppe Jacobs.

Mom, born November 18, 1905.

Many immigrants came to America from the same region with maybe only a passing acquaintanceship with someone who had lived in their neighborhood on the other side of the Atlantic Ocean. Somehow, they settled in the same place in the United States, found each other again, and got married.

The same thing happened to my wife Ruth's grandparents when they both came from the Åland Islands, a huge archipelago in the Baltic Sea halfway between Stockholm, Sweden, and Helsinki, Finland. They had known each other in Åland and probably went to the same church in the Föglö parish, but nothing indicates that they had any kind of personal relationship. When they immigrated to the United States they both settled near Midland, Michigan, where they reconnected and got married.

These reconnections are not surprising. Immigrants frequently ended up close to each other in a strange land. They spoke the same language. Their points of origin were held in common, and the emotional distance between them had already been shortened. They hungered for companionship. Marriage was almost inevitable.

A colorfully illustrated form similar to Dad's, filled out in German, verifies that Marie Antonietta Jacobs, the daughter of Heinrich and Gesena Hoppe Jacobs, was baptized on December 17, 1905, in the Evangelical Lutheran St. Paul's Kirche in Charlotte in Livingston County, Illinois. In a brief autobiographical statement Mom wrote, "My baptism was more important to me than my birthday, as that's when I became at child of God," reflecting solid Lutheran theology.

Mom in 1909. The photo was taken in Pontiac, Illinois.

The baptismal certificate is signed by Hermann Koepp, Evangelical Lutheran pastor. That creates a bit of confusion, because Mom wrote in that same autobiographical statement that the man who baptized her was Pastor Hahn. Whoever officiated at Mom's baptism, the event was exceptionally significant for Mom.

Another experience was a bit different in nature. One warm summer day when Mom was about one-and-a-half years old some of the family decided to spend time outdoors. They brought out the high-chair and tied Mom in with a dishtowel around her waist so she wouldn't fall out. She was enjoying the fresh air when a pig that had been allowed to run in the yard came up to the highchair, got itself under it, raised itself up with the highchair on its back, and took off on a trot. Amazingly, the chair stayed balanced on the pig's back as Mom was bounced along.

Somebody suddenly saw the highchair carrying pig with Mom at the top and took off after it, corralled the pig, and got the chair off its back and solidly on the ground with Mom no worse for wear. From the way the story is told, Mom enjoyed the ride and was laughing all the way through it. After that, the family paid more attention to the whereabouts of the pigs when the highchair was outside.

Mom's family moved from Charlotte to a new farm her father had purchased in Marion Township, six miles south of Dixon, Illinois, in 1914. Their move the next March was a dramatic experience. Even today, moving from one farm to another involves lots more than furniture.

Mom's dad rented three railroad cars for the move. On the basis of frequent visits with my family to Grandpa and Grandma Jacobs' farm and recollections of what I saw there some 25 years and more after the move, those railroad cars were stuffed full.

Most likely, they held at least two (and possibly three) teams of horses and a pony, harnesses, buggies, wagons, cows, milk pails and milking stools, pigs, hog troughs, chickens in crates, chicken feeders, maybe some ducks and geese, a plow and a cultivator, a hay mower and a loader, a grain reaper, hammers, saws, pliers, wrenches, spades, rakes, hoes, brooms, mops, scrub buckets, kerosene lamps and lanterns, and all the furniture, dishes and kitchen utensils in the house they were leaving.

Grace, Welma, and Marie Jacobs.

Their church in Charlotte had given them a farewell celebration. Neighbors they knew near the farm they were leaving helped them move everything out of the buildings and load the railroad cars. Neighbors they would get to know around their new farm south of Dixon helped them unload the cars, haul everything from the railroad depot to the farm about six miles away, and put everything in the appropriate buildings on their new farm.

The railroad depot in Dixon, Illinois, where the Jacobs family landed after moving all their belongings and livestock in three boxcars from Charlotte in February 1915. The photo had been printed as a postcard sent for one cent postage to Herman and Annie Hoppe, Grandma Jacobs' relatives.

Mom and her two sisters, Welma and Grace, made sure that their mom with their six-month-old brother, Clifford, was comfortable on the train. They were accompanied by Claus Ommen, a cousin who was going to be their hired man. Claus brought his family along. They had a two-hour layover in El Paso, Illinois, about 35 miles west of Charlotte, where all the livestock had to be checked to see how they were traveling and make sure they had water. Then they traveled another 85 miles farther northwest to the Illinois Central Depot in Dixon. (Unfortunately, no record remains of the cost of that momentous journey, but it had to be substantial.)

Their dad had gone on ahead to be in Dixon to greet them when they arrived. They got off the train, got into the carriage where he was waiting, and started off on the six-mile ride to their new home. It was a cold ride, but their dad had lit and stoked the coal burner so that they would step into a warm house.

In the light of the next morning they discovered that the house that was going to be their new home was both old and dirty. But, as Mom said, "Mother never left anything discourage her." She and her daughters were soon busy with scrub buckets, and things began to change as the grime and dust disappeared. New wallpaper and fresh paint brightened all the walls within the month.

Their home church would be Immanuel Lutheran in Dixon, but a language problem delayed immediate membership there. Mom, and her siblings spoke what was known as "low German," but "high German" was the language used at Immanuel Lutheran in Dixon. A Lutheran church where services would be in "low German" was established in Harmon, a little town a few miles south of the Jacobs farm, and Mom, her parents, and her siblings attended services there on Sunday afternoons.

Then Pastor Sulchting was called to Immanuel Lutheran and the congregation started holding worship services and conducting Sunday school in English. The family transferred to Immanuel, and Mom was confirmed there in September 1920. Four of the six-member confirmation class were her cousins. Mom's Christian faith and her involvement in the church started when she was a child and did not stop growing until she died.

Horses were essential in those early years on the farm near Dixon. Most farmers did not yet have cars. Mom remembered her first Christmas at Immanuel Lutheran Church. They, and many other members who lived on farms, traveled in bobsleds, each pulled by a team of two horses. The trip took about an hour on a clear, cold night. Her brother, Clifford, only one-and-a-half-years old, was bundled up in many blankets and held tightly by his mother for the entire journey.

When they arrived at Immanuel, the horses were stabled behind the church. After the service, they had another hour-long ride back home, and by now the temperature had gotten colder. When they got home and everyone else was in the warm house, Mom's Dad still had a half-hour's work to do, unharnessing the horses, brushing them down, and giving them fresh bedding for the night.

School and Community

Elementary education started at Duis School, only a mile from home. But after one-and-a-half terms, the school wanted the Jacobs family to pay tuition for their children because they did not live in that district. That was too much of a financial burden so the Jacobs children were transferred to Scott School where they graduated from eighth grade. Scott, as nearly all rural schools in those days, was a one-room school with one teacher for all eight grades. Her name was Agnes Lally, the teacher at Scott for many years.

The learning pattern in Mom's school was not limited to text-books, lectures, and rote recitation. She says that the students learned at Scott, and they received good grades in their Central Exams which they took at Harmon. Mom remembered that school days – and sometimes the evenings – were also filled with community events such as dialogs, singing, and flag drills.

Box socials were also popular. Women and girls brought meals for two they had packed in fancily decorated boxes or baskets. The boxed meals were auctioned off to the highest bidder among the men and boys. If the males had a special attraction to any of the females, they tried to find out which lunch was packed by the woman or girl who was their biggest interest.

Husbands had usually already been alerted to what their wife's box looked like and for the sake of harmony at home, he had better bid enough to buy it. Sometimes men other than the husband created a bit of mischief when they bid up one wife's box until the auctioneer had taken them to the edge of all the husband could afford. Then the mischief-maker would stop bidding and the husband would be able to buy his wife's box – at a premium he had hoped not to pay.

For unattached males, all kinds of signals were devised to help them make pretty good guesses as to which box would pair them up with the woman or girl with whom they wanted to eat their meal. It was an art to try to bid as inauspiciously as possible so that the op-

position or competition was not tipped off. If more than one male was interested in the same box, the bidding could go ridiculously high, at least in those days of scant finances for nearly everyone. Box socials were big money makers because the money did not go to the meal makers. It went to the sponsoring organizations.

Mom traveled the six miles to high school driving a horse-drawn buggy, and she had the company of two neighbor girls. None of them ever thought of coming anywhere close to trying to bully each other or anyone else. Mom's horse and buggy were parked in a stable near a blacksmith shop while the girls were in classes.

Mom's high school photo in 1922. She had made the brown serge dress in second year home economics class.

Mom had one disquieting experience as she and the neighbor girls were on the way home from high school one night when, without warning, the horse dropped dead in its traces. That was more than a bit traumatic. She never said how she informed her dad of the problem, but by the time he had brought her another horse the dead one had already been picked up by the rendering works – standard operating procedure in the twenties.

Mom graduated from Dixon High School in 1924. Two years later she enrolled in nurses training at Milwaukee Lutheran Hospital in Wisconsin. Following graduation in 1929 she returned to Dixon to work in Katherine Shaw Bethea Hospital as a night supervisor in 12-hour shifts for $95.00 a month.

Mom in her nurse's uniform after graduating from Milwaukee (Wisconsin) Lutheran Hospital in 1929.

It didn't take her long to begin moving up the employment ladder. She was night supervisor for only one year before becoming an instructor of nurses. She held that post for the next two years.

Much of Mom's life revolved around two poles – her church and the county extension office.

She taught Sunday school at Immanuel Lutheran Church in Dixon and later at St. Paul Lutheran Church in Gilman, Illinois, for

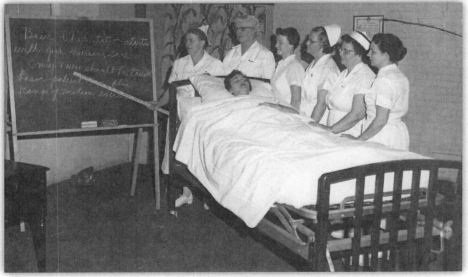

Mom teaching nurses aids at the Dixon Hospital.

a total of 61 years, moving from one age group to another as needs developed for the congregation's children. She was always an active member of the Ladies Aid. That's what the women's group was called until about the '80s, when the name took on several forms of "Women of the Church."

Women of the Church met monthly. The program focused on Bible study with one of the members serving as Bible study leader, often on a rotating basis. The text, suggested commentary, and a guide to helpful discussion questions were supplied in the monthly women's magazine, mailed by the national office to every woman who was a member of the synod's congregations. It was a bold program, and the church depended on it – and still depends on it – for much of its continuing strength and sustenance.

Women of the Church was always mission oriented. Many of the members, and Mom was often among them, met regularly at the church to stitch together quilts that were shipped by boxcars full to mission fields in several countries in India, Africa, and other places in the world that were suffering from hunger and homelessness. Some congregations completed and distributed hundreds of quilts a year.

Not willing to stay home, Mom volunteered and was accepted for a Vista program on the Rose Bud Indian Reservation in South

The Ladies Aid from Immanuel Lutheran Church in Dixon in 1942. Pastor Carl Wagner is in the front row on the right. Mom is fifth from the left in the first row. Grandma Gonnerman is at the left end of the back row. Today Ladies Aid is known as Women of the Evangelical Lutheran Church in America (WELCA).

Dakota for one year in 1975 and 1976. She was able to resurrect her nursing skills to help the Native Americans living on the reservation. Her biggest disappointment occurred when she attended the only Lutheran Church in the area, a conservative Missouri Lutheran congregation, and the pastor denied her communion. She never received the sacrament of the Lord's Supper during her year-long stay on the reservation.

Their New Guinea experience did not go away after Mom and Dad returned to live on the farm in 1968 and Dad died in 1972. Mom continued to show slides and speak about her and Dad's foreign mission experiences in neighboring congregations looking for world mission programs. Mom was host to Ujan and Anilo Talil and their son Seth for a short time in 1977 when the family came from New Guinea in connection with Ujan's enrollment at Wartburg Seminary in Dubuque, Iowa, for a six-year study program.

The Talils and another New Guinea couple were the first seminary students from their country to study in the United States. They spoke at a worship service at Immanuel Lutheran Church in Dixon before a pig roast there attended by members of congregations of the Northwestern District of the American Lutheran Church. Seth,

Mom and Dad preparing for their service in New Guinea in 1967.

four years old, had learned his tribal language, the national language of New Guinea, Pidgeon English, and American English before his visit to the United States.

Mom also played a major role in helping an immigrant Laotian family sponsored by Immanuel Lutheran Congregation in 1979 to set up a home and adjust to life in the United States.

Mom's connections to the Lee County extension office in Amboy, Illinois, ran on two tracks. She was an active member of what was known as the Le Li Lo Club, an organization of farm women in the neighborhood who met monthly in each other's homes to discuss and demonstrate the culinary and needlework arts. They complimented each other on their desserts, centerpieces, hand-sewn dresses, quilting, knitting, needlepoint, and holiday decorations and learned how to do them for their own homes. They also talked prices and bargains and where and when to get them.

Mom was an excellent seamstress. She made dresses for Donna and Mary Ann as well as herself. Her sewing got an unexpected boost during World War II when everything, including fabric for sewing, was in short supply. People learned either to do without or to make do with much less than they would have under ordinary circumstance. Factories that had been making cloth for housewives turned their attention to making uniforms, parachutes, and life jackets for the soldiers, sailors, and airmen. Suddenly, the material that had been made for sewing all those dresses and shirts and pants and jackets was not available anymore.

Then the companies that made food supplements for farm livestock had a great idea. All of the food supplements were sold in cloth bags. Why not put them in bags made of material that could be used for sewing other things? And they did.

From then on, when Dad or Mom went to the grain elevator or feed store they made two choices. First, they picked out the best food supplements for their chickens, pigs, and dairy cows. Then they paid attention to what colorful patterns decorated the bags the food was in. Sometimes they just picked the bag with the most interesting pattern and colorful cloth. Other times they tried to find bags made out of cloth like one or two that Mom already had at home. It took about three bags to make one dress. The cloth was free. And Mom used a lot of it.

Occasionally, Mom tried her hand at decorative touches she saw in magazines, but she frequently ran into problems. First, she never thought she could take the time necessary to do all the little things the creative process required. A rushed project is not necessarily an attractive one. Second, she seldom thought about context or background. The buffet or the top of a small occasional table were almost always full of decorative touches. Once in a while the different objects were visually compatible. More times, they were not.

But that didn't matter to Mom. When she had completed (not necessarily the same as finished) a new decorative doo-dad, she almost never moved other things out of the space where it was to go. Instead, she simply crowded the other pieces more tightly together and created a space just big enough for the new decoration to fit. New creations seldom had the space they required to be visually effective, but Mom never seemed to notice.

On the second track, Mom was a leader of the Nachusa Ever Readies 4-H Club for girls. (In those days, 4-H was divided into clubs for boys and clubs for girls. Dad was a leader of the boy's 4-H club, the Nachusa Nighthawks.) The primary projects for girls revolved around the homemaking arts — sewing, other needlework arts, cooking, baking, and canning. Girls joined 4-H when they were ten and could continue as members until they were 21. Mom tutored them through the regimen of picking projects for the year, filling out record books, preparing exhibits for the county fair, learning the rudiments of *Roberts Rules of Order*, and giving demonstrations and other public presentations.

All of the Gonnerman children were active members of the 4-H clubs, and did well in showing their livestock and their projects in sewing, baking, and home decoration.

Learning from Mom

Mom, like Dad, was also a significant teacher in my life.

- She taught me how to garden, from preparation of the soil to the planting of seeds and seedlings to nurturing the plants toward mature growth to harvesting the produce to preparing the garden space for winter.
- She taught me that little things, such as painting a picket fence, had a big positive effect on not only the

appearance but also the sustainability of a home and farmstead.

- She taught me how to set a table, even though we had the minimum of one knife, one fork, and one spoon (not matching) for each setting. I never knew other kinds of silverware existed until I got to college.

- She taught me the beginnings of my appreciation for the natural world and my collateral responsibilities to nurture and preserve it.

- She taught me through her own life the importance of a spiritual foundation throughout my daily life

- She taught me continuing concern for life, whether it be the lives of friends and neighbors, the lives of the marginalized and the disenfranchised, the lives of people in other cultures, or the lives of the livestock we nurtured on our farm.

- She taught me the necessity for personal charity (apart from pity) and stewardship of what I had so that I could help people who lived on the edges of existence either personally or through responsible organizations with programs that would help them. (Mom did, however, particularly in her later years, have a tendency to send checks of support to some "charitable" agencies with questionable histories.)

Trying "Something Different"

Mom enjoyed cooking. Occasionally, she would see a new recipe in a magazine and decide to try the "something different" that was suggested. Unfortunately, she frequently was not particularly successful when she got away from her usual fare.

Ruth and I had our first daughter Gay during my senior year at Trinity Lutheran Seminary. Mom came to help Ruth with some of the work that new mothers have to deal with, just as she had done when our first son Mark was born during my internship in Detroit.

We had some pears in our kitchen in Columbus, but they had gotten ripe well past their prime, probably because we were preoccupied with getting settled with a new daughter in the apartment and forgot about the pears. Mom always lived with the austerity she and her family had developed during the deprivations of the Great Depression. Food could not be thrown out; nothing could go to waste. She saw those pears and nothing would stop her from putting them to some use.

The day after she found those pears Mom decided to make use of that nearly unreclaimable spoiled fruit. She would bake a pear pie. It would be a first for her and a first for us, but she had seen a recipe in the cooking section of the *Columbus Dispatch* and would not be dissuaded from trying it. She baked the pear pie. Unfortunately, when we sampled this new confection, we discovered that the pie crust – she could make those pretty well – held a not very tasty pear mush. It was undoubtedly one of Mom's least successful culinary efforts. Even she didn't like it.

Mom in her nurse's uniform in 1985.

One Thanksgiving after Dad died, the whole family (her children, the in-laws, and her grandchildren) were all together for dinner at the big house on the farm. Ordinarily, Thanksgiving dinner consisted of the traditional turkey and all the "fixings" and that's what we were expecting. But Mom occasionally was somewhat quixotic.

It was obvious that she had not been roasting a turkey that morning, but when she brought the platter of meat to the table, it was all cut into pieces that had a similar appearance to some kind of poultry. We ate away. The meat tasted somewhat like chicken, but some of us noted that none of the pieces resembled the expected drumsticks, thighs, wings, or breasts that would ordinarily fill a plate of any kind of poultry that we knew about.

I watched Mom. She had a kind of Cheshire cat grin on her face, the grin that says, "I know something that nobody else knows." I thought I knew what we were eating, so about half way through the meal I finally asked her. She responded with the question, "What do you think it is?" "Rabbit?" I answered. She confessed that I was right. She had purchased three domestic rabbits, already dressed, at the grocery store. It tasted quite good. We had often eaten wild rabbits that I had hunted in the winter.

But some of the grandchildren hesitantly put down the pieces they were eating, and didn't pick them up again to finish them. It just didn't seem right to be eating the Easter Bunny at Thanksgiving dinner — or maybe at any other time.

Life in Later Years

Mom finally left the farm in Nachusa in 1987 and moved to a small house in Gilman, Illinois, right across the street from daughter Mary Ann. It was the perfect arrangement. She was independent in her own house and continued to maintain a relatively large vegetable garden, but Mary Ann, also a nurse, was within shouting distance if she needed any kind of help.

She did need help one day. Mom was returning from a shopping trip in Gilman. She opened the garage door with the electronic opener and pulled into place as usual. Then her foot slipped off the brake pedal and landed on the accelerator. Her car leaped ahead, hit the back wall of the garage and went right through. The car was hung up on its undercarriage on the cement block foundation. Mom tried to dislodge the car by stepping harder on the accelerator. The rear wheels squealed. Mom continued to try to back the car off the foundation with more acceleration.

Mary Ann — thankfully, she was a home — heard the commotion in her house across the street. She looked out her window and at first glimpse thought the garage was on fire. Huge plumes of gray smoke were pouring out the still open door. Then she realized that the smoke was coming from the tread burning off the screaming tires on the cement garage floor. She yelled at Russ and they both ran across the street to the disaster in progress. Russ was able to get Mom to stop trying to move the car and turn off the ignition.

Mom was devastated. The wreckage of the garage was bad enough, but she thought more about what would have happened if her foot had slipped off the brake when she was stopped at an intersection with pedestrians in front of her. She never drove a car again.

Mom continued to be active even though she had to depend on others for transportation. She was seriously afflicted with osteoporosis. She had always been short, but she was shrinking to even shorter. She was beginning to be hunched over. Her feet were turning inward so that she was walking, if she walked at all, on the outside edges of her feet.

She was famous in the family for her falls, which happened with increasing frequency as she aged. Nobody knows exactly how many falls she had, but she broke both wrists and maybe an arm several times. Some of her ribs were undoubtedly broken, but she never complained. Once she drove alone to visit us in Northfield with both arms in casts. Even though both arms were in casts, they were not in slings, so she could, with a fair amount of awkwardness and an excess amount of determination, still use her hands to shift gears and steer. Thankfully, she never broke a leg or a hip so she was never immobilized for long.

In 1997, at the age of 91, she was honored with the Woman of Faith Award from the Women of the Evangelical Lutheran Church in America of the Central/ Southern Illinois Synod of the ELCA for her life- *Mom loved reading until the end of her life.* time of service to the church and society.

It was a fitting honor for a woman who had lived a life worth living marked by volunteerism and philanthropy motivated by her strong Christian faith. She had passed that model for living on to not only her children, but also uncounted others who lived alongside and around her. When she moved from Dixon to Gilman and transferred her church membership from Immanuel Lutheran to St. Paul's, Pastor Downs at St. Paul's reported the pastor at Immanuel said, "You are getting a saint." Pastor Downs also said, "I always learned a lot from Marie when I visited her. She made a positive impression on everyone she met."

Mom spent the day in bed on December 11, 1998. Her oldest daughter Donna read to her from *The Prairie Farmer* during the afternoon. Mom had been getting *The Prairie Farmer* for fifty years, so long that they were sending the monthly publication to her free as complimentary copies. Donna left her and went home in the late afternoon to get ready for a Christmas party at the Prairie View Lutheran Home, a home for the aged where she worked.

Mom surrounded by her children: Mary Ann, Paul, Fred, Donna.

While at the party she got a call from her husband Ernie. Mom had been taken by ambulance to the emergency room at the hospital. She was unconscious but alive. When Donna got there someone on the medical staff asked her if they should try to resuscitate her. That, of course, would involve compressions of her chest. Donna said, "No." It was the only response she could give. Mom's bones were so weakened by osteoporosis that any forced compression of her chest would break her ribs.

She died that evening, December 11, 1998, at the age of 93. Mom is buried beside Dad, her husband for nearly 40 years, in the cemetery in Dixon.

LIFE ON THE FARM

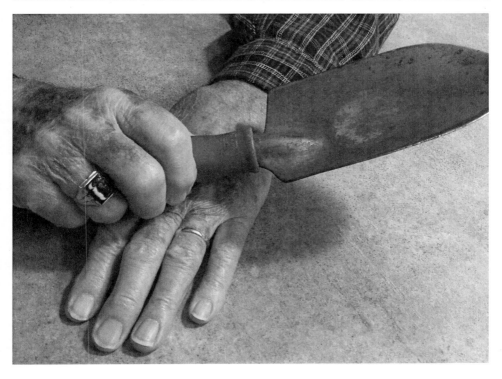

*My siblings and I played it by ear and fended for ourselves.
We learned by our mistakes, but most of the time
we didn't know what our mistakes were
until Mom and Dad pointed them out
after we made them.*

LIFE ON THE FARM

Mom and Dad were products – some might say, victims – of the times in which they lived, their rural culture, the economic uncertainties of the Great Depression, and their German immigrant heritage.

Both were persons of faith, baptized and sustained in the Lutheran church. Both were active in community service. Mom, a nurse, taught Sunday school and was an active member of a variety of organizations related to homemaking. They were faithful contributors to Immanuel Lutheran Church in Dixon, Illinois. Dad was a member of the Nachusa Public School Board. Both he and Mom were always willing to come to the aid of any neighbors within a couple of miles whenever they needed help of any kind.

They surprised family and friends alike when they retired from farming in 1967 to spend the next year as missionary caretakers at the Katherine Lehmann School for Missionary Children in Wau, a town in the mission field in Papua New Guinea. When they completed their term of service in New Guinea they finished circumnavigating the globe with stops in Hong Kong, India, and Germany, where they visited relatives before coming home.

Dad, Marcus Frederick Gonnerman, was the second child born to Alfred (Fred) and Annie Schafer Gonnerman on August 8, 1903. He was the only son and second oldest child of four children. All were born in Ashton, Illinois, where Fred and Annie farmed. Margret was born on November 19, 1901; Dorothy was born on November 20, 1906; and Marion was born on November 30, 1909.

Annie and Fred Gonnerman.

Gesena and Henry Jacobs.

Mom, Marie Antoniette Jacobs, was born to Henry and Gesena Hoppe Jacobs in Charlotte, Illinois, on November 18, 1905. She had two sisters, Welma and Grace, and one brother, Clifford.

Mom and Dad met in Luther League at Immanuel Lutheran Church in Dixon sometime in the mid-twenties. Luther League was a youth organization sponsored by nearly every Lutheran church. They had a sometimes long-distance courtship. First, Mom went to nursing school at Milwaukee Lutheran Hospital from 1926 to 1929. A train ran between Milwaukee and Dixon, but Mom probably didn't use it very often. Dad had been staying with his dad and mom in their new house, built in 1922, while working on their farm.

About the same time Mom graduated from nursing school and came home to work in the hospital in Dixon, Dad went off to school at the Radio Division of Coyne Electrical School in Chicago. He earned his diploma in the two-year program in 1931, but returned to work on the family farm. Dad might have had a car so he could come home on weekends. Otherwise, he also could have travelled back and forth to home by train. They lived near each other for about a year before their wedding.

Marcus Gonnerman and Marie Jacobs were married in Charlotte, Illinois, on June 29, 1932. Neither Mom nor Dad could ever be categorized as romantics, and they had a penchant for personal privacy. They seldom trumpeted details of their relationship and accomplishments to anyone, whether they were family members or neighborhood acquaintances. And few people in their neighborhood were any different.

But that's not surprising. The neighbors were also products of their time – a time where modesty and privacy were expected because they were the norm. I can remember only two or three times when I saw Dad and Mom kiss. Once was when one of them was getting on a train for a short trip, but I don't even remember whether Mom or Dad was doing the traveling, and I have no idea where that parent was going.

They loved and respected each other. No matter what was going to happen in their lives they would be together until death parted them. The most touching and romantic connection I witnessed was just before the lid on Dad's casket was closed by the funeral director for the final time. Mom bent down, gently pushed a wisp of Dad's hair back into place, and gave him a tender kiss on his forehead.

All four of their children were born in Dixon, Illinois: Frederick on June 4, 1933; Donna on April 4, 1937; Paul on May, 29, 1941; and Mary Ann on November 11, 1944.

Note that the children were all four years apart except for Mary Ann who broke the pattern by being born a half a year ahead of the four-year schedule set by her earlier siblings. While that's a nice pattern, it also resulted in the first three children being somewhat distanced emotionally. The age differential was too great. It's hard to get close to someone you become responsible for as a babysitter when you're growing up. With the exception of Paul and Mary Ann, we never really became friends (as

Mom and Dad on their wedding day in front of the house where they would begin their life together.

seems to happen in many other families with shorter birth cycles) until we got older and began to establish families of our own.

The German heritage created its own set of special circumstances. Rightly or wrongly, Germans are noted for their verbosity, their organizational skills, and their systematic approach to whatever opportunity or problem they face at any given time. They also give substance to the meaning of stubborn.

Dad's father, the second generation offspring of staunchly autocratic immigrant German stock, had offered his son and Mom a place to live in a set of buildings on the north side of the L-shaped, 160-acre Gonnerman farm bordering the little village of Nachusa on two sides. Nachusa was five miles east of Dixon in northern Illinois. The Lincoln Highway, then U.S. 30, bordered the farm on its northern edge and ran within 150 feet of our house.

Dad with me and our dog Sandy.

We always had a dog on our farm. Dogs were handy to have around. They helped bring the cows in from the pasture when it was time for them to be milked. They were good friends and playmates for all the kids in the family. They were watchdogs, letting us know at any time of the day or night when something or someone was around that maybe should not be there. Several of our dogs were named Rex. We seemed to like that name more than any other. One Rex was a particularly memorable dog. He was mostly brown with a few streaks of black, a large German Shepherd-Collie mix.

Visitors from the Depression

For nearly ten years after the Depression, thousands of men could not find work. Many of them were homeless. They walked back and forth across the entire country looking for a job and some kind of stability and security. But in most places, no work was available. They often walked past our farm along the Lincoln Highway or jumped out of a boxcar when a train slowed down in Nachusa.

Once in a while they would come to our house, knock on the door, and ask Mom (Dad would usually be working out in a field) if she had any work for them to do. She would always find something – split some wood, straighten up a pile of boards, pick up walnuts, weed some garden – and after they had finished the job she would have them sit on the edge of the porch where she would give them a full meal to eat before they continued on their way.

Those men also needed places to sleep. On some mornings Dad or I would enter the corncrib or the barn and hear a rustling sound and rapid footsteps as a homeless man (it was always a man) scurried out of the place in the corn or the hay where he had slept that night.

One of these visitors was different. Mom, my sister Donna, my brother Paul, baby sister Mary Ann, and I were home alone at night while Dad was away. I think he was working at the wire production company in Dixon, something he did sporadically to provide some cash income. As usual, I was sitting at the dining room table doing my homework with the light of a kerosene lamp. Suddenly, Rex, who slept on the screened-in section of the porch, started a low, continuous growl. A few minutes later, we heard a knock on the door and Rex's growling got louder and more ominous.

It was unusual to have uninvited visitors after dark. Mom and I went to the door, and by this time the man who had knocked was leaning against the door, trying to keep the growling and barking Rex from going through the screen. We grabbed Rex by the collar and pulled him back. Mom told the man whom we had never seen before that he had better get off our farm in a hurry and never come back. With a glance back over his shoulder at a still angry Rex, he ran back to the highway.

Rex's fierce reaction to this visitor was unusual. When others had come to the door before and after this man's visit, Rex was wary, he was alert, but he was not ferocious, and sometimes he even became friendly toward the visitor. But for some reason on this night, Rex sensed real danger to the rest of us in this one man. And Rex made sure that the visitor knew he was in real danger himself when he interrupted our evening to knock on our door.

Rex was a different kind a watchdog the next summer. A white picket fence surrounded our yard, and the younger kids were not supposed to go outside of that yard unless someone else in the family was with them. One afternoon we realized that Mary Ann (then about three years old) was not in the yard. We looked all over, but couldn't find her. Then Mom looked up and down the highway. There she was!

She was walking along the edge of this very busy highway toward our neighbor's farm. But she wasn't alone. Rex was with her. Not only was Rex with her, but he was between Mary Ann and the highway, leaning against her to make sure that she didn't get on the road where she could be hit by passing cars.

The amazing thing was, Rex had been trained so that he knew he was never to go on the highway himself. But in this case he broke the rules of his own training because he saw that the smallest member of our family was in serious danger. Mom rushed across the highway to pick up Mary Ann and carry her back to the house. Then she got down on her knees and gave Rex a big hug. We all did.

Celebrating Memorial Day

We were a mildly patriotic Republican family. Memorial Day was always a day of celebration. The corn had been planted. The oats looked like it would be a good crop in August. The hay could wait one more day before it had to be cut. In other words, Memorial Day was always a good time to take a one-day vacation.

The whole family was loaded into the car by 9:30, and we headed east down the Lincoln Highway the five miles to a cemetery in Franklin Grove. I would be nine years old a few days after Memorial Day in 1942. Donna was five. Paul had arrived very near Memorial Day the year before. The world was in trouble. Adolf Hitler and his Nazis had invaded Poland on September 1, 1939, and began to spread his forces out from there in what he thought would be his empire. The Japanese had bombed Pearl Harbor on December 7, 1941. The Germans were bombing London with regularity. The Allies were reciprocating with massive bombings of German factories and cities.

A speakers' platform was set up in one clear area of the cemetery. Shortly, it would fill with an assortment of political and military personages who were about to provide a half hour or so (if we were lucky) of speechmaking. I and the other children who were there weren't interested in the speeches. A huge maple tree grew in the middle of the cemetery. Its branches extended parallel to the ground and about seven feet above it in all directions. It was a magnet for all the boys because once a person reached the first layer of branches he could climb forever. I told Mom where I would be and headed for the tree. I didn't know many of the other boys – girls didn't climb trees on Memorial Day in 1942 – but I began to work myself up into the branches until all of the climbers hung securely in the space we claimed. From a distance, the tree must have looked like it had just sprouted overgrown fruit, most of it dressed in bib overhauls.

I could hear the speeches, but didn't pay much attention. However, I did pay attention to the traditional things that made Memorial Day a special time across the country. Veterans, mostly from World War I, in their military uniforms solemnly presented the colors. Other uniformed men fired a 21-gun salute with their rifles. Another man in uniform played "Taps" on his trumpet. It was all part of solemn ceremony that paid tribute to everyone who was serving now in World War II as well as those who had served in past military conflicts, particularly those who had died in battle.

When the program was over and the speakers were gone, I returned to my family for the best part of the day. Dad spread a big blanket on the ground between some tombstones, and Mom opened our picnic basket. What a feast we had, starting with the fried chicken, killed and dressed the day before and fried only a few hours earlier. Then Mom took out the potato salad, made that morning and chilled in the icebox until we left the house. That was followed by a bowl of baked beans. All of this was eaten on our oldest china plates (some of them were chipped) with silverware from our cupboards at home. Paper plates had been invented in 1904, but they cost too much money for our family's feeble finances.

Besides, the war had brought us rationing. Gasoline and tires were strictly limited, although farmers had a gasoline exemption so their tractors would have the fuel they needed for planting, cultivation, and harvest. That was a blessing because we sometimes filled our car's gas tank from that supply if we were running short on rationing coupons. Sugar, flour, butter, coffee, and meat were restricted, and purchasing many other products also required ration cards.

But our Memorial Day lunch in the cemetery wasn't over yet. In fact, the best was yet to come. It was too early for strawberries, cherries weren't ripe enough to pick, we didn't grow blueberries, it was hard to grow peaches successfully in northern Illinois, and apples wouldn't ripen until early fall. But rhubarb was in the peak of its season. Rhubarb pie was the Memorial Day dessert, and it was delicious.

After this sumptuous lunch, Mom packed up the dishes and any left-overs, and folded up the blanket. Sometimes conversations would start between Mom and Dad and friends and neighbors who were also attending the celebration. But by no later than 4:00 p.m. we would load up our car and head home to give us time to change our clothes and milk the cows on schedule.

Keeping Busy Weeding

I liked to weed in the garden. My assignments for weeding would usually come when the weeds — big things like button weeds, lambs quarters, pig weed, smart weed, giant ragweed, milkweed, thistles and a few others I can't remember — would get so big they would form a partially shady hiding place once I had worked my way a few feet into the patch.

Usually, I only had to pull them, getting hold of the main stem down close to the ground and giving the plant a strong side-ways yank. Most of these weeds did not have a deep root system and were in loose soil, so it was not hard to pull them out. If they were weeds with a taproot, I had to stand up, grab the weed close to the ground, and pull straight up. If that didn't work, I had a tiling spade handy so that with one, well aimed stroke, I could cut the roots a couple of inches under the ground. (A tiling spade is short handled and has a blade about five inches wide and 14 to 16 inches long.) After I pulled or cut off the weeds, I laid them down in systematic order to form a fresh green pad that I could kneel or sit on.

Two of the weeds — milkweed and bull thistles — were particularly problematic. Whenever a leaf or a stem of milkweed is broken, it oozes a milky, sticky, white sap (hence, its name). That sap was not allergenic, but if it got on my hands, it was a mess. Bull thistles, of course, had large and very sharp thorns. I learned to work up the main stem from the ground, folding the thorny leaves up as I moved up the stalk. That moved most of the thorns out of the way, and I could get the leverage to pull the thistle, or if it were too big, cut it off under the ground with the tiling spade. Weeding these kinds of plants required work gloves. It didn't take long for me to learn that leather gloves were better than cloth.

The weeds themselves were interesting in the way they grew, how big they got, the different shapes of the leaves, and the different colors of green. Although my folks told me the names of some of them right away, I didn't really learn how to identify most of them until I became a member of competitive plant and seed identification teams in high school when I was a member of FFA (Future Farmers of America) taking vocational agriculture classes.

Pulling weeds also gave me an introductory course in entomology. The bugs and worms I uncovered or lifted out of the ground were sometimes as interesting as the weeds. However, to study such creatures for long would make me look like I wasn't busy, so I couldn't do that until I had pulled enough weeds to form a kind of hiding place in the middle of the patch. Most of the weeds I pulled were often three to five feet high.

But the thing that made weeding patches of big weeds the most fun was that my parents and I could all easily see signs of progress. When I would start on a new patch, it might look like it would take days to finish the job. However, because each weed had grown so big that it took up a lot of space, I did not have to pull many to make it look like I had been working fast and furiously for a long time. It was always helpful to leave that kind of impression if I could. Mom and Dad knew that, of course, but allowed this little fiction to continue.

Cracking Walnuts

One of my worst jobs when I was an adolescent was cracking walnuts. Several walnut trees bordered our large vegetable garden on its north edge. The garden was just south of our outdoor toilet.

Every fall those trees dropped hundreds of nuts on the ground, and Mom would insist that they had to be picked up and broken open to get the little black walnuts that hid beneath their husks and their shell. Walnuts were too expensive for us to buy in the store. The only way Mom would have them for baking was for us to harvest them ourselves. (Although English walnuts had a much thinner shell and were much easier to crack, they were far too expensive to enhance Mom's cookies, and they were usually only available around Christmas time.)

The harvesting of walnuts includes several problems. First, when they drop from the trees they are covered with a soft husk about a quarter of an inch thick. That husk is oily. It left a dark stain on my hands and just about anything else that it touched that was almost impossible to wash off. Walnut stains really had to wear off over the course of a couple of weeks.

But removing the husk is only the first problem. The second is breaking through that black shell that is hard as iron. I had to put each nut on a piece of concrete or an iron anvil and whack it hard with a hammer. If I didn't whack it hard enough and dead center it was likely to fly away like a small cannon ball without showing a dent. If I hit it too hard, I had a useless bunch of nut mush in front of me.

But hitting the nut just right didn't really solve all my problems either. Because then I had a couple of hard pieces lying in front of me that had to have the little pieces of nutmeat pulled out of them with a metal pick before they could be deposited in a jar. It took a long time to see much progress. I have to admit, though, that on those few years when my walnut cracking was reasonably successful, the cookies and cakes Mom baked them in were really good.

The Telltale Financial Summary

I knew from an early age that we weren't rich when we lived in the old house with an outdoor toilet, but I never thought we were much different from most of our neighbors and friends, and I didn't really think we were poor. But we were — at least financially.

But I never knew how poor we were until after Mom died and my sisters and brother and I found a one-page, hand-written summary of one year's finances for the farm where I grew up, the one on the north side of the 160 acres. Unfortunately, the page was not dated, but as far as I can determine by studying comparable grain prices, it had to be sometime in the mid- to late-'30s, the period when the country was still coming out of the Great Depression and much of the Midwestern farmland, particularly Nebraska, Kansas, and Oklahoma, was known as the Dustbowl, dried and blown almost out of existence as farmland by the hot, dust-laden winds of the great drought.

A summary of that hand-written financial statement follows:

In the year of the record, Dad and Mom had raised 26 acres of corn, 20 acres of oats, and 12 acres of hay. Three crops from 58 acres, their share of the farm's 160 acres, nearly all of it tillable, made up the total production allotted to Dad and Mom. Fifty-eight acres, their share, was a bit more than 36 percent of the 160-acre farm. Dad and Mom also had about 12 acres of blue grass pasture that bordered a small creek on both sides. That raised the total acreage for Dad and Mom to about 70 acres, a total of 44 percent of the 160 acres. The approximately five acres taken up by the land occupied by the buildings and the garden raised the total acreage allocated to Dad and Mom to 75 acres, or 47 percent of the total farm.

The corn yielded 56 bushels per acre for a total yield of 1,456 bushels; the oats yielded 32 bushels per acre for a total of 640 bushels. They sold 487 bushels of corn for

$191.77 (a little less than $.40 a bushel), and 150 bushels of oats for $36.00 ($.24 a bushel). The total income from grain sales for the year was $227.77.

Dairy products they sold included 1,000 pounds of cream (processed every night with a hand-cranked separator and shipped to Chicago by train in five-gallon cans every couple of days) for $70 ($.07 a pound); two calves for $32 ($16 each); 200 poultry (usually beheaded by Dad with an ax and hand dressed by Mom, although Mom occasionally also killed them) for $150 ($.75 a chicken); 300 dozen eggs (most often shipped to Chicago by truck in 30-dozen crates) for $65 (an average of a little less than $.21 a dozen). The total for dairy and poultry income for the year was $317.

Expenses added up like this: Cash for farm operation, $196; cash for family operating expenses, $144; capital goods purchased, $70.45; paid on debts, $250 (no indication of what the debts were). All the expenses listed totaled $660.45.

The cash for farm and family operating expenses probably included (although it's not itemized) groceries, gasoline and other car and tractor expenses, kerosene for lanterns and lights (we did not yet have electricity), coal for the furnace, fencing materials, and tools. The only fertilizer used was manure from the livestock.

Nothing was included for the cost of housing. Nothing was included for entertainment or eating out because that never happened. However, Mom and Dad still always found something to support their church (Immanuel Lutheran in Dixon) and a number of other charities.

Dad using a borrowed John Deere tractor to pull an early combine trying to pick up oats after wind and rain had flattened the crop to the ground, a procedure that usually yielded only about half the expected crop.

Income from employment totaled $137.00. (The employment is not specified. It might have been income from Mom's nursing at Dixon Hospital and/or from Dad's working in the wire manufacturing factory in Dixon.)

Subtracting the total spent of $660.45 from the total income of $681.77, gave Mom and Dad a balance for the year of $21.32 (not quite $.06 a day). As far as I know, Dad and Mom had no right of ownership in any of the land.

The saving graces were that meat was provided by butchering one or more of our own hogs and other livestock through the year and raising a big garden for fresh vegetables and fruit during the summer and canned vegetables and fruit throughout the rest of the year.

A website called "living history farm," a review of farm life in Nebraska during the Great Depression, reports that corn sold for $.83 a bushel in 1928 and $.25 or $.26 a bushel in 1932. That helps to date Mom's and Dad's financial statement as sometime in the mid- to late-'30s. The website also indicates that some farmers in Nebraska actually lost money every year in the first years after the Depression, probably due to the ravages of the Dustbowl. Even without being effected by the Dustbowl, I'm sure the same was true for many farmers in Illinois.

I learned about chasing chickens and collecting eggs from a very early age.

A quote from the "living history farm" website helps to describe the time: "Most farmers during the '30s grew several crops, a large garden, and a few cows or hogs. As Carla Due remembers, "A farmer's main crop might have been corn or wheat, but in between harvest times cream and eggs were the source of cash during the '30s. 'That was our money flow,' Carla says. Millie Opitz remembers what happened when they spilled the can of cream on the way to town. 'There went our money for gas and groceries.'"

Mom and Dad continued to supplement the farm's income with chickens, eggs, and berries until I was in college. Every weekend they would carry a few dozen eggs, a few dressed chickens, and a few quarts of berries or cherries to long-time customers in Dixon. I don't know how much they sold all that produce for, but I remember that it was usually a few cents less than their customers would have paid in the grocery store.

The Houses Where We Lived

Dad's father was second generation offspring of immigrant German stock. He offered Mom and Dad a place to live in a set of buildings on their farm. The "free" house, which came with a barn, a corn crib, a chicken house, a combination garage and utility shed, and a 35-foot-tall windmill, was part of an unwritten but understood arrangement of shared work and profits. It was neither a good, nor a fair, bargain. The house was without electricity or running water. The toilet was about 75 feet southeast from the back door. Work on the farm was substantial. The profits, going all the way through the Depression, were not.

In fact, it was a nearly feudal arrangement similar to what had been standard in rural Germany in which farmers who did not own any land barely survived contracts and conditions that provided only enough for subsistence.

I remember overhearing snatches of conversation between Dad and Mom. Time after time she pleaded with him to stand up against his father for his right to a bigger share of the profits for a smaller share of the work. But Dad would not – could not – raise the question in any substantive way. Somehow, to Dad it would have been less than honoring his parents to have raised such a significant question and ask for a change in the circumstances.

The status quo remained in force until Dad's father died, and he and Mom inherited all of the farm as their own and were able to move into Grandpa's and Grandma's house. That house had been built in 1922 on the south side of the 160 acres along a road (now

Our house on the Lincoln Highway

blacktop, probably gravel then) that bisected Nachusa and connected highways U.S. 30 with U.S. 52.

I was a junior in high school when we made the move from the house on the Lincoln Highway to what had been Grandma and Grandpa's house. I remember walking around in this cavernous house,

particularly the upstairs, trying to assimilate the knowledge that these large, bright spaces without drafts were now parts of my home, and the upstairs bedroom on the northeast corner of the house would be my very own room with my own bed, my own dresser, my own desk, and a door that

Grandpa and Grandma Gonnerman's house, into which we moved when I was in high school.

closed. This would be the home I would be living in until I went to college in two years, a short time, but better than no time at all.

The new house was tight; no snow would sift through any of those windows to coat my bed at night. It was modern; it had been

The buildings on the farm where Grandpa and Grandma Gonnerman lived, where we moved, were all new in 1929 (l-r): the corner of the barn, the hog shed, the corn crib, the machine shed, and the chicken house. Note that one of the Gonnerman dogs is pulling a child across the yard on a sled. Here the yard is almost completely without trees. That would be remedied with lots of tree plantings.

A barn on the farm of one of Ruth's neighbors in Michigan. The threshing crew is loading bundles of grain into the thresher while another wagon waits with another load of bundles.

wired throughout for electricity that could be turned on and off with push-button switches; and it had both hot and cold running water and a bathroom with a large bathtub standing on balls in raptors' talons. It would be warm in winter with a large coal-burning furnace in the basement that supplied heat to every corner of every room, and cool in summer with many large screened windows that opened easily on both the first and second floors. It even had a large, screened-in, front porch across the whole east side of the lower level.

It was a different world from that place only a mile away which our family had endured for 15 years. Now, we had moved away from that place forever. It was a new beginning and a new lifestyle. We had escaped the deprivations of the frontier and become part of the modern society that lived with comfort and convenience.

In addition to the modern house, the farm site included a two-car garage, a large barn, a corn crib, a machine shed, a hog house, a chicken house, and a milk house, but no windmill. The walls of the garage, chicken house, and hog house were made of an ochre-colored kiln-fired construction block. An electric pump and pressure tank supplied the water from a well. The farmstead also had a large apple orchard and a formal garden — the work of Dad's mother — with a small rock-edged, cement fish pond, and a cherry tree. This idyllic setting also had one more gem — a small grape arbor with red and black raspberries.

The well was deep and the water ran cold, but it had one problem. The water included so much iron that it would turn the inside of a steel milk pail — or any other vessel — red in half an hour. And once a bucket was dyed red by that water it was almost impossible to get clean again. One neighbor enjoyed saying, "Your water is so hard you have to chew it to swallow it." He was almost right.

TALE OF TWO HOUSES

*Together, Dad and Mom lived
through the experience of several
major agricultural changes.*

TALE OF TWO HOUSES

The farm where I grew up was L-shaped, with the top of the L pointed north and the bottom line of the L pointed east. The farm included 160 acres divided just about in half by the Chicago and Northwestern Railroad near the point where the top and bottom halves of the L joined. The railroad included two sets of tracks that carried both passenger and freight trains.

At the top of the L ran U.S. Highway 30, better known in the days when Mom and Dad first lived there as the Lincoln Highway. A small creek, often nearly dry in the summertime, bisected the top part of the L about a quarter of a mile north of the railroad tracks. Two large willow trees grew in a pasture on the banks of the creek. They were located about half way between the two edges of the top of the L and were easy to get to by using a fenced lane that kept our cows out of grain fields as they went back and forth from the pasture to the barn.

My brother and sisters and I, and cousins who sometimes visited, enjoyed playing in those willow trees that had large, low branches almost parallel to the ground. Our play was even more fun if the creek had water running in it. No fish lived in the creek, but it held lots of frogs, toads, a few small turtles, and occasionally salamanders. The area was also home to a few garter

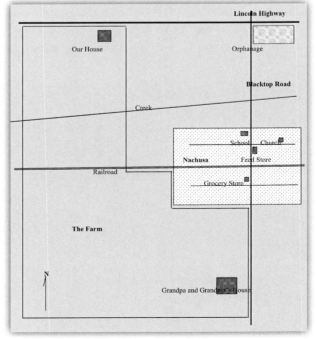

snakes. We spent many hours having fun in and around the willow trees. They also provided just the right size of green twigs (about as big as your little finger) to carve out simple whistles.

The Village of Nachusa

The small village of Nachusa (about 150 people) sat in the inside corner of the L formed by our farm. The town was bisected east to west by the railroad and north to south by a blacktop road that led from Highway 30 to Highway 52 a few miles to the south. Two gravel streets intersected the blacktop road, one on each side of the railroad.

Nachusa included a small grocery store, a post office, a grain elevator and feed store, a Lutheran Church (we didn't go there because it was a Lutheran Church in America (LCA) congregation and that "wasn't our kind") and a one-room elementary school. I don't remember any other commercial or public buildings.

The grocery store was an interesting place. Not even close to the supermarkets that we shop in today, it was a small converted house with a coal-burning heating stove right in the middle of the large room that served as the store. It had one counter to the right as you came in the door. The tin cans, glass bottles, and cardboard boxes (no plastic in those days) that held the food were all arranged on shelves – some of them so high they could not be reached without a ladder – all around the interior walls.

The one-room school in Nachusa was located at the north edge of the village. Gonnerman children studied there for the first six years of their education. Aunt Grace, Mom's sister, was our very good teacher.

Sometimes, I would be sent to the store with a shopping list from Mom. The grocer or his wife (I don't remember their names) would take the list, gather all the items on it and put them on the counter, add them all up, put that amount on the family bill, and put the groceries in a bag for me to carry nearly a mile to home either by walking or by riding my bicycle.

A circle of three or four chairs sat around the stove and people from town often were sitting in them talking about the weather, the crops, who was sick and who had died, and otherwise passing the time of day. Everybody in town knew everybody else, even at a young age, so whoever was sitting in those chairs would always greet me, ask how I was, how my folks were, and what we were doing. It was always fun to go to the grocery store in Nachusa.

Our farm had two sets of buildings.

One set was at the end of the piece of the L that bordered the blacktop south of Nachusa. The buildings included a big, square, two-story, white house with a full basement and a large attic. It had four big main rooms on both the first and second floors, a screened in porch all the way across the front on the east side, and two smaller porches, one on top of the other, in the southwest corner. It had electric lights, running water and a bathroom upstairs. It had been built in 1922 and was like a lot of houses that anchored farmsteads across the Midwest. Grandma and Grandpa Gonnerman lived there.

Our house on the Lincoln Highway was old and primitive. The exterior was covered with a kind of thick tar-paper that was designed to look like light brown bricks. It looked OK until parts of it would tear and be whipped by the wind. Then it began to look tacky.

The house was T-shaped. The top line of the T was two sto-

The house on the Lincoln Highway where the family lived from 1932 to 1949.

The porch ran along the back of the house on the Lincoln Highway, with an area enclosed with screen and a door to the dining room.

ries with a basement (we called it a cellar) under it. It ran north/south. The bottom line of the T was only one story running east/west. A porch ran along the back of the house, running east/west. The far west end of the porch floor had a large door that lifted up to provide access to a staircase going down into the cellar. We could not get into the cellar from inside the house. A small portion of the east end of the porch was enclosed with screen and included a door to the dining room when we faced north, and a door to a kind of wash up room and kitchen/pantry when we faced east.

Between the door to the cellar and the screened portion of the porch was another, smaller door in the floor. When we lifted that door we looked down into a brick cistern that collected water that flowed off the roof when it rained. That water was used for washing and bathing. We got it with a small hand pump in the wash room and kitchen/pantry east of the porch.

A small tool and storage shed stood about 30 feet south of the west end of the porch. When we looked southeast from the porch we saw a very important little building about 75 feet away. It was our outdoor toilet. We did not have a bathroom inside the house. The toilet had two holes so that it could be used by two people at one time – although I never saw that happen. Most of the time, the toilet paper consisted of the pages from old catalogs and magazines that were stacked out there. That saved money since the catalog pages were a substitute for toilet paper and gave us something to read while we were doing our business.

The outdoor toilet wasn't much of a problem during spring, summer and fall. In fact, it could be a rather pleasant place to sit (or sometimes just get out of sight). The winter, however, was a different matter. No one stayed in that outdoor toilet long when the temperature got down below freezing – and sometimes below zero. Thankfully, we were allowed to use a ceramic pot or a tin pail inside at night during the winter. Then someone would be given the chore of carrying that portable pot out to the toilet to empty it every morning.

When we entered the house from the porch, we stepped into a room that was about 16 feet square. To the right was a wood burning cook stove. Mom worked over that stove to do all the cooking. It had a five-gallon reservoir that was used to heat water for our baths as well as for washing clothes. During cold weather, the cook stove was kept hot to help heat the room. To the left was the nicest piece of furniture my folks owned, a buffet on high legs.

Directly ahead against the north wall of the room was a small stand that held our radio. We spent many hours gathered around the radio after the chores had been finished at night, sitting on chairs or on the linoleum floor, listening to a big variety of 15-minute programs. They included "Superman," "The Green Hornet," "The Shadow Knows," "Jack Armstrong: All American Boy," "The Lone Ranger," "Sergeant Preston of the Yukon and His Wonder Dog King," "The FBI in Peace and War," "Fibber McGee and Molly," "Jack Benny," "Amos and Andy," "Burns and Allen," and a few others I can't remember. We didn't need television to see what was happening. The sound effects helped our imaginations envision exactly what our radio heroes were going through.

The center of the room was dominated by a big table. It was almost square and could be extended with extra leaves when we had company. We ate all our meals at that table, and all of us kids did all of our homework there. The only lights we had for anything we did – there or anywhere else in the house or on the farm– were kerosene lamps and lanterns. One lamp was set in the middle of the table to give all of us enough light to read our schoolbooks and write out our assignments for school. One of the subjects I remember most clearly while studying at that table is Latin. (I now have that kerosene "study lamp" in our den as a reminder of those early days.)

If we turned to the right as we entered the dining room, we came to the inside door to the wash room and kitchen/pantry. A counter ran the full length of the room on the south wall with a sink under the pump on the west end. That's where most of the vegetables and fruits were brought from our garden to be washed and prepared for cooking or canning. We used the water pumped from the cistern for washing, but we didn't drink it. Drinking water, kept in a covered pail near that little pump, came from the well under the windmill about 75 yards west of the house. We had to pump that water by hand if the wind wasn't blowing to power the windmill.

Straight ahead, in the northwest corner of the room, the "front door," used only in the summer time, opened onto a small porch on the north side of the house.

Also in the northwest corner, on the west (left) side of the room, was a doorway that took us from the dining room into the living room. The living room included a couch and a few chairs, but the most important piece of furniture was the coal stove with small Isinglass windows in the door. (Isinglass is a thin sheet of transparent mica, a mineral that crystallizes into thin, somewhat flexible layers that are resistant to heat.) The stove was about three and a half feet square and about five feet high. A stovepipe came out the back and went into the chimney in the wall behind the stove.

That stove burned coal, although we would occasionally throw in small logs if we were low on coal and didn't have the money to buy any more right then. It was the only "furnace" in the house other than the kitchen cook stove. Sometimes on winter nights, we could feel the wind blowing through the walls around the windows, sucking the heat out of the room, and we would get cold pretty fast if we got more than eight to ten feet away from the stove. If the winter wind was blowing hard, we could sometimes feel a breeze blowing right through the single pane glass in the windows.

Dad would always "build" the Christmas tree in the northeast corner of the living room. It was the perfect place for it. My family had no extra money when I was growing up. If it wasn't a necessity, we didn't buy it, and some necessities were manufactured from things already available around the farm. That included our Christmas tree.

I can't remember that we ever bought a tree until we moved into Grandma and Grandpa Gonnerman's house. Dad built our tree in a corner of the living room every year. The farmstead where his mom and dad lived on the other side of Nachusa had a spruce windbreak around the west and north sides of the building site. Those spruce trees were all about 30 feet tall. Dad would cut branches off the lower parts of a few of those trees, bring them home and arrange them in layers stuck into a five-gallon cream can. He started at the bottom and built a kind of branch pyramid until the last branch added was standing straight up in the can and formed the top of the manufactured tree.

The result really looked like an evergreen tree that might have been cut out of the woods or purchased in a Christmas tree lot.

When the tree was trimmed, candle holders with real candles were the last decorations added. They took the place of electric lights. The candles were lit only a few times, when all members of the family were present. Either Mom or Dad would be holding a bucket full of water or standing very close to one. The older the tree got, of course, the dryer it became and the more dangerous it was as a fire hazard. Everyone watched it very carefully to make sure the flames on the candles did not get too close to the pine needles. I don't know why Dad never thought to put water in the cream can to extend the life of those branches.

I didn't realize then just how dangerous burning candles were on a Christmas tree. But I certainly remember how beautiful they were.

As we stood in the doorway to the living room, two doors were on our left. The first opened on a stairway that went upstairs. The second opened into Mom's and Dad's bedroom. The only time any of the children got to spend time in Mom's and Dad's bedroom was during a day when we were sick and Mom could look in on us and take care of us easier if she didn't have to run up and down the stairs.

When we went up the stairs, we found two bedrooms. The first, on the south end of the second floor, was the smallest, and we had to go through it to get to the second. It also had a banister running almost its full width so that we wouldn't fall down the stairwell.

The second bedroom was about twice as big as the first. The wall that separated the two bedrooms also included the chimney. The heat that radiated through the brick walls of the chimney was the only heat for both of the upstairs bedrooms except for a little warmth that seeped up through the floor from the furnace in the room below. On really cold nights, Mom and Dad would sometimes let the stairwell door open so a little heat could come up that way.

Each upstairs bedroom had one window. The one in the small bedroom was in the south wall and looked out over the roof of the porch. The window in the large bedroom was in the north wall and looked out over the Lincoln Highway, only about 150 feet away across the front yard. The ceiling followed the roofline, sloping toward the west and east walls and meeting them only about four feet above the floor.

My sisters, Donna and Mary Ann, shared the small room, which was a little warmer on a bright day after the sun had been shining in their window. I got to be all alone in the big bedroom until my brother Paul was born in 1941. It was bigger than my sisters' room, but it was also darker and colder. I slept in a double bed. During the summer it could be pretty warm, even with the window open, so I often didn't use any covers.

During the winter, however, my bedroom could get very cold. When that happened, I slept under several layers of blankets and quilts so I don't remember ever being cold until I had to get out of bed in the morning to get dressed. On the coldest days I would gather my clothes into a ball, rush downstairs, and dress hurriedly while standing close to the heating stove in the living room – or sometimes by the cooking stove in the kitchen if the fire in the heating stove had not yet been poked alive.

The whole house got cold inside during the harshest days of winter. I remember more than once when I woke up and found a fine sifting of snow on the foot end of my bed. It had filtered right through thin spaces around the frames of the window. I also remember that sometimes the first one into the wash room off the kitchen/pantry might find a thin coating of ice on the pail of drinking water. Maybe that's why I like ice water so much.

Bath time was a special time in our house along the Lincoln Highway. First, we bathed only on Saturday nights. Second, our tub was a galvanized metal tub that was only about three and a half feet across and about 14 inches deep. The water, of course, was hand pumped from our cistern into a pail. The pails were then emptied into the reservoir in the cook stove until it was full. Another pail or two of cold water would be pumped to have on hand to cool the bath water if it were too hot. Then we would wait for the water in the reservoir to get hot. It didn't take long.

In the summer, we would sometimes set the tub outside on the lawn and carry the water out to it. That was great, because we never had to worry about splashing and getting the floor wet. Of course, we used a lot more water that way.

But in the winter, the process changed dramatically. The tub would be placed only a few feet from the front of the stove. Then the door to the oven would be left open to provide a little extra warmth. Mom – and sometimes Dad – would use a cooking pan to dip hot water out of the reservoir and put enough into the tub to make it four or five inches deep. If it was too hot, they would add cold water until it was still hot but comfortable.

The youngest child would be bathed first. The younger you were, the more help you got from Mom. She was anything but gentle in her campaign to eliminate dirt from ears, neck, face, hands, elbows, knees, feet, and anything else that looked like it might hold the least little bit of grime. When the youngest was finished, that one would hop out of the tub, be wrapped in a towel, and start to dry off in the warmth of the open oven.

The water was checked for temperature, warmed up as needed with more not quite boiling water from the reservoir, and then the second youngest child would step in. The water wasn't changed, just warmed up.

The process would be repeated until it was my turn. By now, at least after Mary Ann was born, there were four of us and the water had changed to a rather ugly shade of gray. I don't remember exactly when Mom stopped washing me and let me bathe myself, but I'm sure it wasn't until a couple of years after I thought I was old enough to do it alone.

After all of us children were asleep, Mom and Dad would follow the same procedure for themselves. I am certain, however, that they started over with clean water.

We finally got electricity on our farm on the Lincoln Highway about the time I was in eighth grade. However, as far as I can remember the first and only thing we used that electricity for before we moved to the house that had been Grandma and Grandpa's was an electric motor to power the pump instead of the windmill.

Now, we didn't have to depend only on the wind any longer. We could simply flip a switch fastened to one of the legs of the windmill (it was left standing over the well for many years), and we could pump water through pipes and hoses all the way to the water tank on the other side of the barn for our cows and pigs. That was a big improvement over having to pump all that water by hand when the wind wasn't blowing.

It was fun in the summertime to hold the hose that was running into the livestock tank up to your mouth, take deep drinks of that really cold water, and let it splash wildly all over your face.

I don't remember that any of the buildings had electric lights installed in them before we moved away from the Lincoln Highway to the other side of the farm.

I always liked gardening, particularly with flowers.

My inspiration was Grandma Gonnerman and the formal garden she maintained so beautifully. The central point of interest in Grandma's garden was an oblong fishpond with water lilies. The pond was full of tadpoles for much of the summer. All the children in the extended family enjoyed playing in the water while kneeling along the pond's edge, watching the fish, and catching tadpoles in the shallow end of that pool.

The goldfish were always taken in and put in an old bathtub in the basement before the pool froze in the fall. They would be taken back out to the pool in the spring when the danger of freezing was past.

A low grape arbor made up of short posts and smooth wires in two parallel rows was filled with black raspberry bushes as well as grapevines. I used to enjoy going to Grandma Gonnerman's, finding a way to "hide" myself down among the black raspberry bushes, and feast on those plump, black, sweet berries that nearly melted in your mouth.

A red cherry tree always produced lots of slightly sour cherries, and a family of wrens nested in an old coffeepot hanging from a branch year after year. Most of the flowerbeds were rectangular and held what seemed like every imaginable flower that would grow in northern Illinois. One bed was planted exclusively with roses.

The entire layout – about 50 yards long and 25 yards wide, was separated from the house on the north side by an arborvitae hedge. An apple orchard was on the north side of the garden, protected by a spruce tree windbreak. The flower garden was on the east side of the grape arbor. The ground on the west side was reserved for a vegetable garden.

Everything – flowers, vegetables, arbor – was weedless, and the grass around the beds was trimmed in clean, straight lines.

When I was a freshman in high school, two years before we would move to the farm house and yard that Grandmother Gonnerman had tended so lovingly for so many years, I received permission from Mom and Dad to try to establish a similar kind of flower garden where we lived in the old house on the Lincoln Highway. My garden and the landscaping that went with it was an additional 4-H project.

A tall grape arbor, with beams carrying vines over the top to form a kind of roof, was already in place on the west end of the space I was allowed to use. I laid out rectangular beds and planted them with a mixture of perennials and annuals that provided color and cut flowers all year. Most of the perennials came as cuttings or roots from existing plants in other places. Some of them came from Grandma Gonnerman's garden.

The space between the beds was seeded with grass, and by the middle of the first summer, it was good lawn, trimmed carefully in straight lines around each of the beds. I was pleased, and my folks were too.

I did not know it then, but that somewhat formal flower garden was a kind of trial project for the gardens and terraces I was able to plan, plant, and enjoy in Burnsville and Northfield, Minnesota.

My lawn care and gardening experience was not limited to my own flower beds and the grass that separated them. I remember that from the time I was eight or nine years old I was expected to mow the lawn. At first we had a hand mower. Then we finally got a power mower. But whichever mower was available, I enjoyed the work, setting up routes and patterns through the grass to make the work most efficient and effective, and reveling in the change for the better every mowing made.

One part of lawn maintenance, however, was not so enjoyable. Our yard was surrounded by a picket fence that needed to be painted white at least every other year. At first, I painted it working together with Mom and Dad. Then, when I was about ten, it became my responsibility to paint that fence by myself. My brother and sisters weren't old enough to help – in fact Mary Ann wasn't even born yet.

Painting a picket fence is one of the most monotonous jobs a young person could have. Not only did all four sides of every picket need to be painted, but also the two by four supporting pieces. Besides that, the tops of our pickets were cut with a decorative pattern that substantially increased the number of brush strokes needed to cover all the surfaces completely. It might have been one of the few jobs I had that came close to being boring. Progress was always extremely slow.

I vowed then that if I ever had a picket fence of my own I would never paint it. And I never did. (Once a fence is painted it needs to be repainted every couple of years to continue to look good. If it's never painted, natural aging takes its own course.)

My childhood home was certainly humble by today's standards. But when I think back on those days, I remember most fondly that the lessons I learned were not about the disadvantages of poverty or the presumed advantage of privilege. Rather, they were the lessons of sensitivity and acceptance and creativity and independence and gratefulness and faith that I think sometimes Mom and Dad didn't even know they were teaching when I learned them.

Grandma Gonnerman died on November 5, 1950, and Grandpa Gonnerman died almost five years to the day later on November 1, 1955. Both Grandma and Grandpa had moved out of the house in 1949 because of ill health. We moved from our house on the north end of the L on the Lincoln Highway to their much bigger and more modern house that same year. I was a junior in high school.

The move from our house on the Lincoln Highway to the big white house Grandpa and Grandma Gonnerman had built in 1922 was an almost unbelievable transition. We moved from a house that was almost always cold in the winter to a house where every room was comfortable all of the time. We moved from filling and lighting kerosene lights and lanterns to pushing a button on a light switch to turn on a light in whatever room we entered. We moved from a basement that was not accessible unless we went outside to a basement that we could go to easily by simply descending a wide staircase available through a door in the center of the house. Maybe most importantly, we moved from an outdoor toilet to a large bathroom that had not only a toilet but also a sink and bathtub, both with running hot and cold water.

In addition to the house, the farm site included a garage and a chicken house made of kiln-dried umber-colored ceramic blocks, a large barn, a corn crib, a machine shed, a hog house, and a milk house, but no windmill. An electric pump and pressure tank supplied the water from a deep well. It also had, as I've already described, a large apple orchard and a formal garden – the work of Dad's mother – with a fish pond and a cherry tree. This idyllic setting also included a small grape arbor with red and black raspberries.

We had moved to another world.

Suddenly, Mom had traded a wood-fired cook stove for four electric burners and an electric oven. Hot and cold running water splashed from the faucet at her elbow and all of the waste water disappeared into the septic system. She could now store perishable foods in the electric refrigerator without worrying about whether there was enough ice to keep it cold. She had cabinets and drawers in which to organize all of her cooking utensils and all of the dishes that would be used day to day. A little later she had a dishwasher that would wash every dish and piece of flatware and every utensil while she did something else.

The kitchen and the entry (with a sink convenient for cleaning up when someone came in from the fields or the garden) made up one quarter of the main floor. The other three rooms were all about the same size – a dining room with built in china cabinets with glass doors, the living room which held the TV (another new experience) exited to the screened in front porch, and the "parlor" where anyone could play the piano.

The upstairs held four large bedrooms in addition to the bathroom, with a wide central hall and a porch off the master bedroom on the southwest corner. All of the bedrooms were corner rooms about the same size, and all had two large windows. Sisters Donna and Mary Ann shared the room on the southeast corner, brother Paul had the northwest room, and I was in the northeast corner. Making that change and having my own room for the first time in my life was something close to heaven.

A large attic, accessible with a wide staircase, was voluminous and well lit through the windows in three dormers as well as electric lights. It was a magnificent house, particularly after our experiences in the house on the Lincoln Highway.

The other great thing about Grandpa and Grandma Gonnerman's house was the terrific flower and vegetable gardens and fruit orchard I described earlier. Grandma had taken care of the gardens. Grandpa did most of the work on the orchard.

Often, when I had walked into the house when Grandma and Grandpa still lived there, the first thing I noticed was the wonderful aroma of fresh baking. Grandma was always making bread, or cookies, or pies, or kuchen (a German coffeecake with fruit and cream and sugar on the top). Anyone who went in the house soon after Grandma had taken something out of the oven would always receive at least one piece, often with homemade butter.

She also tried to teach me German, but the only thing I remember from those brief teaching sessions is *"brot,"* the German word for bread. I wish I would have spent more time learning German from her. It would have been a great advantage later on, particularly when I took German at Wartburg College.

I never did well in my study of German. I studied the language for a year and half during my first two years at Wartburg College and often wished I had paid more attention to Grandma's attempts to teach me German. Wartburg had lots of students from the Dakotas and Wisconsin. They had learned German from their parents and grandparents when they were growing up and spoke it fluently. They blew the rest of us away in our German classes, and the little *Frau* who was our teacher loved them for it. Many of the rest of us in class did not fare so well.

Ruth and I visited Scandinavia, Germany, and England with all four children (Mark was 15 and David was six) in 1974. The first heritage stop was the Åland Islands from which Ruth's ancestors had immigrated. It was a great stop, not the least because many of the Swedish people who live in this giant archipelago of about 6,500 islands between Stockholm and Helsinki speak English. We found the farm from which Ruth's grandmother had immigrated to Michigan and also found the area from which her grandfather had come. All our children were impressed.

It was a different story when we arrived in Germany and began looking for the ancestral home of my family. I soon discovered that: first, not as many Germans spoke English as the Scandinavians; and second, my three semesters of college German were woefully inadequate. When I really worked at it, I might be able to struggle through the asking of a question, but there was no way I could understand the answer. The result was too embarrassing, and I gave up making the attempt which always ended in massive non-communication.

That came home in spades when we visited the little town of Wommen to learn more about our ancestry. Wommen shows up frequently in the Gonnerman genealogy. We entered Wommen with great anticipation. However, my lack of fluency in German became a major communications barrier. The pastor I found didn't speak English, and I had barely enough comprehension of German to understand that he was directing me to a nearby house and family that might have a connection to us.

As I walked back to the car I began to realize that if the pastor in this little town did not speak English it was quite unlikely that the person to whom he had directed me would not speak English either. I chickened out. I could not knock on the door of a complete stranger who most likely could not speak English and try to make a connection that would illuminate only a minuscule amount of family history. We drove around until we found a cemetery and got out to see if the memorial stones would give us any clues. They did. Some of the stones had familiar names – names similar to those on the membership roll of Immanuel Lutheran Church back in Dixon, Illinois, but no Gonnermans.

Our family had seen the place of our German ancestry, but had not filled in any of blanks regarding the people, the personalities, and the reasons for their immigration to the central United States. The visit had not been a complete failure, but it was a disappointment. Mildly satisfied that we had made some kind of connection to our German heritage, we left Wommen for our "splurge night" reservation in a castle on the Neckar River near Heidelberg.

The Farming Phenomenon

The major changes in farming Dad and Mom experienced added up to an agricultural revolution that took place in less than half a century. It was a revolution that rode on mind-bending changes in both the farmer and the farming.

First, the 160-acre family farm, a standard size in the Upper Midwest, had nearly disappeared by the time Mom and Dad retired. It was being replaced by gigantic farms of thousands of acres displacing hundreds of farm families who either retired or had to find their livelihood in places they had not known, doing work they often did not like.

A farm of only 160 acres, which had seemed more than adequate to support a family even in the Great Depression of the early thirties, just wasn't enough anymore to adequately support many families by the mid-sixties. Many 160-acre parcels were sold to farmers who had the vision and financing to buy up these quarter-of-a-section acreages, putting together single farms of one or more thousands of acres. And if they could not buy the land, they occasionally rented it with an arrangement where the owner and his family that owned it could continue to live in the house. Many farmers who did not have the capital to expand their acreage didn't have any choice except to quit farming and try something else.

Our farm followed that path. After Dad died, Mom rented out their acreage to Chuck Nussbaum, the neighbor across the road, while she still lived in the house. The neighbor's ancestry was Swiss, and he was one of the most efficient farmers I have ever known. He invited me into his machine shed one summer day in 1952 when I was home from college. It was a huge building that held much more machinery (all of it larger) than we had ever had at our farm.

Most astounding were the inner walls of that mammoth structure. They were lined with drawers along most of the building's length from just below my knees to just above my head. Every drawer was labeled, and every drawer held a different size bolt or nut or washer or nail or attachment or repair part that might be needed sometime in the daily work of operating his expanding farm. I have never seen anything to match it.

Mom and Chuck had an unwritten agreement (that's all that was needed back then) that when the Gonnerman farm might be sold he would have first chance at buying it. My siblings and I kept that agreement when Mom died in 1998. Chuck Nussbaum bought our land for a little more than $3,000 an acre, putting his tillable land at just about 2,000 acres.

Second, the costs of everything – machinery, seed, gasoline, insurance, taxes, land, loans – climbed beyond imagination. The larger land holders needed bigger and more powerful machines to work their larger acreages, and sometimes more than one tractor or other piece of machinery was bought at the same time because the landholder was hiring men (and occasionally women) to help him get the work done on time in season.

Third, pastured livestock almost disappeared, and the fence lines went down with them. When the fences went, so did the pheasants, quail, and rabbits. Wetlands were drained and plowed to plant. But wiser people saw that wetlands are necessary for clean water and flood control, so some farmers either did not drain them or put them back. It's a lot harder to put back a wetland than it is to drain one.

Fourth, when the livestock dwindled so did the most popular fertilizer available to the small farmer – manure. You don't have manure when you don't have herds of cattle or hogs or flocks of sheep or chickens. The manure spreader was an essential implement on the small farm. Late in every winter the farmer would park the manure spreader next to the barn door and begin the burdensome task of digging out the manure-laden bedding accumulated in the barn over the past three or four months. His preferred tool for digging out manure was a four- or five-tined fork before barn doors were enlarged and front end loaders on their tractors lessened some of the muscle work.

The manure spreader was a special wagon with an apron of steel bars that moved from front to back along the bottom when it was engaged with a lever. The steel bar apron pushed the manure to the back against three or four revolving spiked reels that tore the manure apart and kicked it out on the field in a broad swath of odorous black gunk as the spreader was pulled across the field behind a tractor. You never wanted to stand anywhere close to the back end of a manure spreader when it was in action. Manure on your clothes is messy and it makes you smell bad. But on the soil that gunk was like gold. It would fertilize the crops – corn, oats, soybeans – that would be planted in the spring.

(I saw a more modern manure spreader on a highway in late winter in 2013. It was a modified dump truck with the spreader mounted where the dump truck box would ordinarily be. It held at least twice as much manure as the spreaders in use when I was a teenager.)

Although some farmers might also add relatively inexpensive lime or phosphorus to the land, manure was free as long as the farmer had the animals to produce it. When livestock disappeared from the farming enterprise, more expensive commercial fertilizers took the place of the manure. From 1930 to 1939, the average annual consumption of commercial fertilizer in the United States totaled 6,599,913 tons. Only three decades later, the average annual consumption of fertilizer in the United States in 1960 to 1969 had increased to 32,373,713 tons, almost five times as much. And the cost had risen exponentially.

Fertilization was one of the primary factors in increased production. In 1930, 15 to 20 labor hours were required to produce one hundred bushels of wheat on five acres with a tractor, a three-bottom gang plow, a ten-foot tandem disk, a harrow, a 12-foot combine, and trucks. (Most farmers did not have a combine. They used a combination of McCormick reapers, muscle power from everyone in the family, and threshing machines.) Thirty-five years later, in 1965, five labor hours were required to produce 100 bushels of wheat on three and one-half acres using a tractor, a 12-foot plow, a 14-foot drill, a 14-foot self-propelled combine, and trucks.

Finally, "factory farms" are gradually (in some places, rapidly) replacing open range pasture in the Upper Midwest. Factory farms can produce a lot more beef or pork or veal or chicken or eggs in much less space with a much more efficient use of time and energy, but the potential for animal or poultry abuse is staggering. Long, low buildings, sometimes five to ten in a row and 100 yards long, disrupt the landscape of what used to be pasture land. They are usually set back a couple of hundred yards from the road because of the odors – noxious to some people – they create. The setbacks also make them less obvious to the expanding group of people who oppose them. Each set of buildings includes wall-to-wall pens with automatic feeding and watering, each holding several more hogs or calves or chickens than is imaginable by family farm standards.

The stench of manure ponds is a continuing community problem. Chickens confined in crowded cages lay eggs that roll to a shelf outside the wire boxes. The hens don't even have the luxury of a laying box. Herds of dairy cows numbering in the thousands are milked around the clock. Beef cattle are fattened in clusters of pens that each crowd in hundreds of animals. The self-sufficient small farm five-crop rotation – oats, hay, pasture, corn, beans – has been replaced on the large farms in the Midwest by a two-crop rotation of corn and soybeans.

Humane societies have become louder and more vociferous in their complaints regarding the treatment of animals housed too many to a too-small pen. Some of those same groups have made surreptitious videos of the crowded conditions and abusive treatment by workers who have not been trained and never before worked with any kind of livestock or poultry.

Incredibly, when those incriminating videos surfaced, the response of the factory farm owners was not to improve the treatment and conditions for the animals, but to seek state legislation that would make it illegal to videotape the horrendous conditions and inhumane handling. Some corporations such as McDonald's and Target have dropped the more abusive factory farm enterprises from the lists of their suppliers. Grocery stores such as Lund's and Byerly's have done the same. But it's a tough fight against many agricultural corporations who own the factory farm franchises.

The ruins of family farms stand everywhere as sad sentinels to the past – monuments to the failure of one of the most significant cultural institutions in United States history. Get off the interstate highways some Sunday afternoon and drive 20 miles in any direction past the city limits signs. Use country roads and count the number of farmsteads that are no longer inhabited or habitable. You will see one unpainted house after another in the Midwest. The glass in the windows is long gone, shreds of curtains flutter out of their openings. The remains of other buildings that once made up someone's farm home might still be there, barns, machine sheds, corn cribs, hog houses, chicken coops. You can see through some of the roofs, some have fallen down in a heap of decaying lumber and have been left where they fell as continuing eyesores and reminders of a different time. Some have been kept sturdy enough to still shelter a massive piece of machinery. Many are almost invisible because trees and bushes have not only grown up around them, but sometimes through the decaying roofs.

Two monumental buildings often mark the landscape as lonely reminders of what used to be.

The first is the isolated corncrib. It stands totally alone in the middle of a field. No driveway leads to its large double doors that used to roll on metal tracks. It hasn't held corn or any other grain for decades. It simply stands there, decaying in the wind and weather. The rain being shed off its leaky roof is almost like tears. Not a speck of paint colors its exterior surface of grey weathering boards rotting a little more every year until it falls in on itself, a tragic death of what had once been one of the most important buildings on a family farm.

The second is the silo. It's 20 to 40 feet high, constructed three quarters of a century ago of kiln fired building blocks in multiple shades of umber. Some still have a metal cap, showing rust but holding up remarkably under the strain of being forgotten. Sometimes a little life still shows on its sides in the Virginia Creeper or other vines that caress its perfectly circular shape. When you see an isolated silo, imagine the barn to which it used to be attached and the small herd of dairy cows that used to be housed and fed and milked there. It is always a marker of a farm site that was the home of a family and of the cows and the pigs and the sheep and the chickens that sustained them in that place nearly three-quarters of a century ago.

You are seeing the ghosts of the family farm.

Let's take a look – both realistic and romantic – at the way farm-

ing was done in the early '30s. That timeframe matches up with the time of the Great Depression as well as the time when Dad and Mom started farming. Together, Dad and Mom lived through the experience of several major agricultural changes.

Grandpa Jacobs was pround of his team of horses, seen here on the family's farm south of Dixon, Illinois.

Crop Farming

Start with haymaking. First, the clover or alfalfa was cut by a two-wheeled mower pulled by a team of horses (later by a tractor). The mower had a cutting bar five to six feet long with a moving sickle made up of a series of small triangular steel plates that were kept very sharp. The mower was powered by the turn of its wheels, and if the power mechanism had not been disconnected, the sickle bar would move when the mower moved. More than one farmer lost a finger when the horses moved an inch or two. The mower left the fresh cut hay lying in neat rows across the field. The rows were as wide as the sickle bar was long.

Next, windrows were made by a machine which was a giant angled turning rake that picked up the cut hay lying flat in the field and laid it gently in billowing rows as soon as it had dried enough not to be a fire danger when put in the mow.

Dad and Grandpa Gonnerman hauling in loose hay. Before bailers, loose hay was stacked in the barn.

To pick up the hay, Dad would start the team of horses down a windrow with one horse on each side. Then he let them go, and the horses would stay on that row until they got to the end of the field. The loader, a machine about ten feet high, lifted the hay over the backboard and dumped it at the back of the

Dad and Grandpa Gonnerman unload silage at the feedlot.

wagon where Dad could use his three-tined fork to lift big, flat layers into places that would balance the seven-foot-high load so it would keep its boxy shape and not lose more than a few wispy stalks on its ride from the field to the barn. It was clean and pleasant work.

Dad enjoyed loading his hay-wagon alone. He knew from experience that the fragrant crop had lain on the ground just long enough — usually two days after it had been mowed — to be fire-safe-dry while it was still green. He also knew that the hay that he was loading would soon be in storage in the barn's haymow. It held all the nourishment possible for his cows.

The technology changed when tractors replaced horses.

Now a tractor pulled a bailer with the same flat hay-wagon — now fitted with rubber tires — behind it. Early bailers required four men. One drove the tractor. Two sat on the bailer, one on each side. One would stick two wires, each with one looped end, between the compressed sections of hay. He would hold on to the looped end. The other would grab the ends of each wire and stick them back through the hay

A Fordson tractor pulling the hay silage maker. Note the steel wheels with spikes on the tractor. Horses pulled the wagon, a not uncommon combination as horses were phased out of farming. The Fordson was the first tractor Dad owned.

about three or three and a half feet from where the wires had first come through. The first man would grab the end of each wire without a loop, stick it through the loop in the other end, and wrap the wires together. Then he would start the process all over again for the next bale, putting two more wires through the hay at the point where the last bale ended.

The fourth man — actually he was often a teenager — rode on the wagon with a hay hook in each gloved hand, lifting each bail and carrying it as far to the back of the wagon as he could and placing the bales two across, four or five bales high, until the wagon was filled. It was not unusual for those bales to weigh 80 pounds each. If a man didn't use hay hooks he could wear out a pair of pigskin gloves in a couple of days by picking up the bale with the wires. From the age of 13 on, I was often that "man" on the wagon. I was paid a dollar a day.

Loading hay wagons with baled hay was a particular challenge when the hayfield was hilly. If I hadn't stacked the bales just right with the slopes in mind, the whole load could shift dramatically when the wagon was pulled from one side of the hill to the other. Conservation measures such as terracing, strip farming, and grass waterways were not yet in vogue — at least not around where we lived. All of those procedures would have changed the terrain while protecting it from the damaging erosion that left deep gullies in its wake.

Bailing was tough work, and even though working on a beautiful summer day, when they stopped for lunch and at the end of the day the faces and arms of all four of the "haymakers" would be black with hay dust kicked up by the bailer.

The hilly farms started just a mile north of our farm. The soil was neither black nor deep, and it had a high proportion of sand and small gravel. We always surmised that the end of the hills marked the edge of the glaciers that had covered the land thousands of years before. But we never asked a geologist whether or not our imaginings were correct. We never knew one to ask. In fact, I'm not sure that some farmers knew what a geologist was.

Horse drawn or tractor powered, all that hay was lifted into the cavernous mow in the barn by either a three-foot wide hay fork with a

Dad on his Allis Chalmers WC tractor pulling the windrower, raking hay. The same tractor earlier had steel wheels; they simply changed the steel wheels to rubber wheels.

rope and a complicated block and tackle system if the hay were loose, or an elevator powered by a tractor if the hay were bailed. Either way, once inside the mow, the hay was stacked so it could be easily accessed and thrown down through a hole in the floor to be fed to the livestock throughout the coming winter. Most children enjoyed playing in the haymow, either bouncing around on the loose hay or building forts and hiding places out of the bales. Everyone in a haymow – adults and children alike –had to know where that hole was and watch out for it so they didn't fall through to the floor below. I never saw a hole in the haymow floor that had any safety railing.

Dairy cows and beef cattle are the biggest consumers of hay. Sheep eat some. Hogs and chickens aren't interested.

After a few years, bailers were developed that tied the bales with twine automatically. Eventually, those bailers even "shot" the bales into wagons that had steel fences all around the edge. Some of those bales weighed only half as much as the ones that had been tied with wire and moved by muscle to their place on the wagon.

One of the most difficult decisions for a farmer when making hay, particularly if the cut hay had been rained on, was how soon it was dry enough to harvest so that it would not spontaneously combust from internal heat generated by too much moisture after it was put in storage in the mow. Too soon might cause a fire. Too late would rob the hay of much of its nutritional value. Spontaneous combustion of hay that was harvested and stored while too wet was always a concern, but it became a particularly critical problem when farmers started baling their hay, packing it into airtight rectangles. The spontaneous fires cost millions of dollars every summer in barns that burned to the ground. A spontaneous combustion fire was usually well underway in the hay mow before it was discovered, and once that kind of fire started the barn was almost always a total loss, together with much of the livestock being housed there.

When we lived in the house on the Lincoln Highway, we all watched helplessly one summer night when our neighbor's barn a quarter of mile down the road burned to the ground, killing many high quality dairy cows. It had been a huge barn with the mow full of fresh hay, and the fire was a traumatic conflagration. I can still see the supporting pillars of that barn, standing like blazing sentinels after the rest of the barn had burned to the ground between them.

We were never quite sure whether that barn fire started from lightning (we did have a thunderstorm that night) or from spontaneous combustion of hay that had been bailed too soon.

In more recent years, haying has changed one more time. Now the hay is rolled into tight round bales that are four or five feet in diameter. The bales are so heavy it takes a fork lift on the front of a tractor to lift them and move them around. They are almost impossible to put in the mow of a barn. Even if you might be able to get them in the mow, those bales would be hard to get out to feed to livestock. Those heavy round monstrosities have become a visual blight on the land, sometimes left for a whole year in the field where the baler dropped them, more often moved into rows that serve as phony fences that begin to disintegrate if they have not been fed to any livestock after nearly a decade.

More recently, two other "crops," both used for wintertime bedding for cattle, hogs, and sheep, have been included in the bailing schedule. Straw and cornstalks, both left out in the field after combining, are also bailed up in those large round monstrosities that clutter the landscape.

In a good year, haymaking is done three times in a summer.

Now consider the once-every-year jobs of planting and harvesting small grains such as wheat and oats. Small grain crops such as oats, wheat, and barley almost always followed corn in the small farm rotation, and they did not need to be planted deep to germinate and grow.

Midwestern farmers started working in last year's corn fields every spring as early as the frost was out of the ground, usually toward the end of March, to prepare the cornstalk-covered-ground for planting. Before small grains were planted, the farmer traveled over the entire field at least twice – once with a disk, and once with the seeder – and sometimes a third pass would pull a harrow (sometimes called a drag).

The machine called a disk (or disc) usually included two rows of round, concave metal plates about a foot and a half in diameter. The sharpened blades were about eight inches apart, and each row was angled at the middle so that the ends of the front row were about a foot in front of the center and the ends of the back row were about a foot behind the center. The angles of the round blades helped them cut through the cornstalks and penetrated the ground to turn it over lightly. Most disks were about 12 to 15 feet wide. When a farmer was using horses, he sat on a seat in the middle of the disk and directed the three- or four-horse team back and forth across the field.

When tractors started to become popular in the early thirties they took the place of the horses, speeding up the process and moving the driver from the middle of the dangerous disk to the more stable seat on the tractor (but still in front of the disk).

When the disking was complete, the farmer would hitch his horses or his tractor to a grain seeder. A seeder was a long wooden box with a wheel at each end. The box was about 12 feet long, three feet deep and 16 inches wide at the top, tapering to about five inches wide at the bottom. A revolving baffle, which would turn only when the machine was moving, ran the length of the box. Slots in the bottom could be set at different widths. The wider the width, the

I started learning to drive our tractor at a very early age. Note the steel wheels with the spikes on Dad's first Allis Chalmers WC, here pulling a disk through a cornfield, preparing the field for planting oats. Although I was not really driving it yet, my time to work in the fields came soon after.

more seed would drop out. (In later years the box was made of galvanized steel.)

The box was filled with oats, or wheat, or barley, or rye. If a hay crop was wanted in the field the next year, clover, alfalfa, or timothy seed, or a combination of two out of the three, would be put in the seeder for a second pass over the ground. When the seeder was pulled over the freshly disked ground the seed would drop out in a random pattern, as thick or as thin as the slots had been set to allow. The reason a second pass had to be done for the hay crop was that the seeds of clover, alfalfa, and timothy are much smaller than oats or other small grains and their drop rate had to be controlled much more tightly. Some farmers planted with a grain drill which left the grain in rows about four inches apart. I can't remember that we ever did.

After the seed was sown, if the farmer wanted a smoother field and wanted to make sure all the seed was covered, he dragged the ground with a machine called a harrow, usually about twice as wide as the disk. The harrow consisted of connected sections, each about six feet long and about five feet wide. Each section included a series of poles that held seven-inch-long pointed metal spikes about five-eighths of an inch square. When the harrow was pulled over the newly sown small grain and hay seed, it buried it a couple of inches deep. Now the small grain planting was done.

Harvesting would begin about four and a half to five months later when the grain was standing straight and tall and had turned from green to a dramatic gold. If any hay seeds had been planted, they didn't develop into a mature crop until the following year.

At the time that Dad and Mom were married, the harvesting process began with a horse-drawn machine called the McCormick Reaper. The reaper had a sickle about seven or eight feet long that was pulled along about six inches off the ground, cutting the standing oats just as it was turning gold. As the oats were cut, a large revolving paddle wheel pushed the stalks of grain backwards onto a canvas belt about four feet wide. The belt moved the grain to the binder that gathered the stalks into bunches about eight inches in diameter, tied them in the middle with twine, and kicked them out onto the ground.

Now Mom and any members of my family who could lift a bundle, and maybe some aunts and uncles, would attack those bundles lying all over the field. All the children were barefoot, and by this time in the summer – late July or early August – the soles of our feet had grown as tough as leather. It was great to go barefoot in the stubble, or any other place. We wore our shoes only during the summer when we went to church or any other social function in the community. Shoes were

Dad shocking oats in the days before threshing machines and combines.

expensive, and if we didn't wear them out, Mom and Dad reasoned, they wouldn't have to buy new ones for four children quite as often.

Unfortunately, that was a false economy with unfortunate consequences. While our shoes stayed the same, our feet continued to grow. My big toes now point to the middle of my foot, and my little toes and the toes next to them overlap each other as they also point inward. The too-small shoes pinched my toes into unnatural configurations that will be with me forever.

Back to the oats.

Our job was to set up the bundles of oats in shocks. Each shock had eight to ten bundles standing upright against each other and one bundle that served as a water-shedding cap. After the shockers learned how to do it, the work became almost automatic. Two bundles would be picked up and stood against each other. Then two more bundles would be stood beside the first two, filling in the gaps where they came together. Then four more bundles (and maybe as many as six) filled in any other obvious gaps. Finally, one bundle would be picked up, held under one arm, and the other arm would fan out both the cut ends of the stalks and the head ends filled with grain. That "cap" would be placed over the other six bundles as a kind of small roof.

All the shockers would move across the field in a line. By the time they were done, hundreds of shocks would dot that field, crisscrossing the acres in curving rows. It was a beautiful sight.

The shocks would stand in the field for a week or two before the threshing machine was available to visit our farm. On most farms,

A steam engine powering the threshing machine (not shown) in the 1920s.

the threshing machine would need only one day to do its work. It would turn all the bundles of oats into clean grain in wagons that would be unloaded into the granary and a big pile of straw that would provide bedding for the cattle and other livestock for the entire winter. Straw does not include enough nutrients to be used as food.

Threshing machines came in several sizes. The biggest ones might extend about 40 feet or more in length. The "apron" end received the bundles or oats, wheat, or barley and moved them into the threshing machine. At the other end, a large metal pipe stretched out to send the straw into a high pile.

Dad gave directions to have the thresher set up where he wanted it. Then a big steam engine would be lined up to power the machine with a long belt that connected the engine's fly wheel with the pulley wheel that powered the thresher's machinery. The alignment of the threshing machine and the steam engine was critical. The belt would not stay on if the pulleys were not in exact alignment. Once the belt was properly aligned and running smoothly, a wagon would be backed into place to catch the grain that would come out of a spout just past the middle of the threshing machine. Now everything was ready. The threshing could begin.

Even while the threshing machine was being set in place, hayracks (wide, flat wagons with a high back fence but no sides) were already being loaded with bundles to be carried from the fields to the thresher.

Every summer, from the time I was about 12 years old until I went to college, I was part of the work crew that helped to load the wagons in the field. Using a light fork with three sharp tines, I would go to a shock next to a wagon, stab the cap bundle just below the twine, lift it and fling it to the wagon. The man on the wagon took the bundle (sometimes even catching it in the air on his fork) and put it in place on the others with the cut end of the straw pointing out.

Those moves would all be repeated until the other eight or nine bundles in the shock were all in place on the wagon. Then we would move to another. An experienced man on the wagon could load it about eight or ten feet high without fear that any of the bundles would shake loose and fall off as he rode them to the threshing machine.

It was great work. I always wore a wide brimmed straw hat in the field, and on really good days the slight breeze in the air would dry off your sweat before you even knew it was there. Sometimes we would hear pheasants or quail in the fence rows. We would often see rabbits. Sometimes they ran out from the shocks when we began to dismantle them. Once in a while we would see a fox, and sometimes a skunk.

The best part of every threshing day was "lunch." It really wasn't lunch, however. It was the biggest dinner anyone could imagine.

At noon all the men and boys pitching bundles hitched a ride on a full rack headed to the thresher. They would jump off near the "horse tank," a galvanized or wooden tank usually about six or eight feet long, three feet across, and two and a half feet high. (A few were round and about eight feet in diameter.) The horse tank was always full of water for horses, cattle, and dairy cows. Sometimes it was also being used as a cooler for cans full of milk or cream. Fresh water was always being pumped into it, and the water was icy cold.

All the threshers would gather along the side of the tank that wasn't in the yard full of livestock, bend over, and splash that cold water on their faces and arms, washing away the dust from the morning's work. Then they all headed to the dinner table.

While the fathers and sons had been hard at work to clear the shocks from the field and separate the grain from the straw, the mothers and daughters had been at work preparing the abundant feast.

First, they set up a long table in the shade. The table was made of sawhorses and wide boards pushed tight against each. Sometimes chairs would be hauled out of the farmhouse. Sometimes the "chairs" were benches made from short stools covered with wide boards. Table clothes were overlapped along the length of the makeshift table and as many china plates as were needed were spaced along its length together with water glasses and the appropriate silverware.

(Paper plates and plastic table ware weren't used much yet back in those days. If one farmer's wife knew she didn't have enough china plates to take care of all the threshers, she would ask neighbors to bring some of theirs.)

Then, as the threshers moved toward the table and found their seats, the women would parade out of the kitchen carrying platters of fried chicken, baked ham, and roast beef. That would be followed by bowls of mashed potatoes and gravy, scalloped corn, and string beans. Plates of sliced tomatoes and jars of pickles would also decorate the tables together with fresh homemade bread, butter, and strawberry jam.

Steaming cups of coffee or cold glasses of lemonade were available for anyone who wanted them. Everything had been grown in the farmers' own gardens or butchered from their own herds. Only the coffee, the lemons, the sugar, and the spices had been bought at a store.

And all of that was always followed with an assortment of pies — apple, peach, and cherry were the favorites.

It was a fabulous feast, and during the threshing season it happened every day of the week except Sunday until every farmer's oats in the community was safely stored for the coming year.

The men would all leave the table as soon as their pie plate was clean and they had decided they had enough coffee. Totally full (sometimes almost uncomfortably so) and completely content, they would sit in the shade around the yard with their backs against trees or lay on their backs in the grass.

The conversation continued from questions first asked at the dinner table. How many bushels to the acre did they estimate this farmer's oats was producing? How many rabbits had been scared up from their hiding places in the shocks? How many pheasants had been heard crowing in the fence rows? Did anyone else see the fox running at the edge of the woods? What were the latest fluctuations in the price of oats, corn, hogs, and beef? Could we finish this farmer's threshing before everyone had to get home to milk their cows?

Then, after ten or 15 minutes, someone would say, "Well, it's time to get back to work," and everyone would get up with great grunts and groans to finish the job begun that morning. The men would leave the yard, and the women would bring out some clean plates and sit at the table to eat from the ample leftovers. Then they carried everything back into the kitchen and washed the dishes.

And that's the way it went threshing oats way back in the thirties and early forties as World War II was ending. It was a satisfying and romantic time.

The production of small grains and corn increased by amazing numbers in the 40 years between 1930 and 1970. In 1930, one farmer supplied 9.8 persons in the United States and abroad with their needed food. In 1970, one farmer supplied essential food to 75.8 persons in the United States and abroad.

In 1930, 15 to 20 labor hours were needed to produce 100 bushels of corn from two and one-half acres of farm land. The farmer used a two-bottom gang plow, a seven-foot tandem disk, a four-section harrow, and two-row planters, cultivators, and pickers. In 1975, only three and one-third labor hours were needed to produce 100 bushels of corn from one and one-eighth acres. The farmer used a tractor, a five bottom plow, a 20-foot long tandem disk, a planter, a 20-foot-long herbicide applicator, a 12-foot self-propelled combine, and trucks.

One of my 4-H projects, a five-acre field of corn planted and harvested in 1950 (I was 17) produced 157 bushels to the acre, the best corn yield that year in the State of Illinois. All the fertilizer was natural. The corn had been planted on an alfalfa field that had been pasture for my herd of hogs the year before.

A major transition in the harvesting of small grains was to a tractor-pulled combine. Farmers waited a couple of weeks longer than they had when they were cutting the grain and shocking bundles. They wanted to make sure the standing grain was totally ripe, but not so ripe that the kernels began to fall out on the ground. Combines cut the grain with longer sickle bars than had ever been used before, fed it into the machine where the wheat or oats was separated from the straw, the grain went into a bin mounted on the combine and the straw was strewn on the field. That strewing part made the operation a lot dirtier than the shocking and threshing had been.

And even as a neighbor was using his combine to separate the grain and the straw, part of the sense of community that had developed and was sustained with the big threshing parties was gone – and would be gone forever.

Today, the combines are bigger, they are self-propelled, and the drivers (both men and women) do their work in air-conditioned, sometimes GPS-directed cabs with radios and power steering. Some of those machines cost more than a suburban house. The grain is off-loaded from the combine into semi-trucks that take it directly to storage elevators that ship it by rail across the country. Sometimes the train terminals end near airports where the grain can be loaded into cargo planes. Other times the rail terminals end at a dock on a river where it is loaded onto barges that take it to ports where it is loaded into ships bound for distant places around the world.

The growing and harvesting of corn had its own set of rituals.

First, the ground had to be plowed. One version of the plow was developed in 1837 by a man named John Deere in his blacksmith shop in Grand Detour, Illinois, only six miles northeast of Dixon on a bend in the Rock River. The surfaces of Deere's plow were polished steel. They went through the soil more easily and dirt did not stick to them. Thousands were sold, laying the foundation for Deere and Company, which developed into one of the major farm machinery manufacturers in the world.

The iron plow was made of interchangeable, replaceable parts. Most important was the mold board, a large curved piece of metal that turned the plowed soil over so that the original surface was upside down. Three other pieces – the share, the landside, and the heel – formed the point and the straight edge which left a straight and clean furrow as the plow was pulled through the ground. Our plow also had a sharp steel disk mounted ahead of the plowshare. It was in line with the edge that defined the furrow and cut refuse on the ground to leave an even straighter, cleaner furrow.

Each plow is called a bottom. Dad started with a two-bottom plow pulled by his tractor, and eventually worked with a three-bot-tom plow mounted to his Allis-Chalmers tractor with a hydraulic system to raise and lower it.

Dad taught me to plow when I was 11 or 12 years old. Plowing is a complicated process. To "open" the field you have to stay in an absolutely straight line. That was easiest when you started along a fencerow. But the second furrow was more difficult. You didn't want to go to the opposing fencerow because that might be a quar-ter of a mile or more away and you would burn way too much fuel just getting from one furrow back to the other. So you divided the field up into strips that were defined by the second furrow about 100 to 300 feet from the first.

That's when plowing gets more difficult. Figuring out where the second furrow would start was no problem, but figuring out where it would end was filled with complications, particularly if the field was not completely flat so that you could not see its end. Sometimes you started that second furrow, stepped off the distance to the first, and then walked to the other end and stepped off the same distance. You had been carrying a stake at least three feet long, preferably with a red flag tied to the top, and you pushed that into place at the stepped off distance. Then you went back to your tractor and plow and headed straight for that stake.

After that, you simply put the big back wheel of the tractor in the furrow and plowed, working the furrows toward each other until all the ground had been turned over. Then you started and plowed other sections until the field was finished.

Two more things happened after the plowing was completed. First, the plowed field needed to be disked so that the clods left from the plowing would be broken up and the field would be flatter. Then the tractor had to be guided over the field one more time, this time pulling a harrow to break up the smaller clods that remained and leave the field ready for planting.

The Gonnerman farm was fertile and the black topsoil went down two or three feet in most places until we would come to clay. Dad insisted that when I had finished plowing a field all he wanted to see was black dirt. He did not want even the tip of any of last year's corn stalks to show on the top. That meant that, in addition to staying in straight lines you had to be sure that the plow was set deep enough to turn all the soil over the refuse, but not so deep that the tractor pulled any harder than it had to. With practice I learned to leave perfectly black fields when I was plowing.

Once the field that was going to be planted in corn or beans had been plowed, it was disked, using the same piece of machinery that had prepared a field for the seeds of small grains, but now breaking up the clods that littered the field after plowing. We used to disk the soil until it was pulverized. Now farmers don't till the soil at all. Today's methods are more economical and environmentally compatible.

Black fields had their drawbacks. We didn't plow much in the fall like almost all farmers do today because in most years, by the time the corn was picked the ground was frozen. But when we did do fall plowing, the wind erosion was substantial if the snow cover

One of the biggest snowstorms ever in Nachusa, Illinois, started at 8:00 in the morning, closed all the roads in the area by noon, and kept Mom and Dad and family from going to Grandma Jacobs' house to celebrate her birthday. Snow banks filled the ditches.

on the fields was light. After days of strong winds, the snow banks along the fence rows and in the ditches along roads would be black with the fine silt from the top of the fields. That was the best dirt blowing away. And if spring rains were heavy, and the fields had a slope or two, rushing water formed gullies where the field had seemed to be relatively flat.

Farmers today, fighting against both wind and water erosion, have changed that substantially. Now many of them practice minimum or no tillage, leaving as much of the refuse from last year's crop on top of the ground as possible. It's a much improved method, but it has taken me awhile to get used to it. Even today, when I see those messy fields left by "no till" farming, my first reaction is still to wonder why they couldn't have plowed those fields better, the way Dad and I did in the '40s.

My brother Paul told me that Dad changed to "no till" farming in the early sixties. That means he didn't plow, disk, or drag the fields anymore. He simply hooked the corn planter to the tractor and planted the seed in fields that had not been worked since the last harvest. It was the new way, approved and recommended by the agriculture extension office, and a sure way to save the cost of gallons of gasoline by cutting the tractor's times around the field from three to one.

Not everyone, however, liked the idea of "no till" farming. One of Dad's neighbors, noted for the preparation time he put in on his fields, took particular exception to the practice. He had a reputation for not planting his corn until the field was flat and smooth as a tabletop. When he finished with a field, the soil had been worked to a texture nearly as fine as salt. He told Dad in no uncertain terms that he was an embarrassment to all the other farmers in the county.

Dad continued with his "no till" planting, saved a truckload of gas, and had a yield every bit as good as his "embarrassed" neighbor.

It didn't take more than a couple of years before many of the other farmers in the neighborhood were also using the "no till" method. The angry neighbor got over being angry, but he never changed his ways. He seemed to like spending lots of extra money for gas for the tractor he had finally started to use instead of his horses long after nearly everyone else had made that transition.

Mom and Dad behind the corn planter that had just been sold at the auction of all their machinery in June 1967.

The progression of improvements in farming is dramatic as new and more powerful equipment becomes available. A test done recently in Nebraska told a significant story. It was done on a carefully marked 40-acre field (a one-fourth mile square).

- A team of four horses, pulling a two-bottom plow making two 12-inch furrows, took 55 hours to plow the field.
- A 1936 Farmall F20 tractor with steel wheels pulling a two-bottom plow took 25 hours to do the same work.
- A 1956 Farmall 450 tractor (50 horsepower) with rubber tires, pulling a two-bottom plow, took 16 and a half hours.

Continuing the test introduced above, when a 1929 John Deere GP tractor (20 horsepower) pulled a 10-foot disk over the same 40-acre field where the plowing tests had been done, it took five and a half hours to finish the field.

When a 1997 John Deere 8100 tractor (215 horsepower) pulled a 25-foot disk over the field it took one and one-tenth hours to finish the field. That's one of the reasons it's possible today for one farmer to farm a thousand acres and more.

When Dad began farming, he rode a corn planter behind a team of horses. The planter had two steel wheels. Each wheel had two pieces of steel that were angled to form a "V" with a space of a couple of inches in between. Ahead of the wheels a small plow blade opened a furrow about five inches deep, a plate mechanism dropped three or four seeds into the furrow from a large can where the seed was carried, and the wheel packed the soil lightly around the seed.

All of our corn was "checked." That meant that the corn was planted at the same intervals in both directions, usually 40 inches. A wire with "knots" or "buttons" in it at 40-inch intervals was stretched the length of the field. Sometimes that wire might be more than a quarter-mile long. The wire would fit in a slot on either side of the planter that triggered the grain drop. It had to be moved 40 inches toward the unplanted side of the field whenever the planter got to the end. The planter also had a marking arm on both sides. A small wheel on the end of the arm marked where the planter should go when it came back along the rows that had already been planted.

When checked corn germinated and came up, it could be cultivated in both directions to loosen the soil and control weeds. Most farmers would cultivate every field three times – twice in one direction and once in the other – if weather allowed. The first cultivation usually took the longest because the shoots of corn were only up three or four inches and if the cultivator went too fast it would throw dirt far enough to cover the plants.

Dad behind the cultivator. Even after he switched to a tractor-mounted cultivator, plowing corn kept us busy until late spring.

Through the thirties every farm could rightfully be called an organic farm. Manure was the primary fertilizer and herbicides and insecticides had not yet been invented. If weed control were needed it was done with a cultivator on a tractor or it was done by hand.

Weeding corn with a tractor-mounted cultivator was an operation that called for precision. If you were driving a tractor with two small wheels right next to each other in front (the way most of them were manufactured), you steered those down the middle between two rows. The back wheels of the tractor would then be between the rows on either side of the front wheels. If you got out of that track, the cultivator would erase sections of two rows of corn in an instant. However, the whole experience of tractor-mounted weeding, done right, was a satisfying accomplishment.

I enjoyed weeding long before I learned how to do it with a tractor. My first weeding jobs were probably given to me shortly after I had started school.

One of the most enjoyable weeding chores of late summer was to take the tiling spade and head out into the pasture to cut down bull thistles. Bull thistles can grow to four or five feet tall. They have thick, hollow stems, spreading roots that go down about seven or eight inches, beautiful purple flowers, and long sharp thorns.

Ideally, the thistles should be cut a while before they began to bloom. If they are cut later than that, the flowers finished their bloom anyway and the blossoms turned to seed. Every seedpod contains hundreds of small seeds, each connected to a white, feathery plume that catches the wind and is carried hundreds of feet away.

When the cut thistles turned brown, the thorns seemed to get stiffer and sharper. They would even penetrate the bottoms of my bare feet that by August had been toughened and hardened so that very little affected them. Thistle thorns hurt, and it wasn't easy to get them out.

In spite of that occasional discomfort, cutting bull thistles was always fun. You could start anywhere in the pasture and within a few minutes see a circle of downed thistles all around you. It worked like this. Staying just out of reach of the thorns, you would go up to a thistle, take one or two swings that drove the edge of the spade into the ground just a few inches from the main stem, and push down to lift up the roots. Then you would drive the spade in again to cut off the roots spreading on the other side. After that the thistle would be lying on the ground, dead. When all the roots had been cut, it would turn brown in a few days.

When I let my imagination roam I would begin to think I was cutting off huge Sequoias or other big trees I had read about. I was a lumberjack, harvesting a large, untamed forest.

A bonus with cutting bull thistles was having a chance to learn about two birds that lived on the Illinois prairie.

The first was the Meadowlark. I always loved the Meadowlark. It had a distinctive song. It also had distinctive feathers. The bird's back and wings were streaked with black and brown. Its breast was bright yellow intersected by a black V. They were a little smaller than a Robin.

Meadowlarks nest on the ground in little round enclosures they fashion out of thick, tall, dead grass that has been bent over by last winter's snow and lies close to the soil. The nests are almost impossible to see, even when you know where they are.

When a person or animal gets too close to a nest with its eggs or baby birds and is thought by the mother Meadowlark to be a danger, she moves quietly and unseen a few feet away. Then she suddenly becomes visible but acts like she is hurt, dragging a wing as she hobbles along away from the nest. When you or an animal follow the Meadowlark, it stays just out of range for 20 to 30 feet. After you have followed it far enough away from its nesting spot the bird blasts off the ground in a whirl of wings and flies to a nearby fence or fence post where it begins to sing its melodious song.

By now, of course, you don't have a clue where the nest is, and the eggs or baby birds are safe.

After a few experiences like that, I learned that I had to ignore the bird with its fake injury and start looking for the nest in the grass within a few feet of where I first saw the Meadowlark. The closer I got to the nest – being very careful not to step on any spot where the nest might be – the more agitated the bird became. It would move closer, trying to get me to move away. When I found the nest, I moved the top grass apart very gently. I studied the eggs or the baby birds for a short time and then returned the covering grass to its original position.

Sometimes I would be able to remember the spot where the nest was so that I could check the progress of the eggs or the growth of the birds every couple of days until they were big enough to fly away. But I never destroyed a single Meadowlark's nest. They were too interesting and too important to harm in any way.

A second summer bird I saw often on the Illinois prairie was the Killdeer. A member of the Plover family, it is mostly brown and white with distinctive black markings. The Killdeer's body is about the same size as a Robin, but it has long spindly legs.

They don't bother with nests. They simply lay their eggs — usually two — on plowed ground. But the eggs are very difficult to find because they look like large pebbles. However, if you or an animal gets close to the place where the eggs lay, the Killdeer does the same thing as the Meadowlark to protect its nest. Suddenly, you hear what sounds almost like a scream of pain. Then you see a Killdeer that acts like it is badly hurt, limping along with a dragging wing. When you follow the bird that looks so wounded, it leads you farther and farther from the nest until it suddenly takes off and flies away. The nest is safe, since neither you nor the animal can remember where the chase of the "wounded" bird began. If you get close to the hard-to-see eggs, the chase starts all over again.

The habits of Meadowlarks and Killdeer, useful to the farmer because of their love of insects as the primary item in their diet, were an important part of the beginning of my education in ecology.

Herbicides and insecticides, chemicals used to kill weeds and insects, were not developed until the forties. Those used on farms can be used selectively to kill undesirable weeds and have made cultivation of corn unnecessary. Consequently, checked corn planting was given up in favor of planting in continuous rows where the rows were planted closer together and the seeds were each only five or six inches apart. The standard space between rows was now only 30 inches rather than 40.

New herbicides continue to be designed to be plant selective, killing broadleaf weeds and certain grasses while leaving the corn or other crops untouched. And as weeds disappear the corn and other grain crops have less competition for soil nutrients and show improved growth and production.

Two of my worst experiences while growing up on the farm both happened in the same cornfield. The first was during the planting season, and the second was during harvest. They were about five or six years apart.

I was about seven years old one spring when Dad was working in our largest field, a 20-acre rectangle that ran along the space between the railroad and the pasture that bordered both sides of the creek. He was planting with an old, two-row planter pulled by a team of two horses. It was mid-afternoon, so Mom made lemonade and a snack for Dad and asked me to take it out to him where he was doing the planting. I enjoyed walking the trip of about a third of a mile in my bare feet down the cow lane and into the field that was already about half planted.

When I arrived, Dad was riding the planter, sitting on the metal seat, heading away from me, almost at the other end of the field. The field was nearly a quarter of a mile long, so I knew it would be awhile before he would get to the end, unhook and move the check-wire, turn the planter around, hook the wire back up, and come back. I set Dad's refreshments down in the grass of the fence row and climbed into a 25-foot-tall choke cherry tree in the field's fencerow.

That's where I waited, keeping my eye on the progress Dad was making with the planter as he headed back in my direction. He got to the end of the row, almost under the choke cherry tree, unhooked the wire, turned the horses and planter around and was just getting off to see if the seed corn cans needed filling.

That's when I dropped to the ground out the tree. I don't think I even said anything, but the sound of my bare feet landing in that soft dirt and the sudden motion of my body coming down out of the tree spooked the horses. In an instant they took off at a full gallop across the field away from me. Thankfully, Dad still had ahold of the reins and was able to clamber back on the seat before they pulled away from him.

I stood dumbfounded as Dad rode the planter, faster than he had ever ridden it before, nearly out of control, all the way across the field, pulling as hard as he could on those reins, trying to stop those runaway horses. He was almost all the way to the other end of the field, nearly a quarter of a mile away, before he was able to slow them down and bring them to a stop. It's a good thing he did. The fence at the other end was barbed wire, and if the horses had run into that they probably would have cut themselves — and Dad — terribly as they went through it.

I knew I was in big trouble, but I stood where I had jumped as Dad slowly brought those horses pulling that corn planter back to where he needed to be to start the next rows. I expected a terrible spanking for such a dumb stunt, but I really did not know any better then. Surprisingly, Dad did not spank me, but he certainly yelled at me a lot, questioning my intelligence and my fitness to be a farm boy.

Then he sat down in the grass in the shade of that choke cherry tree, and drank his lemonade and ate his sandwich.

It could have been worse. If the wire with the buttons had still been connected it would probably have broken more than once and been all tangled up. If the horses had not been stopped when they did, they could have been badly hurt. But I think the fact that Dad had to ride that planter all the way back across the field gave him time to realize that I had not intended any harm. I just didn't know that horses could be spooked so easily, or that they might respond in such a terribly violent way.

The work of picking corn was another job that has been in almost constant transition since Dad and Mom started farming in 1932.

I remember a year or two when I was an adolescent when I helped with the harvest while it was still being done by hand. A team of horses pulled a box wagon – the box was made with wooden boards and rode on four wheels about three feet high. It had a board about three feet high fastened to one side. It was called a bang board and it kept the ears of corn from going all the way over the wagon to the other side. The horses would move along a row of corn slowly without being driven while one to three people would walk along the rows, shucking out the corn ears on the standing stalks and throwing them in the wagon. The sound of the ears bouncing off the bang board and dropping into the wagon was like a rhythmic percussion section in a band.

The pickers wore cloth work gloves that would be worn out in less than a week by the rough corn husks. The right thumb was inserted in a little device made of leather with a rounded metal hook attached. You would grab the ear on the stalk with your left hand, open the husks with a slash of the hook, reach in and grab the ear, break it off, and throw it against the bang board into the wagon. Once a person got the hang of it, picking an ear of corn was one fluid motion. I remember getting so attuned to that rhythm that I didn't even look to see where the ear went when I threw it. When I heard the "thunk" on the bang board I knew the ear was in the wagon. If I didn't hear the "thunk," I knew that I had better adjust the trajectory.

Picking corn by hand was almost romantic, but it was terribly slow when you were harvesting a 20-acre field. And you were always racing against impending bad weather that would stop all picking for that fall.

I must have been about 13 years old when the second bad experience happened. It was in the same cornfield, but on the other end. Once again, refreshments were involved.

This time, Dad was picking corn with a two-row picker mounted on the front and sides of the tractor. An elevator extended out the center of the back, moving the picked corn right into the wagon that was being pulled behind the tractor. It was late October or early November. The weather, as usual at this time of year, had gotten cold and the ground was frozen. This time, Mom sent me out with a thermos full of coffee and a sandwich or some cookies.

Once again I went to the end of the row. The choke cherry trees had been cut down out of the fence row although jumping from one of them now would not have spooked the tractor. We had stopped using horses a couple of years earlier. Dad saw me waiting for him and stopped. I ran over to the tractor to hand him his refreshments so he would not have to shut the machine down.

I wasn't very tall in those days (for that matter, I'm still not), so I stepped up on the top of the bottom side of the back tractor wheel in order to hand Dad his food more easily. The back tires of tractors are big. As I remember, the ones on this tractor were about as high as my head. Some were also filled with a non-freezing liquid to make them heavier and give them more traction. The tires on our tractor were filled with air.

Unfortunately, when I stepped on the lower part of that tractor wheel the valve that is used to fill the tires with air or liquid and to check their pressure was just where I put my foot. When my foot came down, the valve – a little more brittle than usual in the cold air – snapped off. The air was filled with a huge hiss and the tire went totally flat in less than a minute.

I couldn't believe what had happened. Neither could Dad. I had stepped up on tractor tires many times before – in fact, he had, too – and this had never happened earlier. None the less, it happened now, and Dad was not a happy farmer. When you're picking corn, it's important that you make productive use of every hour of good weather, because when the weather starts to turn bad you might not be able to get back in the field and your corn might have to stand unpicked until the snow melted and the ground dried out in the spring. When that happened, much of the corn fell out of its husks and was lost, and the value of the moisture laden corn that was left went down substantially.

But here we were, faced with a totally flat tire. And this tire can't be easily changed like the tire on a car. The tractor – particularly with a corn picker mounted on it – is too heavy to jack up with the usual equipment that most farmers had in their tool shed. And even if you could jack up the tractor, several big men would not be able to move or control the tire when it came off the axle. This flat tractor tire in our cornfield needed to be fixed where the tractor stood with the help of mechanics who had the machinery to do it.

Dad was not pleased. Once again I heard language suggesting that I didn't have what it takes to work on a farm. Then he turned off the tractor, and we walked back to the house together.

Dad called the shop where he usually had the mechanical work done that he couldn't do himself. Actually, there weren't many things he couldn't do, but fixing that tire was one of them. In an hour or so, a pick-up truck pulled into our yard. It had a kind of derrick bolted to the bed of the truck in back. It was also carrying a new tire mounted on a wheel.

Dad and I got in the truck with the mechanic and rode out to the corn picker. He hooked that small derrick to the tractor axle and lifted the flat tire off the ground. Then he put blocks under the axle to hold it in place, hooked the derrick to the old tire, unscrewed the nuts that held the tire to the axle, and moved the flat tire out of the way.

Next, he picked up the new tire and wheel with the derrick, swung it into place to fit on the bolts at the end of the axle, tightened the tire nuts in place, lifted the axle enough to get the blocks out from under it, and eased it back to the ground. Then he picked up the old tire with the derrick and put it in his truck. It hadn't taken him 30 minutes. He was done.

But Dad had lost about three hours of corn picking time and the money it costs for the repair. I don't remember how much that was, but any amount of cash paid to someone else for repairs in those days was always more than our family could afford. But all in all, the flat tractor tire was not as bad an experience as it might have been. Dad survived. I survived. The corn did get picked before too much snow fell. And, probably most important, I learned one more thing to be careful about when I was working on the farm.

As corn was being picked it was put in storage in the crib. Cribs were special buildings. Ours had three sections. First, it had two cribs, each about seven feet wide, 15 feet high, and 30 feet long on both sides. All the walls were made of five-inch wide boards with both edges beveled at 45 degree angles. The boards were all one inch apart. The spaces left air in to circulate through the ears of corn and the beveled edges helped to keep out most of the rain. The inside walls had hinged panels at the bottom, each about 30 inches wide.

Second, the middle section between the cribs was an open space closed by large double doors at each end. A grain elevator, covered with doors made of two-inch thick lumber, was sunk in the middle of the floor. The elevator consisted of metal scoops, each about two feet long, six inches deep, and six inches wide connected to flat chains on both ends that could carry small grain into bins between the ceiling of the center space and the roof of the crib. When the floor boards over the elevator were lifted up, grain could be dumped from the wagon into the elevator and lifted to the overhead bins.

The corn was always stored on the cob. But the livestock couldn't eat it easily that way, so it had to be shelled. Every year, after the corn had been drying on the ear in the crib for a few months, the corn sheller would arrive. The sheller wasn't as big as a threshing machine, but it did the same kind of work. As soon as the sheller arrived, a conveyer trough with another moving bar and chain system would be extended on the floor, tight against the wall of one crib under the hinged panels.

Starting at one end, the panels would be unhooked, lifted to open the crib, and hooked to the wall to keep them from coming down. As the ears of corn tumbled out, they fell into the conveyer and were moved to the sheller where the kernels would be removed from the cobs and deposited in a waiting truck. We would keep as much of the shelled corn as was needed for the livestock. The rest was hauled to the elevator in Nachusa, a trip of only about a quarter of a mile. The cobs would be blown into a large pile. They could be used as a floor covering for older poultry.

When gravity no longer pulled the corn out of the crib into the conveyor trough and all the corn above our heads in the crib had been poked loose, as many men as we had working would climb into the crib and begin to move the ears of corn into the conveyor with wide scoop shovels. That was harder and dustier work than pitching bundles of oats onto wagons. Once the crib was empty the conveyor was moved to the other side and the ears of corn in that crib were given the same treatment.

The sheller was an important part of the cycle of from seed to feed or to sale. But the sheller went the way of the threshing machine when self-propelled combines took the place of pickers, shelled the corn while picking it in the field, and delivered it into the trucks that would take it directly to the closest grain elevator. The corn crib was also suddenly obsolete. That's why so many of them stand unused and rotting in the middle of fields.

Raising Animals

One thing was a constant on the Gonnerman farm – chores. Chores included feeding and watering the hogs, sheep, chickens, and any other livestock we happened to have on the place at any given time. The hogs and sheep were primarily my responsibility since they were my 4-H and FFA projects. In addition to feeding, someone also had to collect the eggs, no small task since we sold about 30 dozen a week.

But the biggest and most demanding chore was milking.

I was seven or eight years old when Dad decided it was time for me to learn how to milk a cow. I was excited, because that meant I was finally going to be trusted with work that big people did. I don't

Dad with a Hereford calf.

think I would have been nearly as excited if I had known back then just how much work milking really was and how relentless the milking schedule was for every day of a dairy farmer's life.

Cows have to be milked twice every day – once in the morning and once in the evening – as close to the same time every day as possible. That meant that no matter what else was going on, you had to stop doing whatever you were doing and go home to milk those cows on time. It also meant that those cows could not be left without being milked. If you weren't there to do it, someone else had to. That's why Mom and Dad never took vacations. In one sense, they were married not only to each other, but also to their cows.

Milking looks like a fairly simple operation. But it takes time to learn all the little things that go into the process. When I started milking, we didn't have milking machines so all the work had to be done by hand.

Start with getting in position. The milker always works from the right side of the cow. You approach the cow from the back, patting her on her rump to make sure she knows you are there, then pushing her over just a bit to make enough room between her and the cow next to her on her right.

If it's a muddy season or a muddy day, you carry in a pail of warm, soapy water and a rag and clean off the cow's udder and teats. If you don't get all the accumulated mud and other dirt off, it will fall into the milk pail and ruin the milk.

Then you grabbed your stool – it was about 14 inches high and usually had three legs – and stuck it under your bottom as you squatted down on it while sticking your head in the hollow just behind the cow's stomach and in front of her back leg.

Now you set your bucket – a clean, shiny, three-gallon steel pail – between your knees and took hold of either the front two or the back two teats. The squeezing was the hardest part to learn. You had to squeeze the teat with the top finger first, then the next, then the next, until you squeezed with the little finger, all in rapid succession. After you did that, you did the same thing with your other hand. And each squeeze produced a stream of warm, white, frothy milk that you directed right into the bottom of that shiny pail between your knees.

After you kept up that rhythm for several minutes, the flow of milk would get less and less until nothing was coming out anymore.

Then, using just your thumb and first finger you would strip down each teat, pulling out the last of the milk. Then you would move on to the other two teats and repeat the process. It usually took between five and seven minutes to finish each cow.

The sound of the milk hitting the bottom of the pail had a nice metallic ring. As the bottom filled up, the sound changed from metallic to liquid, something like the sound of a burbling brook. It was always satisfying to hear that sound change and know that you were making progress.

Cows that were good milk producers would fill the bucket, while some cows would produce only half a bucket at each milking. The goal of every dairy farmer was to have a barn full of cows where all of them filled the bucket every morning and every night.

Holstein cows (black and white) are the biggest producers, but their milk generally has a lower butterfat content. Guernseys (brown and white and a little smaller than Holsteins) usually give a little less milk, but it has a higher butterfat content. Jerseys (the smallest cows with a solid dark beige color and black rings around their eyes) give the least amount of milk with the highest butterfat content. Jerseys were also likely to be a bit more stubborn and sometimes meaner than other cows. Dad's herds always had mostly Holsteins and few Guernseys.

Other breeds of cows that we never had included Brown Swiss (very big and very gentle brown animals) and Ayrshire (medium size cows that are brownish red and white and can have beautiful long horns).

Some cows created complications. A few liked to step in the bucket. When that happened, of course, the milk was ruined for human consumption and was fed instead to the calves or hogs or, if it looked really dirty, thrown away. Once you found out which cows were most likely to try to step in the bucket you could usually keep the bucket far enough forward so the cow couldn't reach it so easily.

Sometimes in the summer, flies were a problem. They would bite the cows while they were being milked and the cow would respond with her natural defense by trying to shoo it away with a flip of its tail. That wasn't so bad if the tail were dry and clean, but if flies were bothering a cow you were milking and it flipped a wet, dirty tail across your head it was not a pleasant experience. Dad and

I both thought that some cows flipped our faces with their tails just to be ornery.

We had one remedy. We carried a short piece of twine. Then if a cow gave us trouble we grabbed the tail, tied the string around it, and tied the other end of the string around its leg. That solved the problem. Some cows had such a reputation for flipping their tails in our faces while they were being milked that we tied down their tails before we even started milking.

We always had cats in the barn. After I had been milking for a while, I got good enough at directing the milk from the teat into the pail that I could sometimes change the direction of the stream and squirt it right into the face of a cat. At first, the cats didn't like that. Then they discovered what had hit them, licked off all the milk, and sat waiting for another treat.

We milked five to seven cows each day while living on the farm on the Lincoln Highway. The barn was old. The original boards had shrunk a bit as old boards do, leaving cracks as wide as a half inch between each one. On a winter day, the wind and snow would blow right through them and the only thing that gave the barn any warmth at all was the heat from the cows' bodies. That's the kind of heat that smells, and the smell of those cows got into all the clothes a milker was wearing.

When you went into town, you could always tell which men were dairy farmers if they were wearing their work clothes. The smell of the cows always gave them away. The same thing was true of schoolmates if they hadn't changed clothes.

Before we had electricity, the only light in the barn on winter nights was the glow of kerosene lanterns. We usually hung two lanterns on nails in the wall, one on each end of the gutters. That would have been just about as much light as two 40 watt bulbs spread across about 30 feet.

Each time we finished milking one cow we would pour the milk into a big funnel set in the top of a five- or ten-gallon milk can. The funnel included a sieve in the bottom made of finely woven cotton to clean out any dirt that had gotten in the pail by accident.

The work in the barn wasn't done, however, when we had finished milking. The milk cows were in stanchions during the late fall, winter, and early spring – about half the year. On the end by the cows' heads, they had to be fed. On the other end, we had to pick up the manure and wet straw with a four- or five-tine manure fork and throw it on a pile outside the barn door. Then we spread out fresh straw under the cows where they would sleep through the night until milking the next morning. If the weather was nice and sunny, the cows were sometimes let out into the barnyard during the day. Dairy farming was a lot less work during the late spring, summer, and early fall months because then the cows were put into the stanchions only to be milked and turned out to pasture the rest of the time.

After all the work was done in the barn, we loaded the cans full of milk on a small wagon or two-wheeled cart and moved them to the door to the basement at the house. The cans were carried down the steps to the cream separator, where Mom would put some of that sweet, warm milk in glass jugs and pitchers. One of us took that milk to the icebox in the kitchen. We drank that milk and put some of it on our breakfast cereal. Every couple of weeks, Mom would also save enough of that fresh milk to be churned into butter.

We had an icebox because we didn't have electricity to run a refrigerator. Someone had to go to the icehouse in Dixon every week to buy a 50- or 75-pound block of ice that we put in a special compartment of the icebox. That ice lasted a long time in the winter. It melted much faster in the summer. A small bucket sat under the icebox to collect the water that melted from the ice. We always made sure that we didn't leave the icebox door open any longer than we had to so the ice wouldn't melt too fast. We also had to remember to check the water collection bucket every day to make sure it wasn't ready to run over.

Every night, once the milk had been taken down the stairs to the basement, Mom or Dad poured the milk into the large metal bowl on the top of the cream separator. When the separator was turned with a crank, the whole milk from the cows was separated into cream that came out one spout and skimmed milk that came out another. Every couple of days the cream was shipped to Chicago by train in five-gallon cans. The skimmed milk was fed to the hogs.

Mom would save a couple of gallons of whole milk that would be used to make butter once every couple of weeks. We had two kinds of churns. The first was a five-gallon crock, 15 inches high and ten-and-a-half inches in diameter. It had a fitted wooden top with a hole in the center for a wooden handle 41 inches long. At the bottom of the handle was a cross-shaped paddle made from two five-eighths inch thick pieces wood, each six and a half inches long and one and a half inches wide.

Mom would pour the milk into the churn and I would start moving the paddle up and down in a steady rhythm. After about five minutes I could feel that the milk was getting chunky. In about 15 minutes big chunks of butter would be floating in a watery liquid. Mom would pull out the chunks of the butter with a wooden spoon. Then she would pour the liquid through a clean white cloth to get the smaller butter pieces. She would pat all the butter pieces together in a small mound, put it in a dish, cover it and put it in the icebox.

The liquid was buttermilk. Dad and Mom liked to drink it, but I never liked its sour taste. Mom would use it sometimes when she made pancakes.

Later on we got a different kind of churn. It was a square, clear glass jar that held about two gallons of milk. But this one had a metal, screw-on top with a gearbox that turned wooden paddles when I turned the crank. It made butter the same way, but was a little faster.

Dad got serious about dairy farming after we moved to the buildings where Grandma and Grandpa Gonnerman had lived. First, Dad built a large milk house and a milking "parlor" on the northeast corner of the barn where the horse stalls used to be. This barn was newer, well built, and tight. It didn't have any cracks between the boards.

The milking parlor included three stalls made of steel pipe. The stalls were end to end. Each one included two gates on the side, one at the back and one at the front, where the cows came in and went out. Those gates could be opened and shut from the control pit where Dad and I worked while doing the milking. My brother Paul, and sometimes my sisters, took my place after I went to college. A large feed bowl was at the front of each stall. A glass pipe about an inch and a half in diameter ran along the entire length of the three stalls. Three sets of automatic suction milking machines were attached to that pipe with hoses and hung from hooks on the side of the stalls.

The space on one side of the stalls was at the same level as the pen that held the cows while they were waiting to be milked. When the door between the pen and the milking parlor was opened with a rope and pulley, the cows could walk in one at a time. Because food – a mixture of oats, cracked corn, molasses, and a protein supplement – had been put in the food bowl before the door was opened, the cows came right in one by one and got into their stalls.

On the other side of the stalls, the space was about three feet lower than the floor where the cows stood. That meant that when we were milking Dad and I had the cows' udders right in front of us a little below eye level. Each cow came into the stall to eat while getting milked, her udder was washed and dried, the milking machine suction cups were put on all four teats, and the milk went right into the glass pipeline while the cow ate. In most cases, the whole operation took only about three minutes for each cow.

Most farms had flocks of chickens. Here Dad opens up a shipment of chicks that had just come by mail. Each box held 100 chicks. Eggs were a cash commodity, usually supplying money needed for grocery shopping.

Then the front gate of the stall was opened with a lever, the door to the exit pen was opened with another rope and pulley apparatus, the cow that had been milked left, the front gate of the stall was closed, fresh feed was put in the food bowl, the back gate was opened, the holding pen door was opened, and another cow walked right into the stall to be milked. They almost always came in the same order.

At one point, Dad was milking about 40 cows twice a day with this system and when

A brood of well-protected chicks. A mother hen protects them on the right and the dog watches out for them on the left.

he and I were working together the whole milking operation was finished in about 30 minutes.

That glass pipe carried the milk to a large, stainless steel holding tank that took up about two-thirds of the space in the milk house. The holding tank was refrigerated and had a large paddle inside that kept the milk moving slowly. A large tank truck visited our farm every couple of days. It sucked the milk out of our tank in the milk house and carried it, along with the milk produced by our neighbors, to the creamery where it would be pasteurized and packaged for sale in grocery stores.

The milk house also included the compressors that made those three sets of suction cups work. One of the big concerns in this kind of milking operation was to make sure the milk never became contaminated. That meant that all of the equipment – particularly the glass pipeline – had to be absolutely clean all the time. It was cleaned before and after every milking by forcing boiling hot water with special disinfectants through it. The holding tank also had to be washed out every time the tank truck emptied it.

Inspectors came around to check the milk for its purity several times a year. If tests showed that our equipment had any kind of contamination, our milk might not be accepted by the creamery where it was being sent or the price we received was downgraded to a lower class. Either way, that was serious because it was a severe loss of income.

Turkeys were another source of food and money. Here Aunt Margaret feeds a flock.

The price of milk was calculated on the basis of how much the cows produced, the butterfat content for each shipment, and the grading at which our milking operation was ranked. The milk was sold by the pound.

A Farming Revolution

Lots of things had changed in the 35 years between 1932, when Dad and Mom began farming, and 1967, when they retired to go to New Guinea. Lots more has changed as the world charged into the twenty-first century.

The changes amount to a revolution, particularly in the size of the farms and the size and cost of the machinery needed to operate them. Look at the 2012 prices of machinery manufactured by John Deere, one of the major manufacturers of farm machinery in the world.

The basic 5045D utility tractor with a 45 horsepower gasoline engine has a base price of $16,000. But that's not a big enough tractor for much more than a hobby farm. Move up to the 5075M utility tractor and the cost is $44,500. Even that is not adequate for pulling the heavy machinery needed to work thousand-plus-acre farms. Go to the 8310R tractor, big enough to handle just about everything, and the price climbed to just under $290,000. (To put that price in perspective, it equals the cost of a dozen moderately priced automobiles.)

If you are one of those thousand-plus-acre farmers, you are going to need a corn combine. The base machine costs more than $293,000 plus accessories, but you can't pick corn with that unless you buy the "corn head." An eight-row corn head costs $65,500; an 18-row head sets you back $149,000.

If you need to harvest wheat, oats, barley, or rye you need a "small grain" combine that will top out at more than $336,000. Set it up with a 25-foot "cutting platform" and it costs you another $56,000. If 25 feet isn't big enough, you could get a 40-foot "cutting platform" for close to $77,000.

If your farm is a major producer of hay, you might want a 956 center-pivot rotary mower-conditioner at a cost of $45,000, and, of course, you will also need a 569 premium round baler costing $57,000.

Preparing your soil for planting was also an expensive proposition in 2012. An eight-bottom 995 reversible moldboard plow costs a little more than $26,000; and a 20-foot, nine-inch long folding disk costs almost $40,000. If you need a bigger disk, a 40-foot, eight-inch long folding disk costs more than $94,000. If you want to be more ecologically correct, a 22 foot long, three-section flexible C-shank chisel plow costs $34,500, or you can go really big (if you have the tractor to pull it) and get a 61 foot long model for just over $84,500.

Also, if you don't have one, you need a secure machine shed big enough to include all of that expensive machinery under a leak-proof roof. That shed needs to have enough space so that the farmer can also service his machinery – greasing, oiling, welding cracked or broken parts, replacing worn out parts – before every season it will be in use.

Income is always uncertain. However, the average corn yield that could be expected in Rice County, Minnesota, in 2013 would be 180 bushels per acre which might be sold for $6.80 a bushel. The average soybean yield in Rice County in 2013 would be 50 bushels to the acre with a possible sale of $5.05 a bushel.

Obviously, anyone who farms today needs both lots of capital as well as lots of acres. Of course, no farmer has to make investments in every piece of machinery listed above (and more), but most farmers need financial help to lay down a couple of hundred thousand dollars on the machinery dealer's counter for a piece of machinery. Furthermore, none of those outlays for machinery includes the cost of gasoline or diesel fuel needed to make them go, or the cost of the quality seed that gets everything underway for the growth and harvesting cycles.

Before the machinery, the farmer needs the land. In 2013, the average cost of land in Rice County, Minnesota, was $8,000 an acre. The average cost to put in an acre of corn – fuel, fertilizer, herbicide, and seed – was $800 an acre in Rice County, Minnesota; the average cost to put in an acre of soybeans was $300 an acre.

Today, payment for machinery is handled just like the purchase of a new car. The franchise making the sale also sets up the financing: so much down, so much a month at a relatively low rate of interest. Depending on circumstances, the local bank might lend up to 75 percent on the cost on machinery, and up to 80 percent on the costs of seed. The interest at the bank would be higher than the agency that sells the product.

Farming in the twenty-first century is a very expensive business.

But capital is not the only concern of today's farmer. More things than you can count – or expect – can go wrong in any given year. Maybe it rained too hard and too long before you had your crops planted in the spring, and that cut down the length of your growing season by three weeks. Maybe it didn't rain enough and your seed did not germinate like it should have. Maybe it didn't rain at all during the peak of the growing season in June and July and your crop began to whither in the field, producing lots of stunted stalks of wheat that never developed a seed head, or small ears of corn with only a few kernels filled out, and you decided it wasn't worth the time or cost to harvest it at all. Or maybe the wheat looked great going into the beginning of August when you had a torrential rain with 30-mile-per-hour winds that flattened the wheat field and made it impossible to harvest. Or maybe it looked like the corn would average 200 bushels per acre until an early September hail storm completely destroyed it. Or maybe your corn was only three weeks away from maturity in mid-September when you had an early frost that stopped its growth in its tracks.

That's why nearly every farmer today invests in crop insurance. It's available to farmers in the upper midwest for $30 an acre for corn and $20 an acre for soybeans. Hail insurance can be added for $5 to $15 an acre more.

Every farmer – small acreage or large – will tell you that successful farming is always partly luck, and that Mother Nature plays an unpredictable and sometimes devastating role. That's just the way it is – and always has been. Dad and Mom knew all about that . . . from experience.

GROWING UP

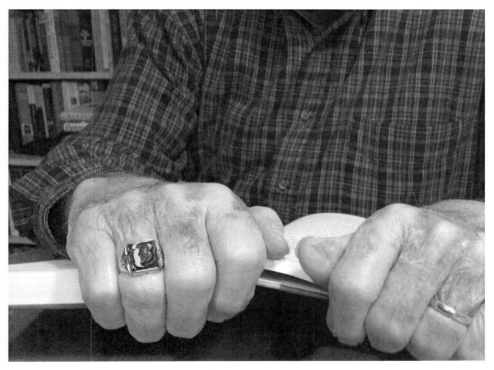

*Farm parents make sure their children know
that chores are a way of life on a farm.
Neither Mom nor Dad could tolerate
simply relaxing for any sustained period of time.
After we reached school age, all of the children
in the family had to look busy all of the time.*

GROWING UP

School Adventures

I began my own schooling in a one-room school in Nachusa in 1939. Aunt Grace, Mom's sister, was my teacher and she was a good one. She had her two-year teaching certificate from Wartburg College, then in Clinton, Iowa. I experienced firsthand one of the great advantages of a rural one-room school. Mine had only the first six grades. But as soon as we had finished first grade and were promoted to second, we became tutors for the children in the grade below us. Consequently, we were constantly reviewing the material we had learned so that we could help the children coming behind us by a year or two to also assimilate it. I wouldn't trade the one-room school experience for anything, particularly under the tutelage of my Aunt Grace.

All the classes were small. My class ranged from four to six students through the years, and all of us were friends. All the parents of all the students knew each other. They also knew, and kept track of, all the students. A little more than half the children came from homes in Nachusa and the rest came from farms in the surrounding countryside.

Nachusa's one-room schoolhouse where Donna and I spent the first six years of our education. Aunt Grace was our very good teacher.

I liked school, and I was interested in just about everything. Arithmetic (that's what we called it back then instead of math) was fun. I also liked grammar and reading, and I read a lot.

One of my favorite classes was geography. Our United States geography textbook took us to all 48 states (Hawaii and Alaska were not states then) by moving us along a route that started in New York, ended in San Francisco, and always came back to travel along U.S. Highway 30, better known as the Lincoln Highway. That was exciting since the Lincoln Highway ran east and west only about half a mile north of our school and was the northern boundary of our farm.

The Gonnerman children: Fred, Mary Ann, Paul, Donna.

Recess offered its own excitement. Everyone in the school had recess at the same time, so older and younger kids played together. That worked out well most of the time. I have to admit that sometimes, after I got older, the smaller kids could be a pain to have around and older students sometimes took advantage of them.

Tag and hide and seek were popular recess activities, although hiding wasn't that easy on the flat expanse of playground. We also played a game called Alli, Alli, Auxen Free in which we divided up into two teams. Someone on one of the teams threw a ball over the roof of the large garage on the school grounds. Sometimes it took three or four tries to get the ball over the roof. When it did go over and a member of the other team caught it, that team ran around the garage to tag members of the team that had thrown the ball who tried to get to the other side of the garage without being tagged. Back in those days, that was pretty exciting.

In winter, we always organized into two sides for snowball fights. Each side built its own elaborate fort, and made stockpiles of snowballs that were stored in strategic places. Then each recess would be a battle to see which side could capture the other's fort. It was great fun, and I don't remember that anyone was ever hurt.

The most exciting game, however, was made possible by the farmer's fence at the edge of his pasture on the north and west edges of the playground. The fence had woven wire at the bottom and a six-inch board along the top. On the side of the board away from the schoolyard, the neighbor had placed an electrified strand of barbed wire. Most farmers in our area used electric fences to control their livestock and keep it in the right fields. The shock was enough to keep a cow or pig from going through or over the fence, but not enough to be dangerous.

Sometimes during recess, the older kids would start a "snake dance" where everyone grabbed hold of someone else's hand and then the whole line would twist its way back and forth around the schoolyard. After this had been going on awhile, the person at the head of the line would reach over the farmer's fence and take hold of the electric wire. The first people in the line would feel hardly anything, but as the electrical charge ran down the line of kids it got stronger. People near the end closest to the fence would feel a slight kind of "buzz" as the charge went through them. But the last couple of people in the line really got zapped.

It probably was not the smartest thing to do, but it was fun if you could stay in the middle of the line. And if you knew what was going to be happening, you could "accidentally" lose your grip on the person who was closer to the fence, and the electrical charge would stop with him or her. I always thought we were kind of lucky being kids from a farm community in a one-room school. That game with the fence taught us something about electricity. City kids had a chance to enjoy that experience only when they visited a farm.

Our one-room school wasn't big enough to hold everybody after my class was promoted to seventh grade, so the school board – Dad was on the board then – made arrangements to send us to school in Franklin Grove, about five miles to the east, for seventh and eighth grade.

That meant that I got to ride the school bus morning and night. It picked me up right at the end of our driveway. School in Franklin Grove was fun. Our teacher was Byrle S. Fish. I liked her almost as much as I liked Aunt Grace. Ms. Fish introduced me to an appreciation of the study of history. That introduction began an interest that continues growing yet today.

All the kids were either in seventh or eighth grade, and we had opportunities that simply were not available in Nachusa. We had a gymnasium and a softball field. I liked basketball, but I had never played it before and it showed. I wasn't very good. However, I had played softball, and I played it pretty well, but I was still one of the last people picked when we formed teams. All of the students from Nachusa were new at the school. Nobody knew us.

The gymnasium had a stage, and the seventh and eighth grade used it to put on musical productions once a year. One of those productions was *Tom Sawyer*. I auditioned for the part of Tom. I really wanted that role and thought my audition was as good as anyone else's. I was quite disappointed when I didn't get it. It went instead to a classmate who lived in Franklin Grove. He was also the basketball and softball star.

He also did not wear glasses. I had worn glasses since I had been about ten years old. I was very nearsighted, and I needed glasses badly in order to see, but I really disliked the bother they caused. Both the lenses and the frames were broken frequently (neither were fortified against breaking back then, and they broke easily and often). In a time when money was constantly short, both Mom and Dad always blamed me for not being careful enough. Most important, I thought my glasses held me back from participation in some of the more active things that I enjoyed and wanted to do. But the "star" of the class always seemed to be in my way on the road to that kind of success.

What I really liked at Franklin Grove was the shop and art classes once a week. That's where I learned about power saws and lathes – something we never had at home until I had gone to college – and where I had my first real chance to work creatively with wood, paper, and paint. Dad later accumulated quite a workshop for himself in our basement and became adept at using the tools, particularly the lathe.

I also became interested in girls. Unfortunately, none of them was interested in me. I remember when I spent a lot of effort and a fair amount of money to pick out a very fancy Valentine's Day card for the girl I thought was the prettiest and smartest in my class. (I always shot high.) I watched expectantly as she opened it at her desk a little ways in front of mine. She looked at it, got a surprised expression on her face, and showed it to her closest girlfriend who sat next to her. They started to giggle. I could see they thought it was a bad joke. I was crushed. I didn't give another Valentine to any other girl until I had already established at least the beginning of a relationship with her.

When Mom started high school in Dixon in 1920, one of her teachers was Myrtle E. Scott, who taught history and what we called "Civics." When I entered Dixon High School in 1947 as a freshman, 27 years after Mom, Miss Scott was still on the faculty. I was in her American History class during my sophomore year and in her Civics class during my junior year. I loved both subjects. Miss Scott was a good teacher. She was thorough and expressed the relevance of history and her ideas with great clarity. Those classes continued my initiation into the study of history that has kept me interested in that subject to this day.

Democracy in the United States would be much better off today if every high school student had the kind of intensive study in civics provided by Miss Scott, study that moved students toward good citizenship and an understanding of the workings of democracy for the rest of their lives.

Dixon High School was ahead of many in the country in preparing its students for college. English classes introduced us to research papers in our junior and senior years. We learned where and how to do research, how to incorporate information we had found, and how to footnote material so that we gave the original author credit and did not try to pass it off as our own. I knew what plagiarism is. When I arrived at college I soon learned that the research paper had not been part of the curriculum of many of my classmates. I was well ahead of most of my college class in this area, and that was an incredible asset.

I was 14 when I attended a week-long camp known as Leadership Training School during the summer of 1947. The camp experience was a program of the American Lutheran Church. It brought together girls and boys – all about the same age, to consider the possibility that God was calling us into positions of leadership in the church. Boys, of course, would be considering whether or not they might become pastors. Women would not be allowed to be pastors in the Lutheran Church for another three decades, so the girls at Leadership Training School were urged to think about becoming a parish worker or a parochial teacher.

I liked the Leadership Training School's format. After an early morning devotional program we were assigned a Bible passage and told to find a spot where we were isolated from everyone else so that we could meditate on that passage for a couple of hours while we tried to figure out what it might mean for our own lives.

I always went to a spot in the woods where I could not see anyone else, sat down with my back against a big tree, and began by reading the scripture passage. I would read it several times as we had been instructed. Sometimes I read sections on both sides of the assigned passage to give myself the context and more perspective. Then I would simply sit and think about what I had read, about the world around me, about my place in the world, and what I wanted to do with my life. We did that for a week. It was an intense time.

I had already been thinking about being a pastor. This experience made it a certain decision about what I would be doing with the rest of my life.

A couple of days after I got home, Mom and I were in the basement running the cream separator. We were talking about my experience at Leadership Training Camp and what it had meant to me. I had already given an enthusiastic report to the whole family. But here, while the cream separator whirled, doing its work separating the cream from the skimmed milk, I told Mom that I had decided to be a pastor. She was overjoyed, and tears streamed down her face as she hugged me. My commitment was complete. At that point I had in mind being pastor of an idyllic rural parish where maybe I could raise a few sheep on the side. That never happened.

About four years later, I enrolled at Wartburg College in Waverly, Iowa, to study in the pre-theological curriculum in the liberal arts. I graduated with an English-Speech-Journalism major in 1955 and enrolled that fall in The Evangelical Lutheran Theological Seminary (now Trinity Lutheran) in Columbus, Ohio. I graduated with a bachelor of divinity degree in January, 1960, and was ordained at Immanuel Lutheran Church in Dixon, Ill., the following month. My first call was to Resurrection Lutheran Church, a mission congregation I established in Painesville, Ohio.

Not quite two years later I was called to become assistant director of public relations for the national office of The American Lutheran Church in Minneapolis. That was an interesting place to be at a time when many church members and some leaders were not sure that churches should be practicing public relations at all. Public relations meant manipulation to them. I was convinced that the church's ministry has always relied on public relations for its basic ministry of world and domestic missions, stewardship, and evangelism, and no manipulation was or is involved. Public relations in the church is direct communication that helps people hear, know, and act upon the Gospel of Jesus Christ.

The rest of my ministerial career was spent in positions where I focused on the specialized ministry of communication in church-related institutions – St. Olaf College for 23 years and Luther Seminary for nine.

I was never quite sure whether Mom and Dad ever accepted the fact that I never stopped being a pastor in this specialized ministry. But I know that in this ministry of institutional communication to which I was called I had a larger influence on more people than I could possibly have ever had if I had remained a pastor who served only parishes.

Learning the Joys of Public Speaking

I always enjoyed the challenges of public presentations, and while in seventh and eighth grade in the Franklin Grove school, my teacher, Byrle S. Fish, encouraged me to enter the annual "Women's Christian Temperance Society Speaking Contest." The contest involved memorizing one of many speeches published in a small booklet and then giving it in front of a relatively small audience, including, of course, some members of the Women's Christian Temperance Society. I don't remember the specific language of the speeches anymore, but I do remember that all of them were little essays – probably no longer than a 300 words – on the evils of drinking alcoholic beverages.

It was a competitive venture with contestants from a small number of area schools. My biggest competition, however, was always a girl in my class named Carolyn Herbst. I had a crush on Carolyn from the first time that I saw her. I tried to sit close to her in class (not too hard since G and H are close together in the alphabet), but she really never gave me the time of day.

She was, however, *the* competition in the temperance speech contest. As I remember, she placed first and I second one year, and I placed first and she second in the other.

When I think about those temperance speeches now, they were terrible little diatribes against alcohol with everything being "Yes" or "No," white or black, without nuance or even the hint of shades of gray. The temperance speech contests did, however, give me helpful experience for 4-H demonstrations that I was able to give at the Illinois State Fair. I remember three of them.

One was a team demonstration with another 4-H member. We built a fairly elaborate model of a farmyard and moved toy machinery around on it. I think our subject had something to do with farming efficiency, but I can't remember for sure. I do remember that the other member of the team was extremely nervous in his part of our presentation and had a difficult time answering the judge's questions directed at him. We got a red ribbon for our efforts, and I vowed that I would never do another team demonstration.

Both of my next two demonstrations were much more dramatic – and successful.

The first involved proper ways to prune and trim trees and bushes. I had prepared all kinds of posters to show the basics and had lots of branches of many kinds as well as well sharpened pruning shears and saws to demonstrate proper procedures.

The big climax was a four-inch-diameter tree branch in the form of a Y. I had mounted that branch on a board, and I stood it off to the side on the table for the whole demonstration as a kind of visual teaser until I got to the finale. Then I sawed off the branch using the standard three cuts (once underneath the branch a half dozen inches from the main trunk, then on the top of the branch an inch or so further away from the trunk until the branch fell off, and then right next to the trunk to cut of the remaining stub) to avoid any tearing of the bark when the branch came off. The demonstration won a blue ribbon.

The second involved one way to solve the problems of soil erosion – a big problem that continues even now on many Midwestern farms. I made four pieces of equipment (two sets) to demonstrate both the problem and the solution. The first involved two sloped metal troughs. One held loose black dirt. The other held a large square of sod. When I poured water on both of them at the same time the results were dramatic. Nearly all the loose dirt was swept off the trough into the pail below almost immediately, while the water went down through the sod and came out the end of the trough just as fast but nearly clean. And the sod was still all in place.

The second set of equipment involved four one-gallon glass jars (we didn't have plastic jugs back then). First, I taped two lids together and punched them full of holes to form a sieve. Then I took two pieces of string and tied each of them in a circle slightly smaller than the circumference of the two jars that would be the tops of my "hourglasses." After soaking the strings in kerosene, I laid them around the bottom edge of two jars, set them on fire and let them burn. When the fire got hot enough, the bottoms cracked cleanly out of the jars. Now, when I screwed them together with their lids, I had two large hourglasses with the tops cut out. I put tape around the cut edges so that I wouldn't cut myself as I was working with them.

I put a piece of sod in the bottom of the top part of one of them. Then I filled the top half in the other one with loose black dirt up to the depth of the sod. Now, when I poured water in each of these "hour glasses" the water on the sod went through to the bottom jar almost at once. And it was also nearly clean. The water on the dirt, however, didn't go down at all for a while. Then you could see it slowly start to seep through the dirt creating little rivulets on the inside of the glass. When the water finally came through the sieve, it was muddy and carried quite a bit of dirt with it.

The demonstration effectively and impressively proved that grass waterways on slopes in farm fields could prevent serious erosion, preserve the original soil, and keep the ground water running into rivers and streams nearly silt free. It won a blue ribbon.

I had a totally different experience when I entered the FFA (Future Farmers of America) speech contest my senior year in high school. In this competition, each participant had to write, memorize and present his (girls were not in FFA back then) own speech that was about five minutes long.

The speech I wrote was on the dangers and costs of farm fires. It was a good speech. Early in its introduction I wrote that farm fires cost farmers in the United States about three and a half million dollars a year (this was back in 1950). I remember that the text I typed said "$3,500,000."

When I gave the speech at the regional level (a win here would have taken me to the state contest) I thought everything went very well. The first question the judge asked when I had finished was, "How much do fires cost farmers every year?" I told him exactly what I had said during the speech — "three thousand five hundred dollars." The judged asked me another question that I answered easily. Then he asked again, "How much do fires cost farmers every year?" I thought it strange that I was being asked this question again, but responded as I had memorized my text, "three thousand five hundred dollars." I answered another question or two before the judged asked one more time, "How much do fires cost farmers every year?" Now quite confused by the repetition, rather than thinking about a different answer, I was locked into the wrong response and I answered, "three thousand five hundred dollars" one more time.

I placed second, and a friend named Tom Foster, who, according to our advisor, Mr. Reed, had not done as well in the presentation of his speech, won the contest. When the judge explained the reason for his placings, I was crestfallen. I learned that night to be careful when reading numbers with commas and decimal points. It was a horrible learning experience, but I had no one to blame but myself.

The Odyssey of the Extra Cupcake

Attending a one-room school gave me some education that was not at all related to studies in the classroom. It related totally to the discipline that Mom and Dad enforced whenever they thought it was needed. I will never forget the episode of the extra cupcake. It happened this way.

I was in third or fourth grade when the PTA (Parent Teacher Association) planned a social occasion at our one-room school in Nachusa. Those occasions were frequent community gatherings and always called for ample refreshments, usually fresh baked goods supplied by the mothers. My Mom made cupcakes for this affair, put them on a plate, covered it with waxed paper (Saran Wrap hadn't been invented yet) and asked me to deliver them to the school for use that evening.

The person I delivered them to – Mrs. Krayenbuhl – fawned over me and the way I handled this simple assignment. As I was about to leave she said the magic words, "You deserve to have an extra cupcake tonight."

I remembered those words, and that night after the serving of refreshments was well underway, I went to Mrs. Krayenbuhl and said in a clear and loud voice, "May I have my extra cupcake now?" My question was heard by all the people within 15 feet. I thought my question was perfectly in order on the basis of my conversation that afternoon. Most of the people who heard smiled or laughed. A tray full of cupcakes was pushed toward me and I picked out the best looking one that was left. It tasted really good. Mom, however, was one of those who overheard that brief conversation, and she was not laughing. She was mortified at her son's bad manners. She was sure that I would now forever have the reputation as "the one who had asked for a second cupcake." As far as she was concerned, the whole family was embarrassed and would be forever ostracized by my request.

As soon as we were all in the car to go home (it was only about a quarter of a mile), Mom let me know in a loud voice about my poor taste and lack of etiquette. No matter how much I tried to explain that it had been promised to me earlier that day, Mom insisted I should have known better than to ask for a second cupcake. Mom and Dad were sure my greediness was a blot on the whole family. The Gonnerman name had been stained beyond repair. I don't think I ever asked for a second cupcake – or anything similar – again. The learning curve for all of the Gonnerman children was a very shallow one.

Blowing the Chance to Sit with Friends in Church

Everything we learned about manners and personal relationships had a very small but expandable laboratory in which to be tested: Mom, Dad, and siblings, of course; two sets of grandparents; multiple aunts, uncles, and cousins. After that, it broadened out to the other students at school and the members of the families at Immanuel Lutheran Church in Dixon. We almost never socialized beyond those circles.

Generally, moving in those circles was an easy relationship. One Sunday worship service, however, was a personal disaster.

I had just gotten old enough – about 12, as I remember – to have permission along with other boys my age to sit together in the back of the church on a couple of short pews under the staircase that accessed the bell tower. On this particular Sunday, about six of us were sitting together in this rather isolated place. Our parents were sitting in pews throughout the sanctuary.

As children will sometimes do, we became more interested in being together and what we had done the week before and what we were going to do in the week to come than in the worship service and the sermon. In fact, we lost track of the sermon altogether as we talked back and forth to each other in ever louder whispers.

Then, about half way through the sermon, we slowly realized that it had gotten very quiet. We looked toward Pastor Carl Wagner in the pulpit. He was not saying anything, but he was looking directly at us. In a carefully measured and obviously irritated voice he said, "If any of you boys think you can do a better job of preaching this sermon, come up here and do it now."

Everyone in the congregation — particularly all of our parents — turned around where they sat and stared at their trusted progeny. We were totally humiliated. Pastor Wagner finished his sermon. We slunk down to try to be less visible in our pews under the staircase and never said another word we were not supposed to say for the rest of the service.

None of our parents let any of us sit together in church again for several months. Once again, I had put an indelible blot on the Gonnerman family reputation.

I can't remember ever going to a restaurant to eat as a family. Mom and Dad simply didn't have enough money to go out to eat, even only by themselves. When we went on a day-long trip, Mom would always pack a lunch which we would eat as a picnic in a park along the road, and if we couldn't find a place to picnic we ate that lunch in the car as Dad drove along the road. That was a lot less expensive than stopping at a restaurant. Besides, restaurants were not that easy to find before the era of fast food. (Dairy Queen hit the Midwest in 1940, Kentucky Fried Chicken followed in 1952, and McDonald's started its climb to being the largest fast-food chain in the world in 1954.)

Other Adventures in 4-H

Mom and Dad had encouraged me to become a member of the Nachusa Nighthawks 4-H Club in 1943, the year I became ten, the earliest age I could join. (By "encouraged" they meant "you will be a member.") My sisters and brother were also all "encouraged" to 4-H membership, and each found the experience as significant in their lives as I did in mine.

My membership, of course, meant that I had to have a project. I chose pigs. Dad, working through a broker, bought my first pig for me. It was a Spotted Poland China gilt (female), the first purebred livestock that we had ever had on the farm. It weighed a little more than 40 pounds, and cost $25.

That pig came on the train that stopped at the station in Nachusa. On the day it arrived, Dad and I stood on the train platform as the steam engine puffed past, blew its whistle, and came to a stop. We moved to stand in front of the baggage car, and when the door opened my pig was looking right at me through the slats of her wooden shipping crate.

She was mine; I was a farmer at the age of ten. Dad and I loaded the crate that contained my pig into our wagon and pulled it home behind the tractor. Her fenced-in pen was a small piece of pasture. A small farrowing house stood in one corner.

That first gilt produced two litters of pigs (averaging about nine to 12 pigs per litter) every year for six years. She won ribbons regularly at

Pigs were my 4-H project for several years growing up.

county fairs in the region. But when she grew to a weight of about 600 pounds I knew I had to ship her to market. At that weight, she was prone to die from the summer heat. She was also getting to be a risky mother since she was so big she could easily crush or suffocate little pigs by lying on them during their first ten days of their life. She wasn't as mobile as she had been when younger, and she had gotten too heavy to move quickly if the pigs were under her when she would lie down.

My own herd of pigs had grown to about 50 when she started to be a problem. She had to go. I shipped her to a meat processor at the Chicago stockyards where she provided one last surprise. The check from the processor was supposed to read $111.11. But when it came in the mail, and I opened the envelope, I was astounded. The check was made out for $1,111.11.

That presented quite a moral dilemma for a 16-year-old boy. I asked Dad and Mom what to do. They thought I should only get the $111.11 that the processor intended, but they had not seen many thousand-dollar checks in their lifetimes, so they knew what a bonanza it would be if that extra thousand dollars was legally mine. But even though it might be legal, it didn't seem right to take that much money. What a conundrum!

I decided that I would have the bank make the decision. I nervously took that check to the bank with the bill of sale and explained the situation. The bank teller said it was a legitimate check, and I could cash it for the full amount. I still had to make the decision, but by now it wasn't as hard as I thought it would be. I cashed it for only $111.11, the amount my pig was supposed to be worth. The money was immediately deposited in my bank account. I expected to receive some kind of note of appreciation for my integrity from the meat processor, but I never heard a word. Disappointed, I never shipped livestock to that processor again.

That 600-pound sow had been the start of my own small farming business when she weighed only a little more than 40 pounds. By the time I went to college, I had a purebred herd of 65 hogs, a purebred

flock of 45 sheep, and my own corn acreage. That's what financed most of my undergraduate education at Wartburg College in Waverly, Iowa.

Having livestock could give a teenager and his parents one unexpected learning experience after another. One year I had one lamb that became something of a pet. Most farm livestock is thought to be utilitarian, grown to produce meat as quick-

I put my agricultural experience to good use two summers during college when I fed out a train carload of feeder pigs. I bought the pigs when they weighed between 40 and 50 pounds. They were put on pasture and fed shelled corn and a high protein supplement through the summer and weighed about 200 pounds, the ideal market size, when I shipped them to Chicago before going back to college.

ly as possible or milk in abundance every day or wool once every spring or breeding stock that will improve and enlarge every herd and flock. But this lamb, a purebred Oxford ram, had been rejected by its mother when it was born and had to be fed milk with a bottle until it could move to the usual grain, hay, and pasture diet. That almost always made a pet out of an animal, at least in the early months of its life. And pets were sometimes given special privileges like living outside the pen where the rest of the flock was, having the run of the entire farmstead.

This particular ram lamb was a good one. I knew it would be a winner in the show ring that August. I also knew it would sell for a good price to another Oxford farmer as a breeding ram.

One morning in early summer I was horrified to find this lamb staggering around the yard, just barely able to keep its balance. Something was drastically wrong. When I looked around I found the source of the trouble. We had a 50-gallon gasoline barrel on a small stand at the edge of the yard. As I walked past that barrel I realized that gasoline was running out of the spigot into a pan.

The small bit of wool on the handle of that spigot was the only clue I needed to know what had happened earlier that morning. My lamb had rubbed against the spigot and opened it enough to start the gasoline running. Then, thinking the gasoline collecting in the pan was a new kind of beverage, it drank its full.

Gasoline is poison. My lamb was dying. I rushed into the house, told Mom – Dad was already working in the field – and called our veterinarian. I explained what had happened and, with tears in my eyes, asked if there was anything I could do.

He said, "Take a large pop bottle, fill it half with orange juice and half with castor oil, and make your lamb drink every bit of it."

Luckily, we had everything we needed in the house. Mom helped me mix the orange juice and castor oil and pour it into the bottle. Then she rushed out with me to try to get that smelly concoction into my lamb.

We held the lamb's head up while I stuck the bottle down its throat, clamped my hand around its jaws, and didn't let go until every drop had drained into that very sick, poisoned animal. After that, all we could do was wait.

It didn't take long until that lamb started to urinate. It just stood there, with the urine flowing out. It stood there for much of the rest of the day, urinating. I put a lock on that gasoline spigot and turned over the dish under it. But there was nothing else we could do that night except hope the remedy had worked. It did. The next morning, that lamb was walking around as if nothing had happened.

Later that summer that young ram strutted its stuff and took top ranking in every show ring. He was sold at the end of the fair season for $200. I was a little afraid that the gasoline poisoning might have made him sterile. If that had been the case I would have had to return the money. But I never heard a bad word about that ram, and the money went into the bank.

My love of fairs took root when I joined 4-H. The climax of every 4-H project – whether it was animal husbandry or home economics – was the excitement of showing something at the county fair that represented what you had done and what you had learned during the year.

More important, I began to learn something about the art of showing an animal and how significant the way an animal was shown was to how well it placed. I noticed that some exhibitors had small boards – about two feet high by two-and-half-feet wide, made of three-eighths inch plywood, with a handhold cut into the top. The boards were always painted. Some of them had a 4-H emblem or the exhibitor's name on them. It was used to move the pig around the ring, keep it away from other pigs (they often wanted to fight each other), or keep it from going where it wasn't supposed to go.

I noted that some exhibitors who had more experience and had spent more time training their pigs for the show ring didn't use a board but had a short whip instead. The first two-and-a-half to three feet of the whip was stiff and covered with leather. The six to eight inches of the whip at the end was a continuation of the leather, braided together with a fringed end that could be flipped in front of your pig or against its ears to make it turn or stand still.

The second year I showed my pigs – I now had enough pigs to enter more than one class – I had made myself a board and purchased a showing whip. I used both of them, and they helped with my poise in the show ring.

Until I got to be a teenager with a driver's license my fair experiences were limited to Lee County where I lived. Within a couple of years after my first fair experience I had added sheep to my list of projects and was showing both pigs and sheep in several classes.

Sheep were shown differently than pigs. Pigs moved around in the show ring and the judge walked among them, sorting out the best and sending those he knew were not going to place out of the ring and back to their pens.

But sheep were brought into the ring with the exhibitor's hand grasping the wool under the sheep's neck. When you got in the ring with your sheep you put it in a line with the rest of the sheep in that class, continuing to hang on to the neck wool and using your other hand to spread and place the sheep's feet to give it its best look. Then the judge walked back and forth along the line, sometimes asking exhibitors to turn the sheep so that he could see it from the side, and then turning the sheep back again.

As the judge made his decisions about the order in which he was going to place the sheep he told the exhibitors to move the sheep to different places in the line. You had a pretty good idea about how your sheep would place as the judge moved you and your sheep from one end of the line to the other. It was pretty exciting, particularly if you stayed near the head of the line.

Whether it was hogs or sheep that were being judged, after the decision had been made for how the animals would place, the judge would take a microphone and explain the reasons for his placings to the exhibitors and all the other people watching this competition. That's where you found out what kind of breeding and feeding you had to do to improve your herd or your flock.

I was raising two kinds of sheep, Oxfords and Cheviots. Oxfords were medium size with bodies that were quite compact. They had faces and legs covered with dark brown wool that was almost like hair. They were rather quiet, quite gentle, and seldom got excited. Cheviots were a little bigger than Oxfords. They had white faces and white legs. They were quite excitable and could run like deer.

Once, when I was showing my Cheviots at the fair in Dixon, one of them got away from me while I was moving it to the show ring. Not only did it get away from me, nobody could stop it before it got out of the tent. It took off down the street, ran across one of the bridges over the Rock River, and dashed into the parking area between the bridges. About a half dozen of my friends and I took out after it on a dead run. We could not catch that sheep. All we could do was keep it in sight.

Finally, it tired of running around between the cars in the parking lot. And it was scared. We cornered it and I was able to grab it by the neck. Getting it back to the fairgrounds was quite a bit of work since the sheep wanted to go in the opposite direction. But with help, I finally got it back in its pen. That sheep had run away from its chance to be shown. It didn't win anything at that fair that year.

As I got older and more experienced, I began to enter my hogs and sheep in the open class as well as the 4-H and FFA competitions. That was even more fun. Now my livestock was competing against the "professionals." The prize money was bigger, too.

My fair experiences expanded greatly after I was able to borrow our neighbor's small truck, load up the best hogs and sheep I had, and haul them around to several county fairs in Northern Illinois. Each fair lasted a couple of days, and I enjoyed sleeping on cots in empty pens next to them or in special accommodations that the better fairs provided.

After the last of the county fairs, I drove my animals to the Illinois State Fair near the campus of the University of Illinois in Champaign-Urbana. There, I showed my livestock in both the 4-H and open class categories. By this time I knew a lot of the other teenagers and many of the adults who also traveled the county fair circuit before the state fair.

We showed our animals against each other in a friendly competition. I soon learned that different judges did not always place animals in the same way, so there was always some exciting mystery left when I brought my hogs or my sheep into the show ring. That meant that just because your animal had taken a championship ribbon at one fair did not mean it would take championship ribbons at all of them. Sometimes the competition changed and a new animal was in the ring. Sometimes a ribbon-winning animal simply didn't show as well at one fair as it had the week before.

I also learned that fairs were good places to buy animals that would improve your own flock or herd. More than once I bought a gilt that had placed well against my hogs so that I would be able to upgrade my own stock.

However, I also learned that practice had risks. One year, I saw a Spotted Poland China gilt that I really liked in the open class at the Illinois State Fair. It placed well in the competition. As soon as I could find time I looked up the owner and asked if her pig was for sale. It was, and we agreed on a price of $125.

When the fair ended, I put that pig in the truck with the rest of my livestock and headed home. The next spring I noticed that some of my pigs seemed to have a strange problem. Their noses began to look like they had been pushed back into their face. The worst case was on the new gilt – now a sow that had given birth to a litter of pigs.

I called the veterinarian. He came out and confirmed the worst. The gilt I purchased at the Illinois State Fair had a disease called rhinitis. That prize-winning pig had not only passed the disease on to her own pigs, but probably had also infected the rest of my herd and contaminated the ground of my hog lot. I would not be able to sell any more of my pigs as breeding stock, but I would be able to ship them to market.

It was a big blow, but I was going to college that fall and was planning to get rid of most of the herd that year anyway. The biggest problem was that pigs that are shipped to market to be butchered into pork chops, bacon, ham, and sausage were not worth nearly as much as if they had been sold individually to other breeders as gilts or boars.

The love of fairs has stayed with me since that first time I showed my first pig. Ruth and I went to the Ohio State Fair every year that we lived in Columbus. We went to the Michigan State Fair when I was interning in Detroit. And we went together to the Minnesota State Fair every year but one after we moved to that state in 1961.

I remember the excitement of preparing for the Rice County Fair when our children were active members of 4-H and I was a 4-H leader. And it was fun to be a judge of 4-H photography for 20 years at the Minnesota State Fair.

Fairs are in my blood – and always will be.

Get Rich Schemes That Weren't

I and many of my friends in 4-H and FFA were always looking for something a little off-beat that we thought would make us lots of money. I tried three ventures. None of them was successful.

First, I noticed that no one in our area was growing peanuts. I also noticed that peanuts were pretty expensive to buy in the store. So I read about peanut culture. I learned, first of all, that peanuts grow in the ground like potatoes. I also learned that they prefer sandy soil. The soil on our farm was heavy black loam – anything but sandy. None-the-less, I was not going to be convinced that I could not raise peanuts and get in on what I thought was that rich peanut market.

I plowed and disked a couple of acres. Then I banked that soil into long, foot-high mounds about two feet apart and 50 yards long. I ordered the peanut plants from a seed catalog and planted them according to instructions as soon as they arrived.

They did well, and that fall I harvested them by pulling them gently, bringing the peanuts up from the ground with the plants. The nuts in the shells were fastened to the ends of the roots. I stacked the plants with their nuts still attached in one of our empty cribs. The crop made a large pile, and the peanuts tasted good.

But now, as in many of my enterprises, I didn't know how to market the crop. Somehow, I had to let someone who would be interested in buying them know that I had them to sell. Then I had to get them to that person or company in a form that they wanted. I didn't know whether I could sell the peanuts in the shell, whether I had to shell them first, or whether they needed to be roasted and salted. So I didn't do anything with that crop in the crib until I finally decided, just to get rid of it, to feed the whole mess to my pigs.

No big profit there.

Next, I decided that popcorn would be a good cash crop that no one else in our community was growing. Planting this crop was a lot simpler than the peanuts. I simply used the corn planter we usually used for other corn. The harvest was good, and I piled the ears, still in their husks, in the same place in the crib where the peanuts had been.

But once again, I didn't have a clue about marketing. I didn't know how to find a person or company that was willing to buy the ears of popcorn and process them for sale. The popcorn lay in the crib about as long as the peanuts had the year before. Then I fed that crop to my pigs.

No big profit there, either.

Finally, I read about angora fur and saw in catalogs how expensive angora sweaters were. I decided I could make a lot of money growing and selling angora fur. So I bought Angora rabbits. I already had a couple of rabbit hutches from an earlier interest, so that wasn't a problem. Those fuzzy, white, pink-eyed bunnies were cute. But, even though the floors of their hutches were open hardware screen, they kept getting that expensive fur matted with their manure. It was frustrating to see that matted mess and know that it wasn't close to marketable in that shape.

Finally, the rabbits seemed to get themselves cleaned up. When their fur was now about two or three inches long I decided to shear them. That was another unexpected adventure. First, the fur was so fine that it was hard to keep it from flying all over the place after it was sheared from the rabbit. Second, rabbits don't sit still like sheep when they are being sheared, so cutting the wool off without cutting the rabbits' skin was a real challenge. Third, angora fur is sold by the pound, and after I had sheared a couple of rabbits and put what fur I could keep from flying away into a shoebox I still did not have enough for any appreciable weight at all. It seemed like I would have to shear hundreds of rabbits hundreds of times to have enough fur to sell.

No big profit there either. I got out of the Angora rabbit business.

Three ideas. Three adventures. Three failures. One valuable lesson: You can't make money with any venture if you don't know how to complete the job with intelligent and informed marketing. However, one of the most significant things about all of these failed projects was that Dad let me do it. And while he never said so, I think he was quietly hoping they would succeed.

The Lutheran Orphanage and the Boy Scouts

A Lutheran orphanage stood at the southeast corner of the intersection of the Lincoln Highway and the blacktop road that led to Nachusa. The orphanage (that's what it was called instead of a children's home until after World War II) consisted of three large brick buildings and a barn plus the nice brick house where the superintendent lived with his family. I never lived at the orphanage, but it was an important place in my life.

First, the Nachusa Boy Scout Troop held all of its meetings there so boys who lived in the orphanage could be members. Boy Scouts was an important organization for me. I advanced as far as Life Scout, but never earned enough merit badges to become an Eagle Scout. My interest in scouting waned as 4-H began to claim more of my time, enthusiasm, and energy. I was, however, made a member of the Order of the Arrow during one of the Boy Scout camps that I attended nearly every summer.

The initiating ceremony for Order of the Arrow was infused with mystery and included elements of a Native American ritual. After it was totally dark, all of the more than 100 scouts at camp made a large circle around a blazing campfire. Then a small group of scouts moved slowly around the inside of the circle. One held a bow. As they got to a scout who had been selected for the Order of the Arrow, an arrow was shot into the ground between his feet. Only six to ten scouts were selected each year and they were never told in advance that they had been picked.

The arrow between your feet was only the beginning. All the initiates were told to bring their backpacks with blankets or a sleeping bag, their compass and their knife to a meeting late the next afternoon. Each of us was given two matches. Then we were all taken on a hike together and one by one left off alone in different parts of the woods. That's where we spent the night. Those who could build a fire with two matches did. I did. It was kind of cold. The next morning we had to find our way back to camp headquarters. The whole experience was a great, somewhat scary adventure.

I have been disappointed and chagrined at the anti-gay stance the Boy Scout organization has taken in recent years. That position is extremely ill-informed, and, bordering on bigotry, actually goes against the tenets of scouting's own pledge. They made one move toward improvement in the spring of 2013, when they ruled that gay boys could be members of Boy Scouts. The next year scouting leadership, responding to extended negative response, also moved to allow gay men to be scout leaders.

Boy Scout First Aid

However, while I was a Boy Scout I learned most of what I still know about first aid as I participated in first aid contests. The contests worked this way.

We were in teams of four scouts each. Each team would be given a first aid problem that spelled out the symptoms a person had after he (we only dealt with boys) had been in some kind of accident. One of the members of the team (designated by a number on the sheet that spelled out the symptoms) had to play the part of the in-jured person. That meant he could not participate in the diagnosis or treatment. The other members of the team had to diagnose the problems and figure out the treatment they could perform before professional help would arrive to take over.

The problems ranged everywhere from bumps and cuts on the head, to broken arms and legs, to deep cuts that were bleeding pro-fusely, to shock. We had to use things we would have with us or could find nearby under ordinary circumstances if we were hiking in the woods or working in a farm field. We would decide what needed to be done and then would rig up and apply tourniquets, slings, and even makeshift casts to the person who was designated as the patient.

We had great training. Since Mom was a nurse, when our team got together for practice she helped us diagnose what was wrong, figure out what we had to do, and decide how to do it without mak-ing things worse or hurting the patient even more. David Hockman, my best friend, was one of the members of the team. The other two members were usually two of the boys from the orphanage. We all worked well together and won several contests. David, now retired, went on to become a doctor in Galena, Illinois.

Each team was judged on the correctness of its diagnosis, how well it applied the appropriate first aid remedies, how fast the treat-ment was completed, and how neat and secure all the bandages, slings, and other treatments had been tied on.

Another reason the orphanage played a role in my life was that it had the only softball field in the community. I didn't use it much until I joined 4-H and became a member of the club softball team. We had a good team that played well enough to be Lee County champion at least one year. I loved to play the left side of the infield, and was named as all-league shortstop one season.

The third reason the orphanage was important came later. It had a school bus to take the children who lived there to school in Dixon. I rode that bus back and forth to Dixon nearly every day during the four years I attended Dixon High School. Earlier I had ridden a bus during seventh and eighth grade to attend school in Franklin Grove. Dixon was five miles west of our farm. Franklin Grove was five miles east.

Bicycle Accident

I had a bicycle from about the age of 12 through high school. It was particularly important because the two sets of buildings on our farm were about a mile apart on opposite sides of Nachusa. I don't remember that any of my bicycles were ever new when I got them. They were all second – or maybe even third – hand. Dad got my bicycles for a few dollars from one of the neighbors when one of their children had outgrown them. That usually happened when they got their own car. (I wouldn't get my first car until I was a junior in college.)

Bicycles were different back then. They had balloon tires, not the narrow tires on most bikes today. They also had coaster brakes what worked by rotating the pedals backwards. I had never even heard of hand breaks. Nearly every bike had a wire basket attached to the handlebars. The basket could be used to carry lunches, softballs and bats and gloves, groceries, books, and anything else you couldn't hang on to while riding your bike. Some bicycles even had baskets that hung on both sides of the rear wheel.

I rode my bike a lot. Sometimes I even used it to go to the pasture in the late afternoon to get the cows for milking. Mostly, however, I used my bike to ride back and forth to Nachusa and a little farther to Grandma and Grandpa Gonnerman's house.

One evening I was riding to a Boy Scout meeting at the orphanage about half a mile from our house. I was riding east on the Lincoln Highway – riding fast because I was late to the meeting.

For reasons I can't remember, I put on the brakes hard and fast. The bicycle stopped. Unfortunately, I did not. I went flying over the handlebars. In a flash, I landed on my face on that rough cement of the Lincoln Highway. My glasses were bent all out of shape. My mouth was bleeding. Most frightening, however, I knew from feeling the rough edges with my tongue that I had broken at least one of my front teeth.

I pedaled back home in tears, and I must have been a bloody mess when I came through the door. Mom was able to clean up the blood, patch up the cuts, and help to straighten out my glasses.

But the teeth were another story. One of the middle ones on the top was broken off about an eighth of an inch. The other one seemed to be OK. However, we didn't have the money to get them fixed properly, so the dentist ground off the rough edges on the broken one and tried to even my two big front teeth up a bit.

About 35 years later the one that had not been broken began to turn gray. That's when my dentist in Northfield recommended that it was time to have both of them capped. By now, I had insurance to cover most of the cost so ever since that time the two large teeth in the top of my mouth have been porcelain caps.

The Joy of Chores

Farm parents make sure their children know that chores are a way of life on a farm. From the time that a boy's dad thought his son was old enough and big enough to help, he was assigned chores. Girls were assigned chores inside the house by their moms and did outside chores if they had 4-H livestock projects of their own. The first assignments were usually made when children were between the ages of six and eight. And once an assignment for chores was made, those chores were expected to be done every day, morning and night, whether it was sunny, rainy, snowy, warm or cold.

Most of the chores for boys on a farm when I was growing up involved something to do with the care of animals. One of the first things any farm child learned when chores were assigned is that the animals depend on you. If you didn't do your chores, the animals would be hungry, thirsty, and uncomfortable.

Chores might include anything Dad or Mom thought needed to be done. It might be making sure the water tanks were full for the cattle, hogs, sheep, and chickens. If they weren't, we filled them. It might be collecting the eggs that hens had laid during the day from their nesting boxes and carrying them into the house in a basket. It might be feeding the calves and making sure their pens were clean. It might be "slopping" (feeding) the hogs. It might be shelling corn with the small, hand-cranked corn-shelling machine. It might be filling the chicken feeders with cracked corn and protein supplement and making sure the eggshell feeder was full.

During the summer, my chores might include going to the garden to pick peas or beans or tomatoes, pulling radishes, or cutting lettuce for dinner that night.

The chores were assigned on the basis of how much I could lift and how hard the work was. The older I got, the harder the work would be and the more I was expected to do as a part of the family.

At the age of ten, after I had gotten my own livestock for a 4-H project, my chores took on a more personal nature, because now I was taking care of my own animals. Dad would not do those chores for me unless I was sick.

I was always in trouble whenever I didn't do my chores at the time that was expected. No excuse was acceptable.

One winter day when I got off the school bus I noticed as I was walking up the driveway that the whole barnyard was covered with about a quarter inch of clear ice. It had rained late that winter afternoon and all the water turned to ice as it hit the frozen ground. I went in the house, told Mom I was home, and changed my clothes for chores.

I knew what chores I was supposed to do, but that slippery ice all over the yard was too good to pass up. I grabbed my sled from the porch, ran across the driveway toward the barn, belly slammed onto that ice, and slid like the wind across the yard – for about 50 feet.

Then one of the metal runners of the sled hit a small clump of dirt that had not been covered with ice. The sled stopped at once. I didn't. Instead, I slid headfirst off the sled and onto that ice, slicing my chin open as I went. It didn't hurt much, but when I got up, blood was all over the front of my chest. I had ripped a hole in the skin of my chin, and blood seemed to be rushing out.

I ran yelling into the house. Mom could not help but see my problem. She grabbed a towel and pushed it up against my chin, telling me to hold it there. I did, but the bleeding did not stop. Mom knew I needed more help than even she could provide, so she found Dad in the barn, told him what had happened, and said she would have to take me to the doctor.

I got in the car, still holding the towel under my chin, making sure I didn't get blood all over the front seat. The rain had not frozen on the highway, so Mom could drive pretty fast going into Dixon to the doctor's office. When we got there, Dr. Murphy took a look and had a nurse clean up the laceration at the bottom of my chin. Then he sewed the wound up with four stitches and put a bandage over it.

It was pretty quiet in the car as Mom drove home. As I expected, Dad was without sympathy. I knew what Dad would say, and he did: "That cut on your chin is your own fault. If you would have done your chores first like you were supposed to, it wouldn't have happened. I did most of your chores, but you still have to feed your pigs." I did.

After the stitches were taken out, I had a small scar about an inch long. It never went away. When I got older I would often nick it when I shaved and draw a little more blood. That's one of the reasons I've worn a beard for the past 45 years.

Hunting and Target Practice

I bought my own rifle when I was about 13. Dad had a Remington that stood in the broom closet behind the cook stove in the house on the Lincoln Highway. I was entranced by that gun, as most young farm boys would have been. It was totally harmless. The firing pin had broken off and there was no way it would ever fire a bullet unless it was repaired.

The rifle I bought was a .22 caliber, bolt action Marlin with a tubular magazine under the barrel. The magazine held 18 long rifle or 22 short rifle shells. I usually used long rifle. I also fitted the gun with a leather sling. The gun and sling together cost about $25.

It was a good rifle. Sometimes, for target practice, I would nail Campbell's soup can lids to a wooden fence post and try to shoot the nail out of the lid from about 25 feet away. After some practice, I was proud of the fact that could do that consistently with one shot.

A few years ago I was going through a small box of memorabilia. To my surprise, I found a shoulder patch for the National Rifle Association (NRA). I think it came with the purchase of my rifle. However, given the recent history of the NRA, and its more and more mindless opposition to any restriction on gun ownership, I want nothing to do with that organization today. The membership patch went into the garbage.

Even after one massacre after another by demented gun owners, the NRA never softens its stance. Instead, it insists on making its pronouncements more unreasonably rigid, particularly in its fight against background checks with gun purchases. Furthermore, they use the Second Amendment as an excuse to encourage the arming of the entire populace while stimulating the paranoia that makes many people think their government is out to get them and take away their armory of weapons. They seem not to see, nor to understand, the introductory words to the Second Amendment: "A *well regulated* militia ..." The NRA takes offence at any regulation at all.

I had one major problem when I learned to shoot. I could not shut my left eye and hold my right one open. I still can't. That made it hard to sight the rifle when I tried to shoot right-handed. I could, however, shut my right eye and hold my left one open. So I simply shot left-handed, sighting with my left eye. That was awkward with a bolt action rifle when the bolt opens on the right, but I adjusted, and that's the way I always used that gun.

Dad showed me how to use the Marlin, gave me some basic safety training, and then I was on my own. That's the way it was for most farm boys back then. What I remember best about those days with my gun were several incidents related to hunting. Apart from the times when I went after pests such as rats, skunks, gophers, and crows, I only hunted rabbits.

The best time to hunt rabbits was after a light snowfall when I could see their fresh tracks in the snow and follow them to where they were hiding. Sometimes the tracks led into a large brush pile in the orchard. When that happened, I would stomp loudly around the hiding place, yell a little, and hit some of the brush with a stick. Usually, a rabbit would dash out the other side, run a little ways and sit down. Sometimes I was able to keep it in sight and was able to take a shot at it where it sat. Other times, I had to track it to its new hiding spot where the rabbit was always easier to see than it had been in the brush pile.

When I shot a rabbit, I would pick it up by its hind legs and either tie it to my belt with a piece of twine while I looked for another one, or would simply take it back to the house to skin and dress it. After it had been dressed (that means that it was now ready to be roasted) I would put it in a paper bag, tie a string around the top of the bag, and hang it on a nail outside the house to freeze. Mom thought that a wild rabbit always tasted better after it had been frozen for a few days.

Then Mom would bring it in, thaw it out, stuff it with dressing made mostly from pieces of old bread, and roast it in the oven. Rabbit tastes a lot like chicken. It was always good, and it didn't cost us any money.

Sometimes when rabbits are hiding and you get too close, they simply bolt from their cover and run away to another hiding place. When they break out of their hiding place right in front of you it's usually a startling experience, and I was never very good at shooting a running rabbit with my rifle. Other times, a rabbit, when it thinks it's in danger simply "freezes." It sits absolutely still. No part of it moves. And if it's sitting in dry grass or weeds that match the color of its fur, it's very hard to see.

Once when I was hunting, I saw a rabbit sitting in the grass right in front of a wooden fence post. I'm sure it thought that I couldn't see it. I did, however, and slowly raised my rifle, took aim and squeezed off a shot. The rabbit never moved. I thought that was a bit strange – usually they fall over after they have been shot – but I went over and picked it up by its hind legs. Just as I was lifting it up to examine it, it jerked, surprising me so much that I dropped it. It ran off, and this time I couldn't follow its tracks to where it stopped again.

When I went back to the fence post where the rabbit had been sitting I discovered that the bullet had gone into the post just a whisker above its head. The bullet never touched it, but it scared the rabbit so much that it "froze" to the point that it let me pick it up before it realized that now it was in even greater danger and made its get-away.

My best friend David Hockman and I often got together with our rifles for target practice. He also had a Marlin, but his had a clip magazine. (David lived in a big, white, house in Nachusa, right across the street from the feed store, only about a quarter of a mile from our farmhouse.)

One day, after we had been shooting at targets on fence posts for a while, we walked out in a field to see what might attract our attention. A group of crows flew up and we both took a shot or two at a couple of them. (Crows are considered to be major pests on a farm.) When we brought our rifles down from our shoulders, David said to me, "Did you see that? You shot one of those crows right out of the sky."

Both David and I were pretty good marksmen, but neither of us ever expected to hit anything on the fly with our .22s. That's just too tough a shot.

But we went out into the field another 75 yards of so, and sure enough, there was a very dead crow. I had aimed at it, but as I hit it my rifle barrel must have lifted above the target and I didn't see the crow fall. That was probably the best shot I ever made, but it was certainly more luck than skill.

Thinning the Crop of Gophers

Gophers were one of the worst pests we had on the farm. After a field of corn had been planted, gangs of gophers could start at one end of the row and dig up and eat every seed in the ground for 50 to 75 feet. Poisons didn't help much. We didn't like to use them anyway (we never knew for sure what was going to eat them), so Dad thought it was just fine for me to spend an hour or so a day right after the corn had been planted trying to thin out the gopher population.

Gophers are crafty little animals, a lot like prairie dogs. When they take over a territory they fill it with tunnels that run in all directions about five inches under the top of the soil. As soon as anyone came around, all the gophers would disappear down their holes. But gophers also are not too smart. They whistle to each other, and it's pretty easy to imitate that whistle.

So I would go to the spot in the cornfield where I knew the gophers had begun their feasting on the seed corn, lie down, tighten my sling, and whistle. It didn't take long before a gopher would stick its head out of its hole to see which of its friends was calling. It made a target that was hard to miss. So one after the other I would whistle them up and shoot them down. It was pest control at its best.

A Skunk in the Chicken Coop

One night, just before we went to bed, we were startled by a horrible squawking from a small chicken coop about 50 yards from our house. Dad and I both had a pretty good idea what it was, but he told me to check it out. I loaded my rifle with long rifle cartridges, found a flashlight and headed out in the dark to the chicken coop, being careful not to get too close when I shined the light in the open door.

Sure enough, there in the light from the flashlight inside the coop was a skunk with a dead chicken in its mouth. Skunks are a problem to get rid of. I had read that if you shot a skunk in the head its muscles would relax and it would still spray its awful smell as it died. The only way to avoid that problem was to shoot a skunk in the spine, paralyzing its muscles. Of course, that is not an easy shot, particularly when the skunk is facing you and you are aiming at it while holding a flashlight under the barrel of the gun.

Working very carefully, I moved the flashlight around until it illuminated the front sight of the gun, aimed just above the skunk's head at the center of its back, and squeezed the trigger. The skunk dropped instantly and never released its smell.

I went back into the house, unloaded, and put away my rifle. Then, as nonchalantly as possible, I announced that I had taken care of the problem in the chicken coop. Dad was impressed. I buried the skunk the next morning.

Rats in the Basement

The old house on the Lincoln Highway had an assortment of inconvenient problems. Not only was it drafty, had an outdoor toilet, and was lit only with kerosene lights, it also had rats in the basement. Sometimes we could hear them scampering around down there when we were sitting in the living room.

One cool fall night I decided I could be the family protector and asked Dad if I could take my rifle into the basement and see if I could shoot them. I had shot rats in other places around the farm — wood piles and under the corn crib — many times.

Dad said, "Yes," so I loaded my gun with long rifle shells, lit a kerosene lantern, open the door in the floor of the porch, and headed down into the dark cellar which we used for food storage and cream separating.

I hung the lantern on a nail that had been pounded into one of the wooded beams and waited. It didn't take long. Pretty soon I saw a rat scampering along the top of the stone foundation beneath the supporting beams. I had been holding my rifle with the barrel pointing up. When I saw that rat, I began to bring the barrel down to aim, but in my excitement I squeezed the trigger too soon. The noise was horrendous as the gun went off in that small room while it was pointed at the basement ceiling, which was also the living room floor. I hoped with all my might that the bullet was lodged in one of the floor's supporting beams.

For a moment the conversation my family was having above me in the living room stopped and it was very quiet. Then it started up again as if nothing had happened. The accidental firing scared me, and I decided I was done trying to shoot rats in our basement that night.

I tried to be relaxed when I went back upstairs, blew out the lantern, and unloaded my gun. Dad asked if I had killed a rat. I said I had seen one, but missed it. Then I tried to rejoin the conversation with my family. Mom said that the stove had jumped when they heard the shot. That scared me even more, but I tried to act like it was no big deal.

The next morning, when no one else was in the living room, I looked under the heating stove. There, lying on the metal-covered, fire protection board under the stove, was the lead slug from my bullet. It had come up through the floor only three inches inside of one of the legs of the stove, hit the bottom of the stove, and dropped back down to the board while leaving a round hole with little triangles of metal all around it under the stove.

I felt weak all over as I realized that if that bullet had come through the floor only a few inches from where it did it might have missed the stove and hit my brother or one of my sisters who were gathered close by. A guardian angel had been watching over everyone in the family, including me, that night. I found a screwdriver and used it to push those little telltale metal triangles back over the bullet hole. I never hunted rats in the basement, or fired my rifle in the house, again.

The Dust Puffs Mystery

A strange thing happened one summer. Some of us in the family began to see little puffs of dust "exploding" near us as we were walking across the barnyard.

Dad and I both saw it. We talked about it but couldn't figure out what was causing these little disturbances. Then, as we were wondering about the mystery, we also began to hear our windmill, which sat in the northwest corner of the yard, make some unusual pinging noises. At first, we didn't make any connection between the two.

But one day, when the wind was blowing from the west, we also heard what sounded like gun shots. Our closest neighbors lived less than a quarter mile to the west on the opposite side of the road. We could see their farm clearly whenever we looked in that direction.

When we looked at our neighbor's farm on the day we heard the gun shots we saw our neighbor's oldest son Richard out in the yard with his .22 caliber rifle. He seemed to be aiming in the direction of our farm. Then everything came together.

We heard the sound of the rifle firing, at almost the same time we heard the pinging sound from the windmill, and an instant after that a bit of dust puffed up a short ways from our feet.

Dad and I looked at our windmill with its large steel wind vane and figured out what was going on. Richard was using the wind vane for target practice. Sometimes, if the vane was at just the right angle, when he hit that metal vane the slug from the bullet ricocheted into our yard and kicked up a puff of dust.

Dad went right over to the neighbors and talked to Richard's father, Frank. We never heard any pinging sounds from our windmill, and we never saw any unexplained puffs of dust in our barnyard again. Those slugs probably weren't dangerous after traveling a quarter mile and bouncing off steel, but we were glad that none of them had ever hit anyone in the family.

Manners, Courtesy, and Family Rules

Mom and Dad, especially Mom, paid special attention to rudimentary manners, and made sure all the children knew how to hold and handle their silverware. We asked for a dish of food to be passed with "Please" in the asking and "Thank you" when the dish was received, and we didn't even think of reaching past another person to pick up a dish of food on our own – at least not more than once – if we knew what was good for us.

But silverware at our house never went beyond knife, fork, and spoon, usually not with matching patterns, so we did not know the mysteries of dealing with multiple forks and spoons. If any eating utensil showed up above the plate we just assumed that it was left there by accident. I was never even introduced to that conundrum until I got to college and began to move in other circles. In fact, most children who grew up on farms never had the opportunity in their childhood to solve those kinds of puzzles.

Lots of things were "no-nos" while I was growing up, but two things were particularly bad and could get any of the Gonnerman children in trouble fast.

The first was a meal-time thing, and it did not deal with dinnerware. All the children in the family – Mom and Dad did it, too, setting the example – could not leave the table until their plate was clean. That included several rules. First, everyone had to put at least a spoonful or a piece of every food on the table on their plates, no matter whether it was familiar or totally new (we didn't get much of anything "new") or whether we thought we would like it or not. Second, everything on our plates had to be eaten. This rule was called the "clean plate club."

If, in an almost unthinkable surge of rebellion, we tried not to eat something on our plates, we would sometimes have to sit at the table until we did eat it, or we would not get any dessert (when there was dessert), or we would have to go to bed early. We would also hear about "the starving children in India," as if our eating everything would somehow keep them from starving. Of course, before we developed our capacity for critical thinking, the "starving children" anywhere had the emotional effect Mom wanted. How could we possibly threaten their livelihood by our lack of appetite for foods we thought we didn't like?

We also all stayed at the table together until everyone was done. No one was excused from the table ahead of the rest of the family without a very good reason.

One of the occasional "delicacies" in our diet was called "cracker souppie." Most often, it was a snack before we went to bed. Occasionally it was dessert after dinner. Here's the recipe: take a handful of soda crackers, put them in a dessert dish, pour milk over them, and add sugar to taste. It doesn't sound like much when I write it down like that, but it was delicious, particularly when Mom and Dad didn't have the money to buy anything fancier.

The second of the "sins" was getting caught looking as though we were not busy. Neither Mom nor Dad could tolerate simply relaxing for any sustained period of time. After we reached school age, all of the children in the family had to look busy all of the time.

Consequently, we all learned that if we weren't working on some particular chore, or doing homework, or practicing a musical instrument, we either had to stay out of sight or be doing something that looked like it might be work. We all learned ways to look busy while doing as little as possible.

The Good and the Not So Good at High School

High school was a totally different experience from everything in my education that preceded it. I continued to go to school on a bus, but this bus went west to Dixon instead of east to Franklin Grove. It came from the Lutheran Orphanage just a half mile east of our farm. It picked me up in the morning at the end of our driveway. In the afternoon we caught the bus at the Dixon Public Library about five blocks south of the high school on the opposite side of Rock River that flowed through the middle of town.

The best thing about meeting the bus at the library was that while walking there I went past an ice cream shop that served great malts for 25 cents. The malts were cold and creamy and so thick both a spoon and a straw stood straight up in the glass. And you got the whole can, which amounted to about two full glasses. I almost always had pineapple, my favorite flavor back then.

The second best thing about meeting at the library was that while waiting for the bus some of my friends and I could find and check out books that we took home to read just for fun.

The high school was a beautiful, light stone, four-story building, made to look something like an English castle with five-story towers on both sides of the main entrance. The towers were topped with parapets as if someone might stand up there and protect the place with bows and arrows. You reached the entrance doors by climbing up a long flight of wide stairs that was nowhere close to handicapped accessible. Nobody worried about that in the '40s and '50s. Handicapped persons were pretty much invisible.

It was a large building, longer than a city block, with a gymnasium on the west end and an auditorium on the east. The Rock River ran in front of it on the south. Both the gymnasium and the auditorium could be entered from the school, but they also had separate entrances for fans coming to sports events and audiences coming to performances and concerts. Those entrances, with their own towers and parapets, were similar to the main entrance to the school.

I loved high school classes, but had real trouble trying to fit into the social structure. Most of the more than 600 students had grown up together in Dixon's elementary school system and knew each other well. The few of us who came from other school systems — almost all of them in farm country — were not welcomed all that eagerly and had a hard time fitting in.

From the beginning I enrolled in classes that would prepare me for college, with one exception. That exception was the four years of classes I took in vocational agriculture. I have never been sorry I did that. It gave me invaluable information about plants, animals, and the conservation of the land. I used much of that knowledge in my flower gardening until failing legs and knees would not let me do that anymore.

Vocational agriculture classes also made it possible for me to develop my 4-H and FFA (Future Farmers of America) projects to the point where the livestock in those projects paid for most of my education at Wartburg College in Waverly, Iowa.

Unfortunately, two of the most embarrassing classroom experiences I ever had happened in vocational agriculture. The first was personal. It happened during the late winter of my freshman year. One of my sows gave birth to a litter of pigs one night in late February, and I was up with her (as I usually was with most of my sows when they were having pigs) to make sure everything went all right. This time, to impress the teacher and the rest of the members of the class, I also kept complete records of the birthing (known in pigs as farrowing).

I wrote down exactly what time each pig was born, how much it weighed, and whether it was a gilt (female) or a boar (male). I also cut all the umbilical cords and cut off each pig's "wolf teeth" (one extra-long, very sharp incisor on each side of the pig's mouth) with a nippers so that they would not cut each other up while fighting for space at their mother's nipples. Then I cut small notches in their ears in a particular pattern so that I would know the heritage of each pig if I wanted to register it later as a purebred. Ten pigs were born in that litter that night.

The embarrassment came the next day when I was reporting on this experience to the class. I was reading the information on the time of birth, and the weight and sex for each pig, and had gone through about three of them when I realized that laughter was building in the room. I stopped reporting and looked up from my notes, wondering what was so funny. George Reed, the teacher, said, do you know you're calling each of those pigs a boy or a girl? I hadn't known. And I don't know why I had used that language. From then on in the report all the male pigs were reported as "boars" and all the female pigs were "gilts." But I felt pretty ignorant.

The other embarrassing experience happened when I was a senior. One of the boys in the class had the habit of falling asleep almost every day. He didn't try very hard to hide it. Our desks in vocational ag were large black laboratory tables with stool-style seats that swung out from under them. We sat two to a table, facing the teacher. The boy with the sleep problem simply put his arms up on the table shortly after class began, laid his head on them, and went soundly to sleep several times a week. Sometimes he slept so soundly that he snored.

Most of the students thought it was kind of funny. Mr. Reed didn't. In one class he warned the sleeper that if he didn't stay awake, he would do something to help him remember to stay alert in every class. Sure enough, not many days after the warning, the boy fell sound asleep in class again. Mr. Reed had prearranged with another member of the class, the first string quarterback on the football team, to do the dirty work. He went into a small lab at the side of the classroom, ran warm water into a glass, came out and poured the water into the student's ear.

The student sat up in shock amid peals of laughter from everyone in the class, ashamedly in hindsight, myself included. Then the student had an even more shocked expression on his face as he wet his pants. That's the natural, automatic, and unstoppable reaction when warm water is poured into anyone's ear. The student, now very wide awake, ran out of the room with his hands between his legs.

When he ran out, the class became very quiet. It was inhumane treatment. Mr. Reed got away with that back in 1951. Today, at least he would be given a serious reprimand. He might even be fired. As far as I know, no one, including Mr. Reed, ever bothered to find out why that student was always so sleepy. That would have been the sensible and sensitive solution to the problem. He was not the brightest boy in class, but I suspect that he was in a home situation where he had to wake up too early every morning to do chores on his family's farm and it simply wore him out.

I had liked Mr. Reed. I had learned a lot in his classes and had earned straight A's. But my respect for him disappeared on that day.

Many of my high school teachers had been around a long time. In fact, some of them had been Mom's teachers when she had gone to the same high school. Some of them made the connection when I was in their classes. I was glad that most of them did not.

My freshman English class was particularly helpful. The teacher, one of the youngest and prettiest in the school, was Elizabeth Shoaf. She had an interesting procedure to help us improve our verbal communication. We were graded in her class not only on the basis of our tests, but also on how we responded verbally in class. Every time any of us answered a question, we were under the gun to make sure the response was absolutely perfect grammatically and structurally. This teacher had devised a point system that rated every kind of grammatical mistake, or structural awkwardness, or the use of a wrong word or phrase. All of us started at 0, and if we made a grammatical mistake, she added and recorded the appropriate number of points. Points would be added if we paused with an "Ah" anywhere in a sentence. Saying "Yeah" instead of "Yes" earned you points. To say, "I mean," and, "You know," was out of the question. Even starting a sentence over when you knew you were in trouble with syntax added penalty points to your score. At the end of the semester, the students with the fewest number of points "won," although I can't remember what the prize was, or even if there was one.

Mary Ann Gibson and I were tied with the fewest number of points at the end of the semester. The lesson had been to learn how to think quickly and clearly about how a response should be phrased and constructed before we spoke. That skill has been invaluable to me throughout my life.

Later, a teacher named Alice Richardson introduced me to great literature and acquainted me with the works of William Shakespeare. I loved literature then, and I still do. She also introduced me to the proper way to do a research paper.

Algebra under Ada West and geometry taught by Wallace Coon were great fun. Chemistry with L.E. Sharpe was more difficult, but I managed to get through it reasonably well, even serving as a mentor in the subject for some of my friends. Physiology – the study of the human body and all of its parts – was the science class I liked the best. I still remember a great deal of what I learned from Olive Cotta.

Latin – two years of it – was difficult, but I liked it and the language proved to be a big asset in my love of literature and pursuit of skills in communication. The downside to Latin was that in my sophomore year Christine Bessmer marked my report card with my first B. That wasn't really a shock – I knew I hadn't been doing well – but it was a disappointment.

History and Civics and Government, both taught by Myrtle Scott, were two of my favorite subjects. They still are. If more high schools today taught more Civics and Government, I think we would have less citizen apathy and more thoughtful political participation than we have now.

Two other classes were important. One was a business law course taught by A.P. Hammersmith that I found absolutely fascinating. It still helps me occasionally when I am thinking about finances and individual rights. The other class was typing, taught by Evelyn Arnould. Without it, I don't know how I would have survived college and seminary, or how I would have progressed through a most satisfying ministry in communication. It has been an absolutely indispensable skill.

My attempts at athletics were not particularly memorable. Basketball in junior high had been a lost cause, I had never seen a football game until I got to high school, and my experiences in softball were limited to playing on 4-H and church teams. But I had a few experiences in athletics that were memorable.

We were learning the game of soccer outside on the football field. I knew nothing about this game until we started playing it in gym class. I liked the game and got fairly good at dribbling the ball with my feet. Then, one day, I took a pass near the opponent's goal, dribbled right up to the football goal posts (we didn't have nets) and slammed the ball through with my left foot as I slid out of reach of the goalie. I can still hear the gym teacher as he shouted to the rest of the class. "Did you see that? That's the way to score." That really felt good.

I tried out for the track team for two years before I decided it wasn't much fun finishing towards the back of the pack all the time. I thought I was a dash man, and I was fairly fast, but not fast enough to make my races in high school competitive. Also, I always had to make sure I left practice early enough to catch the bus home from the library. If I missed the bus I had to walk, and five miles is a long way. Not only that, but Dad was never happy if I got home late to help with chores.

If I had been smarter, I would have dismissed the idea that I was a dash runner and worked instead at being a long distance runner.

Then I could have run that five miles home every night in training for the mile and half-mile races. I've always wondered whether I might have been more successful doing that. It would have been fun to know. I simply thought about that possibility way too late.

Early in my senior year I learned that on the basis of my grades I was one of the top students in my class. I also learned that the valedictorian – the student commencement speaker – would be chosen from those with the top six grade points. I wanted that honor, not the least because it would show both the faculty and the students that one of the farm kids who was often left out of social circles could compete with anyone, even with the kids who came from the city.

The procedure went like this. At the end of the first semester of their senior year, the six students who had the highest grade point were invited to prepare a short speech. The speech had to be submitted in writing. Then everyone who wanted to participate was to give the speech to a faculty committee. That committee would decide who the valedictorian would be.

I was the one selected. That was really a proud day for Mom and Dad as well as for me. I began work on my valedictory speech almost at once. The year was 1951. Two atomic bombs had been dropped on Japan in 1945, ending World War II, and the unanswered questions regarding atomic power and its effect on the nation as well as the world were still on most people's minds. I no longer have the original manuscript, but that's what my speech was about.

It was a success, well received by the class and the Commencement audience.

Summer Jobs

After I was old enough to be hired for a job other than farming I decided that I could make more than the standard one dollar an hour farmers usually paid.

One summer, I was hired by the telephone company in Dixon as a part of its line crew for $1.25 an hour. I was assigned to a truck that included two linemen. We set poles, strung new line, installed phones, and trimmed trees to keep the lines clear.

Sometimes I was sent up poles that were already fitted with "steps" made of steel pins with the ends bent up to form an "L" that would keep a person's feet from slipping off of them. I was given a safety belt, and sent up the pole to pull a line tight and fasten it to an insulator. That was great fun.

Most of the time, however, I stayed on the ground, throwing special tools up to a lineman who had already climbed to the top of the pole. I had to practice in order to learn just how hard or how soft I had to make my underhand throw to get the tool just to the point where the lineman could reach out and catch it without having to lean too far over or reach too far up or down.

We used a lot of ropes on most of the work. One rule our foreman had was that once we finished a job, the truck would not move until all the things we had used were put back in the places designed for them. That meant that all the ropes had to be coiled, wound up to keep them from unraveling, and hung back on the hooks where they had been.

That's how I learned to roll up electrical cords and ropes for storage. That skill alone has probably saved me hours of frustration I might have had if I had to unravel tangled piles of ropes or cords.

The most dramatic job I had that summer involved tree trimming. Trees and brush that overhung a telephone line and had to be cleared away were right next to a small stream. I was told to go up the biggest tree to saw away the branches that were giving the line the most trouble. I grabbed a safety belt and went up the tree to the point where I could reach most of the troublesome branches with my saw.

Then I made the mistake of looking down. The trees were along an elevated bank and after I had made my climb I was about 60 feet about the water in that shallow creek that carried a trickle of water only five or six inches deep. I double checked the latch on that safety belt before sawing off the branches and letting them fall. After I finished and climbed down I really felt like I belonged in that crew of telephone linemen.

The next summer my best friend, David, and I saw a "Help Wanted" ad from the Borden's Milk Company in Dixon. We each applied and were both hired. The pay was $1.44 an hour. That seemed like a fortune back in the early '50s.

Each of us did the same work, and sometimes we even worked together. The Dixon Borden's factory made the tin cans that were used for condensed and evaporated milk. The cans were complete except for their labels and a single hole about an eighth of an inch in diameter in the top of each can.

David and I stood in an empty railroad boxcar, facing in opposite directions. The cans came roaring down two steel conveyor tracks to the center of the car. We had each been given specially made metal forks. If we were loading condensed milk cans, the forks could pick up 32 cans at a time. Evaporated milk forks picked up 16 of the larger cans at a time.

Our job was to stick the fork into the spaces between the cans when they got to the end of the track, lift them up, and carry them to the end of the railroad car. We laid them in place and went back quickly to pick up the next row of cans, carrying them back and laying them next to or on top of the cans we had already put in place. We did that all day long with a 15-minute bathroom and coffee break (I didn't drink coffee then) each morning and afternoon and a half-hour break for lunch.

The noise was awful as those empty cans banged into each other while rattling down the steel conveyor track into the boxcar. That noise rang in my head even after I went home at night. I even heard it in my sleep. The company never even suggested that we should wear any devices to protect our ears from the noise. I doubt if anything like that had even been invented back then. (It's probably why I'm wearing hearing aids today.)

At first, both David and I had some trouble sticking the fork in exactly the right spot, and sometimes when that happened we knocked a whole row of cans unto the floor. That made even more noise, but we couldn't stop to pick them up because the cans kept filling up the conveyor track. After a day or two, we both got pretty good at sticking the forks in the right place and hardly ever knocked cans onto the floor.

We filled the boxcar with rows of cans as high as we could reach all the way up to the edge of the door in the middle. Then the conveyer tracks would be pulled out, other workers would fasten wooden walls in place to keep the cans from moving, and the car would be added to a train that took it to the factory where the cans would be filled. After the cans were filled, the little hole in the top was sealed with a drop of solder, labels were glued on, and the dairy product was sent to grocery stores all over the Midwest.

David and I worked well together and we seldom had cans backed up on the conveyor track. That caught the attention of the foreman. Pretty soon we were "promoted" to a conveyor track that put the cans in boxes.

That was not quite as noisy. Now we were inside the factory. At the end of our new conveyors evaporated milk cans were automatically forced into clusters – two layers of five rows of four each. I had to take cardboard boxes that were folded flat and stacked on one side of me, open them up and fold the bottom shut, press the open end against the end of the conveyor, and step on a switch that shot all 40 cans into the box. Then I folded the top flaps of the box shut and set the new box full of new cans on a conveyor that took it to a worker who put that box with others in a bigger box.

The tricky part of this operation was making sure that the box was lined up exactly right to catch all 40 cans. If it wasn't, the plunger simply pushed the box in my hands out of the way and all the cans fell to the floor.

Working at Borden's was hard and monotonous work. I earned my $1.44 an hour. I had learned to complete the work assigned working for Dad all those years on the farm. That summer I also learned that whatever I did for the rest of my life, it was not going to be working in a factory.

My best summer job was working as a door-to-door salesman. I was employed by a small animal feed and building maintenance and repair company in Franklin Grove. My job was to drive all over Lee County visiting as many farms as I could. I was working on commission, which meant that I didn't get a salary but I earned a percentage of the cost of every job that I sold.

It was interesting work and I met a lot of interesting people. I never knew what I might sell when I turned down a farmer's driveway. Often times I did not sell anything. I didn't try too hard to sell feed very often unless it was a last resort because I didn't earn much of a commission from feed. What I looked for most was bad roofs on houses and barns.

It wasn't hard to tell when a farmer needed a new roof, so that was the idea I would approach him with. If he was at all interested, I would measure the roof and give him a free estimate on the basis of the different qualities of shingles my company offered and the amount of labor I thought it would take to finish the job.

Many of the old barns on farms had corrugated steel roofs that were badly rusted and made the whole farm look bad. I often offered a product that my company could paint on the old, rusted roof and give it the shiny silver look it had when the roof was new. I sold a lot of those jobs, too.

By the end of the summer I had become very familiar with most of the roads and many of the farms in Lee County, and I had sold enough jobs to earn about $700 in commissions. It took the owner of the small company in Franklin Grove most of the rest of the year to finish all the jobs that I had sold for him.

I had other profitable work going during the summers I was in college. Two summers I "fed out" a "carload" of feeder pigs. One summer I "fed out" a "carload" of feeder lambs. Here's the way that worked: Using a broker, I would buy a stock truck full of pigs when they weighed about 40 pounds each just after they had been weaned. I would fence about five acres of alfalfa pasture, build a shelter to protect the pigs from the summer heat, move in an automatic watering tank and an automatic feeder, and turn the pigs loose in their new home as soon as they arrived. The goal was for those pigs to grow up to about 200 pounds and be shipped to market by the time I went back to college for the fall term.

Because of the automatic feeder and waterer, the work was minimal. Each of them had to be filled only a couple a times a week. The feeder was divided into two sections: The larger section was always filled with shelled corn, and the smaller was kept full of a high protein food supplement.

I can't remember exactly how much I earned on feeder pigs for the two summers I raised them, but I do know it was a nice profit for only three months of relatively easy work.

My experience with feeder lambs, however, was a different story. I bought half a carload of Corriedale and Western lambs through a broker and tried to apply the same principals of care and feeding that I had used for pigs. However, I knew something wasn't right about half-way through the summer when it became obvious that they were gaining way too little weight while eating far too much food.

When I checked with the veterinarian I learned that every lamb had worms. I should have run all of them through a worming tank as soon as they got off the train. It was a hard lesson. By now, it was too late for worming to do much good. I had the sheep sheered before I shipped them to market, and the price I got for the wool helped me to barely break even.

All of those summers were important in my life. I learned something about different kinds of work. I learned something about the kinds of life led by other people. I made some money. But most importantly, I learned something about myself – who I was and what kind of person I wanted to be. And those kinds of things are the most important.

Wartburg College

I was still feeling pretty good about having been the valedictorian of my class at Dixon High School when I entered Wartburg College in the fall of 1951. Then I found out that most of the people in my class at Wartburg had also been valedictorians. That brought me back to reality in a hurry. This farm boy from Dixon, Illinois, was now in a totally different academic world. However, the field was more level because many of my Wartburg classmates were also from farm backgrounds, and everybody was starting even because only a few in the class knew anyone else in the class before we arrived on campus.

The choice of Wartburg College was not the nerve-racking experience that many students go through today. First, Aunt Grace had received her teaching certificate there. That was enough of a recommendation. Dad and Mom thought Wartburg was a good idea. I never applied anywhere else. Furthermore, it was one of the five colleges of the American Lutheran Church. (Ruth graduated from one of the others – Capital University in Columbus, Ohio.)

We met our roommates the day we arrived. We had no hint of who they would be until we were on campus. Unfortunately, I was assigned to a room with two bunk beds and with three other freshmen. A quad is not a good experience for a freshman. Getting used to one roommate is hard. Becoming acquainted with three at one time is a horror. I had little in common with any of them. One was a jock, one was going to be studying art, and the third one just seemed to be there.

The second day was a surprise. The entire class (it numbered only a few more than a hundred) sat at tables in the gymnasium to take a day-long test. Almost none of us knew what the test was for, and I don't remember that anyone asked. As I think back, it was probably something like today's SAT or ACT, but only to find out whether we needed any remedial work and how we might be placed in some classes. Nobody in the class needed any remedial work. That would have insulted our high schools.

The third day I decided to find an extra-curricular activity. I tried out for one of the choirs called The Castle Singers. I didn't make it. In hind sight, that was providential because the next extra-curricular activity I decided to try to become involved in was *The Wartburg Trumpet*, the weekly newspaper. I started as a reporter – forcing me to take journalism courses – and ended up as editor my senior year. The journalism courses turned out to be one leg of my triple major, English-speech-journalism, the foundation for my ministry in public relations and communications in institutions of The American Lutheran Church (The ALC) and its successor, the Evangelical Lutheran Church in America (ELCA).

Almost all the men at Wartburg began to learn about the nitty-gritties of life – such as laundry. I had never washed my own or anyone else's clothes when I was home on the farm. Sadly, I still haven't, even after becoming an octogenarian. Grossman Hall, my dorm at Wartburg, didn't even have a washer or dryer. Or if it did, I never found them. It seems to me, however, that the dorms for women did. That's chauvinism at its best.

But our clothes were laundered regularly none the less – by our mothers. Most of the men had brought a big box with them when they came to college. It was made of a kind of pressed board (a precursor to plastic) and had canvas straps with buckles going around it in both directions. It was approximately 18 inches long, about 14 inches wide, and six inches deep. It was actually two boxes that fit inside each other and since each box was six inches deep it could be expanded to almost a foot.

About every two weeks I would stuff all my dirty underwear and shirts that I could into that box, strap it tight, change the address card from mine to Mom's, and carry it to the campus post office to be mailed. Only a few days later I would get that box back, now filled with all the laundry I had sent, clean and neatly folded. Often Mom found enough room in that box to include a bag of cookies.

It was a great system. The only thing it did not do was teach me how to do my own laundry. It did give me a regular contact with home in case I wasn't writing as many letters as Mom and Dad were expecting.

Even though I never learned the intricacies of washers and driers, laundry detergents and bleaches, when to use hot water and when cold was demanded, all of my children (two boys and two girls), and all of their children (five boys) not only learned how to do the laundry, but do it. They are the richer for it.

I loved college. One of my favorite professors was Gerhard Ottersberg. He taught history as the one continuous story it is. He never used a note. Sometimes he sat on the front edge of his desk, lifted one leg, put his heel on the desk, and held it by clasping his hands around his knee. Most of the time he paced back and forth in front of his desk, wearing a path in the floor that has been preserved in that classroom. His tests were straightforward and to the point: four questions, one hour. Write everything you know that answers the questions. The love of history runs in our family. Mark and David were both history majors at St. Olaf College, and some of our grandsons have similar interests.

Margaret Wolff was another teacher with a massive impact on my life. She taught journalism and creative writing as well as being the advisor to the weekly newspaper (*The Wartburg Trumpet,* known popularly as *The Trumpet*), the yearbook (*Fortress*), and the literary magazine (*Castle Tales*). She taught the basics of all kinds of writing, and her students seldom forgot them.

My journalism experience under Ms. Wolff was incredibly practical. After starting off as a freshman reporter for *The Trumpet*, I moved up the ladder to be assistant editor my junior year and editor-in-chief when I was a senior. Wartburg had a great relationship with *The Independent-Democrat*, the local weekly newspaper. It not only printed the *Trumpet* and set the type for body text on their linotypes, they also let *The Trumpet's* senior staff work on the printer's "stone," setting headlines letter by letter from the type cases on "pica sticks" and locking the lead lines that formed the type together in the steel forms that defined the pages. The format also included the metal engravings that would print as photographs. Then it was ready for printing on the letterpress.

I cannot imagine better training in determining the appropriate size of headlines, learning dimensions in picas, and figuring out how many points of space between stories, heads, and text were appropriate for the greatest readability. Everything I learned in that special laboratory was transferrable to the offset printing processes I learned to deal with while producing publications for The American Lutheran Church, St. Olaf College, and Luther Seminary as printing made astronomical leaps into the digital age. It was also helpful when printers discovered I could speak their language as they printed for me one publication after another that I had designed, written, and edited.

An old frame house, officially the Publication House but better known by journalism students as the Pub House, was the on-campus heart of Wartburg's journalism department. Ms. Wolff's office was there. In addition to the *The Trumpet*, the *Fortress* and *Castle Tales* were also edited in that small building. Sometimes the lights in that house would burn until 3:00 or 4:00 in the morning as editors put their publications together. But when we finished for the night, a bunch of us (almost always exclusively men) would head to Roy's Place for his infamous egg sandwiches.

Roy's Place was one of those off-campus institutions that play a significant role in a college student's education. It was a hole-in-the-wall eating establishment on Bremer Avenue, Waverly's main street. Roy's was only half-a-dozen blocks east of the Pub House. It was a compact place with one counter running its length in front of a row of about ten elevated stools. Roy always stood between his counter and his grill. He was the only one I ever saw working there.

His egg sandwiches were good, but they were overloads of cholesterol and fat. Roy's grill was continuously flooded with about an inch and a half of hot cooking oil. To make a fried egg sandwich he simply broke an egg into that steaming oil, broke the yoke so that it spread around, then lifted it out with a spatula when he thought it was done and laid it on a hamburger bun. Those sandwiches probably did not let us sleep right away when we got back to our dorm, but they sure were good.

The Evangelical Lutheran Theological Seminary in Columbus, Ohio

Seminary was also a great experience, not least because that's what made meeting my wife possible. The year I entered Trinity Lutheran Seminary Ruth was a senior at Capital University, which happened to be across the street. It was providential that she was a senior. She had stayed out the year before to take care of a pastor's family of five boys while his wife was in a tuberculosis sanitarium.

I had enrolled at Trinity rather than Wartburg Seminary in Dubuque, Iowa, because I had received a providential letter the month before the seminary year started. The letter was from Edward Schramm, the editor of *The Lutheran Standard*, the national monthly magazine of the American Lutheran Church (ALC), published in Columbus. Dr. Schramm offered me a position on his magazine as part-time editorial assistant while I was attending seminary in Columbus. It was a great opportunity, marrying my two biggest interests – theology and journalism.

Had those two providential events never happened, Ruth and I would never have met.

The offices of *The Lutheran Standard* were in the building that housed the Wartburg Press, the publishing arm of the ALC. *The Lutheran Standard* was only one of a stable of publications published there. After a while I began to be moved around so that I ended up editing weekly Sunday School papers for different age groups when their regular editors were away for a while. Part-time turned out to be about 35 hours a week, so it took me an extra semester to finish seminary. I didn't mind.

One of the publications produced at Wartburg Press was a monthly for youth called *One* magazine. I knew both of the editors. They had been students at Wartburg a few years ahead of me. Ruth Harper, a student at Capital University, worked part-time for *One*. Omar Bonderud, editor-in-chief of *One*, invit-

Ruth at her college graduation.

ed me to dinner at his and his wife Minnie's house shortly after I arrived in Columbus. He also invited Ruth.

That was the beginning of a friendship and a marriage that is now 58 years old. Ruth graduated from Capital in 1956. We were married on June 16, 1957, two months before my internship began at Salem Lutheran Church in Detroit.

Our Inexpensive Wedding

Our wedding needs a little elaboration. Most of what I was earning at *The Lutheran Standard* was going for the costs of my seminary education. Ruth's salary as a social worker at the Lutheran Orphans and Old Folks Home in Toledo, Ohio, was not large. Neither of us was able to save much. So we went for a wedding that would be as inexpensive as we could make it. Some would say, "On the cheap."

Ruth asked a friend in Ottawa Lake, Michigan, to make her dress. Ottawa Lake was the town where Ruth had taken care of a pastor's five boys while their mother was in a tuberculosis sanitarium. Ruth provided the material. The dress was beautiful.

Ruth's dad had a few miniature rose bushes at the edge of his yard. I found a pattern to make what looked a little like a miniature rose from pink paper ribbon. We took two silver colored rings, fastened them to a round card so that they stood up, and filled in the space around them with lots of our handmade miniature roses. That was the decoration for our wedding cake. With our handmade decoration, the cake cost $28.28. It was beautiful.

We spent $17.56 for a dozen white roses, a dozen white carnations, a half dozen pink miniature roses, ivy strands, florists wire and tape, and I made the bridal bouquet and necessary corsages and boutonnieres. The flowers on the altar were lilacs from Ruth's dad's bushes.

Our wedding ceremony was held at Trinity Lutheran Church in Midland in the afternoon on Trinity Sunday, June 16. During the morning worship service Ruth and I attended together there, she wrote a few notes on the back of her bulletin:

> "Let's tell Harold and Paul (the ushers), if it gets hot, to open all doors, outside and inside."

> "Who lights candles?" I responded with my own note: "I think we do before the ceremony."

> I wrote down a question: "Do they have any fans to put in the lectern and pulpit?"

We obviously were not thinking much about the worship service.

It was hot that afternoon. Very hot. Pastor William Kiether, also a friend, changed his shirt five times during the day because he was sweating so much. During the ceremony Ruth and I were a little distracted because he had a drop of sweat hanging from the tip of his nose and each earlobe. We had three bridesmaids and three groomsmen. The bridesmaids' dresses were coral in color. Everybody in the wedding and in the congregation was very hot. This was before the advent of air conditioning in most churches. We had to depend on large fans. They were not adequate.

The reception after the wedding was a partial potluck where many of Ruth's relatives brought dishes of food for our guests' refreshments. After everyone had eaten, Ruth and I opened all the presents. The patience of our guests in that hot basement was amazing as they stayed to witness our gift opening down to the last package. But that was the tradition back then. Thankfully, the cards included about $200 in cash, and we would use almost all of it on our honeymoon. We began our married life together living on love and faith. We had very little cash of our own. We did not have any credit cards, and if we would have had them, most motels, restaurants, and stores would not have accepted them. Credit cards were still too new an idea.

We created a little mystery regarding which car we would take on our honeymoon, always important to keep your vehicle from being garishly decorated by your friends and relatives. Ruth's Dad and I kept secret the place where we had hidden my '49 Chevy, but when we left on our honeymoon we were driving Ruth's Dad's '57 Chevrolet, a car that became a classic.

We stayed at the "completely modern" El Pancho Court in Bay City, Michigan, our first night at a cost of the going rate of $3.00. Then we drove on to Traverse City, Michigan, where we stayed for a week in the Bay View Motel and Cabins, a motel where Ruth and her dad had stayed a few times. We had a fantastic time and came home via way of Wisconsin, timing a stop in Illinois to help celebrate my mom and dad's 25th anniversary.

We returned to Midland where we lived with Ruth's dad for a month and a half before moving to a first floor flat in Detroit to begin my internship at Salem Lutheran Church, a block and a half away.

Life at the Seminary and After

I enjoyed seminary and the eight professors who taught there.

Edward C. Fendt, dean of the seminary, taught dogmatics, the study of theology. He had never married and his classroom discourses on family life often left students, many of whom were married, both amused and bemused.

Theodore Liefeld taught New Testament, and Herbert Leupold taught Old Testament, both in the style of storytellers. The study Bibles I still have in my library are filled with notes in the margins, jotted down so I would never forget the nuances with which they brought those stories to life. Dr. Leupold was a very formal man. I remember one morning when I was a few minutes late. I tried to sneak in the back door of the classroom. Dr. Leupold interrupted himself in mid-sentence. "Good morning, Mr. Gonnerman," and then continued his thought as if my entrance had not been any interruption at all.

Frederick Meuser taught church history. I will long remember the first paper I wrote for him. I thought I had become a pretty good writer, but I became more than a little careless with that paper. Dr. Meuser knew I was supposed to know something about writing. He justifiably cut that paper apart with more red ink than I had seen on any other paper I had ever produced. I will never forget the look of that paper and never wrote so carelessly again.

Gerhard Doermann taught education. His first assignment was to write a Sunday School lesson plan for Isaiah 6:1-8, a passage overflowing with descriptive language of God on his smoke-shrouded throne with seraphim worshipping him. One of those seraphim goes to Isaiah, touches his lips with a burning coal, and calls him to be God's messenger. The passage sets up a tremendous challenge to translate all that power and majesty into language that will be instructive to children. It was a great assignment. Dr. Doermann also introduced his students to a law they would remember many times from experiences in their ministry: "If anything can go wrong in an audio-visual presentation, it will." And that was in the days of flannel boards, filmstrips, and slideshows.

Arthur Becker taught counseling. First, we were assigned hospital calls throughout the city of Columbus with people who most likely had not been called upon by any pastor. We reconstructed those calls in writing, and then we role-played the experiences. It was great teaching.

Stanley Schneider, a superb preacher, taught homiletics, the art of preaching. From him we learned the structure and organization of a sermon and the most effective methods of verbal presentation. He assigned texts and demanded an outline for every sermon we worked on. By the second semester of our junior (first) year we were preaching occasionally in daily chapel and filling needs to supply pulpits and conduct worship services in Lutheran congregations throughout Ohio. Dr. Schneider is one of the few seminary professors I have known who resigned his teaching position to return to a full-time call in a parish.

Leonard Ludwig taught pastoral theology, also known as practical theology. A former pastor (as all Lutheran seminary professors were), Dr. Ludwig spoke with a deep German accent and overflowed with cautions, advice, and admonitions that would serve the future pastors in his classroom well. He was one of my favorite seminary professors. He preached the sermon for my ordination at Immanuel Lutheran Church in Dixon, Illinois, on February 7, 1960. The text was 2 Timothy 4:1-8; the theme, "Fulfill Your Ministry."

Every seminary student spends a year of internship between his or her second (middler) and senior years. My internship was a more than interesting learning experience. Two weeks after I was assigned to Detroit, the pastor who was there took another call and left. I was alone in a church of about 1,500 members for the first three months of my internship. A person learns a lot in that situation, much of which is "don't try it that way again." The church was a beautiful small cathedral that seated about 900 people. The parochial school that had been operating for 69 years was closed at the first council meeting I attended. That left a lot of empty classrooms and a full-sized gymnasium. Facilities also included a large kitchen and four bowling allies.

Mark, our first son, was born in Detroit in April. When we returned to the seminary for my senior year we lived in the new apartments for married students across the street from the seminary. They were comfortable except in the summer. It can get very hot and humid in Columbus, and none of the apartments was air-conditioned.

First Call

I graduated from the seminary in January 1960 and was ordained in February. Our first parish was a mission congregation in Painesville, Ohio, northeast of Cleveland along Lake Erie. Lake Erie was terribly polluted. We (a daughter, Gay, born in Columbus, was also now part of the family) went to the beach once and never again. The Cuyahoga River that ran through Cleveland was so polluted it caught on fire and burned.

I had been told that 13 families were worshiping in someone's basement. That sounded like a good start toward the core of a new congregation. What I was not told was that the 13 families were a splinter group from a congregation across the river. That changed the equation of quick growth substantially. But we built a church and education unit on a ten-acre plot and about 140 people were worshipping regularly within the first 20 months.

Then I received a call from the public relations department at the national church office in Minneapolis. That call set the direction for the rest of my ministry. We moved to Minnesota in November 1961, and have lived there ever since.

I had been assistant director of public relations for The ALC for five years when I received a call from St. Olaf College in Northfield to establish and direct a new office of information services. When I moved into that office I had a news service director and a secretary, both full-time. When I left there 23 years later, the staff included four and half full-time people and 30 part-time students. It was a great staff.

I left in 1989 to accept a call to Luther Seminary in St. Paul to establish and direct its first office of public relations. My office at Luther made great inroads in putting Luther Seminary, the largest Lutheran seminary in the world, on the map. We also oversaw the changing of the seminary's name – from Luther-Northwestern Theological Seminary to Luther Seminary – and the introduction of a whole file drawer full of new programs.

Ruth and I both retired in 1998. How many people have the fun of establishing a new congregation and building its church building, establishing two new communications/public relations offices for non-profit institutions, and shaping those offices around the things they know are most important? It has been a great ministry – and a great life.

RITUAL & REVOLUTION

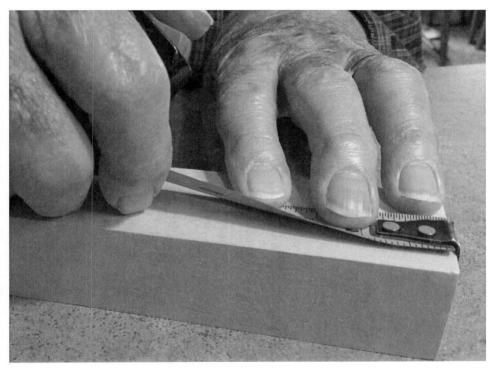

*Conversations were incredibly predictable,
especially when they happened almost every week.
The weather and the status of the crops came first.
Car talk followed with the usual argument about
whether Fords or Chevies or Plymouths were the best.*

RITUAL AND REVOLUTION

They didn't know it was happening, any more than any of the rest of us know the big picture of social, cultural, and technological changes when we are a part of them, but Mom and Dad both were participants in spectacular social and cultural revolutions throughout their lives. They – and we – lived through a period of time when more world-changing things happened in a couple of generations than in any other span of history.

The continuing revolution in relationships – between spouses, other races, religious groups, the changing natures of agriculture and medicine, the effects of both war and peace, the development of technologies not even imagined when they were born, the creation and use of leisure time – challenged both of them personally at the same time it had both small and extreme effects on the communities where they were active participants.

The amazingly massive advances in agriculture are handled in another chapter.

The changes in medicine that Mom experienced between the time she graduated from nursing school in Milwaukee in the late '20s until the time she last practiced the art of medical care as a Vista volunteer on the Rosebud Indian Reservation in South Dakota were monumental.

The routine practices she had learned in nursing school were modified more than once. The sensitivity to poverty, hunger, and homelessness was learned first-hand not only by Mom and Dad, but also by countless citizens during the Great Depression and stayed with the country in a more limited but no less dramatic degree into the present day.

Unfortunately, the current political spectrum overflows with men and women who carry millionaire status into office and never had the leveling experience of the Great Depression. They seem to be free of any feelings of compassion for those who are less fortunate financially. The cutting of food stamps and unemployment benefits for the masses of people who need them for subsistence is nothing more than an unfeeling financial calculation without any concern for the social and physical well-being of millions of men, women, and children who depend on those programs for life itself, let alone any kind of social satisfaction in their poverty stricken existence.

The art of medical care saw the universal use of inoculations, the discovery of miraculous antibiotics, the nearly complete disappearance of diphtheria and tuberculosis. John Crandon discovered the cause of scurvy in 1939. Jonas Salk produced the first vaccine to prevent polio on July 2, 1952, paving the way for nearly wiping out that disease around the world

But the most astounding medical breakthrough might have been the first heart transplant on December 3, 1967. The place was Groote Schuur Hospital in Cape Town, South Africa. The surgeon was Christiaan Barnard. The patient was 53-year-old Lewis Washkansky, a South African grocer dying from chronic heart disease. The transplant was not an overwhelming success. Washkansky died 18 days later from double pneumonia. But the transplanted heart had functioned normally until the patient died. Better anti-rejection drugs were developed in the '70s and later in that decade many of Dr. Barnard's patients lived up to five years longer with their new hearts.

Organ transplants were here for good and patients since have received new kidneys, livers, lungs, faces, and nearly every other organ except the brain. When the knees, hips, and shoulders we were born with wear out today, they can be replaced, and many of them are.

Magnetic resonance imaging (MRI), colonoscopies, electrocardiograms, electroencephalograms, mammograms and a multitude of other procedures that were just coming on the scene enhanced diagnoses and treatment when Mom was reaching her mid-eighties. She lived through nearly all of those momentous advances in technology, always learning as she worked throughout more than a half century of medical advances.

Research on DNA had been going on since the '40s, but in 1972 Paul Berg and Herb Boyer produced the first recombinant DNA molecules. The Human Genome Project was begun in 1988 with the goal of determining the entire sequence of DNA composing human chromosomes. It was successful.

And in the time since Mom died in 1998, the vast strides in the mapping of our DNA have become a major tool in the matching of organ donor and donor recipient as well as the identification and capture of criminals, outstripping identification by the time-honored matching of fingerprints. And the wonder of stem cells is a whole new frontier with uncounted promises for future rehabilitation.

Soldiers who were wounded in any way during the Civil War had a minimal survival rate. With every succeeding war – World War I, World War II, the Korean Conflict, the War in Vietnam, the wars in Iraq and Afghanistan – the survival rate has increased beyond dramatic, and the development of always better prosthetic devices to replace hands, arms, feet, and legs has made thousands of wounded soldiers almost physically whole again. One sprinter in the 2012 London Olympics ran on prosthetic feet that appeared to be like steel springs. Men and women who have had their legs blown away walk without a noticeable limp and don't even need crutches or a cane. Plastic surgery today can hide many of the most grotesque physical scars.

However, we still are not dealing anywhere close to adequately with the psychological damage that the trauma of war inflicts on more men and women in the armed services than we know. And we are just becoming sensitized to the damage concussions do to the brains of everyone from combat soldiers to high school football players. Soldiers returning from the First and Second World Wars didn't talk about their post-traumatic stress (those terms weren't even being used when they came home from their wars), but we know now that some of them suffered horrendous stress for years. Veterans returning from the War in Vietnam gave physicians and psychiatrists their first hints of the problem.

The Ritual Sunday Feasts

Nearly every Sunday dinner was a family reunion at the home of Grandpa and Grandma Jacobs. Mom and her family – her sister Grace, her brother Clifford, and his wife Bernadine – would usually all come together for a big dinner as soon as we had left Immanuel Lutheran Church. Cliff and Bernadine weren't there as often since they lived 20 miles to the west in Sterling. Occasionally, Mom's sister Welma joined the group with her family, but that happened only occasionally since they lived almost 50 miles east in Sycamore.

Before they retired, Grandma and Grandpa Jacobs had a farm about six miles south of Dixon. Going there was always a treat, especially since all the cousins took turns riding the brown pony that Grandpa kept in the pasture. Grandpa didn't have a saddle (or if he did, we never found out about it) so we simply put a bridle on the pony and jumped on bareback.

Grandma and Grandpa Jacobs surrounded by their grandchildren from the Gonnerman and Mundy families in 1948.

Grandma and Grandpa Jacobs retired from farming at about the time I entered high school. Then we all gathered at the big white house on the east end of Dixon to which they had moved. The most memorable thing about that house was the long cement staircase we had to climb from the street to the front porch. (Access was considerably easier at the back door, but even that had a three-step staircase. We didn't pay much attention to handicapped accessibility back then.)

After Aunt Grace married Vernon Near, we sometimes went to their house. It was a newer house, closer to the church. And it didn't have a long outdoor staircase.

The only times I remember that the Jacobs clan gathered at our house when we lived on the Lincoln Highway were for summertime picnics. Our house was a lot smaller, was without electricity, didn't have a modern kitchen, and had no drinkable running water except what was pumped by the windmill to the watering tank for the cattle and horses, or carried in a bucket to the house for our own consumption.

No matter where we went, however, the procedure was almost always the same. The younger cousins would try to find someplace to play by themselves, out of the way and out of the eyesight of grandparents, parents, uncles, and aunts.

The men and older boys all went into the living room where they divided up the Sunday *Chicago Tribune* and traded sections back and forth as they read the whole thing. No one in our family had television, but sometimes someone turned on the radio to listen to the Cubs or White Sox baseball teams.

Conversations were incredibly predictable, especially when they happened almost every week. The weather and the status of the crops came first. Car talk followed with the usual argument about whether Fords or Chevies or Plymouths were the best. It was always the same argument and no one ever changed his mind. (Women did not participate in those conversations.) Sometimes the conversation might drift to politics, but since everyone was a rock-hard Republican everybody generally agreed with everybody else. No one liked Franklin Delano Roosevelt, and nothing he ever did could be right. After Roosevelt died, Truman was even worse in the minds of the Jacobs and Gonnerman clans. (The only possible exception might have been Aunt Grace, but I can't remember that she ever voiced any disagreement.)

The women and older girls all gathered in the kitchen. Then they set the dining room table after adding a leaf or two to make it big enough. After the children got old enough — about ten or eleven — four of the oldest sometimes sat by themselves at a card table that was set up in the living room just off the end of the dining room table. It was a big moment when we got to sit with older kids at the card table for the first time.

The women always prepared the meal together, and it was a wonder. In the summer and early fall, it usually started with chicken — killed, plucked, and dressed the day before and fried that morning before church. In the late fall, winter, and spring the meat was roast beef, roast pork, or ham. Once in a while we would have roast turkey with dressing, but that special dish was usually reserved for holidays such as Thanksgiving and Christmas.

A big bowl of mashed potatoes and a ladle filled with gravy was always alongside the meat on the table, as were at least two vegetables. In the summer and fall those vegetables were fresh from someone's garden. We seldom had a tossed salad, but Jello with mixed fruit or sliced bananas was often on the menu as a substitute.

Big sliced tomatoes and cucumbers were on the table as soon as they ripened in the gardens. The tomatoes were eaten with sugar, and the cucumbers were eaten with salt. Fresh creamed peas were a staple early in the summer. Bowls of fresh green string beans were devoured in July and August. Buttered carrots were always good later in the year. I don't remember seeing much broccoli or Brussels sprouts in any season.

But the biggest success of the season was sweet corn on the cob. In most years that delicacy would stretch out for only two Sundays at the end of August unless Mom had planted plots of sweetcorn a week apart. Then we might also have sweet corn available for an extra week and maybe even two in September.

Mom would pick about three dozen ears early on Sunday morning and put it in paper grocery bags to carry to Grandma's house. There it would be shucked of its husks, rubbed clean of its silk, and boiled for a couple of minutes in a huge kettle before being placed on a pair of platters, one for each end of the table. Dishes of butter, most often homemade, and salt shakers would be near the platters of sweet corn.

Table grace was said by everyone in unison, "Come Lord Jesus, be our guest, and let these gifts to us be blessed."

Then you selected an ear, moved it to an edge of your plate, spread it liberally with butter and sprinkled it lightly with salt. Then you raised that sweet-smelling ear to your mouth for your first taste. After that initial satisfying taste test you filled the remainder of your plate with the meat, potatoes, gravy and other vegetables being offered that Sunday before giving your attention back to your ear of corn.

Sometimes a little butter escaped both your corn and your mouth and ran down your chin when you ate it. That's what napkins are for. Eating corn on the cob usually follows one of two forms. Some eat around the ear, collaring it with mouth-wide bites. Others eat along the length of the ear, taking three or four rows of kernels at each pass. I have always been a length of the ear eater. But whichever way you ate it, fresh sweet corn on the cob was (and still is) culinary heaven toward the end of summer.

When summer-fresh vegetables weren't available any more, the women went to their supply of home canned beans, peas, and sweet corn. The vegetables had been canned in quart or pint jars with a pressure cooker and were lined up on ten-inch-wide wooden shelves built just for that purpose in the basements (sometimes called cellars). Every family at those Sunday dinners had their home-grown and home-canned supply in their own basements at home. Canned vegetables were seldom bought in the store, and frozen vegetables had not yet become popular. When they did, every family had a big freezer that they filled with vegetables and fruits in bags and meat they butchered themselves wrapped tightly to avoid "freezer burn."

Fresh bread had been baked the day before. The butter had been churned by hand (two of those churns are still in our family), and the strawberry preserves had been canned during the previous strawberry season.

After everyone had eaten their fill, the dishes that still had food in them were always passed around a couple of times until very little remained as leftovers. Grandma Jacobs, a big woman, was always sure that every child at the table could eat "just a little bit more." And we usually did. But none of us got fat. Apparently, we just ran the calories off with exuberant play (and as we got older, strenuous work).

But we always managed to leave just enough room for dessert, almost always pie. It would have been made the day before by Grandma, Mom, Aunt Grace, or Aunt Bernadine. The kind of pie was also determined by the seasons. When the cherries were ripe that's the kind of pie that would be brought to the table. Rhubarb pie would appear during the short rhubarb season. Apple pie would show up during the apple season. We couldn't grow peaches easily in Northern Illinois, but sometimes someone would splurge to buy them in the store for the few days they were available. Peach pie was one of my favorites then, and it still is.

Families helped each other with seasonal tasks. Here Mom and family members peel apples with a hand crank peeler, perfect for apple pie.

On some days we would get the bonus of large dips of ice cream alongside the pie. Sometimes the ice cream had been homemade in a wooden ice cream maker. It was powered with a hand crank and had a metal can with a beater that had wooden slats. First, the ingredients – lots of milk and cream, with eggs, sugar, and vanilla – were mixed together and cooked on the stove. Then, before dinner, it was poured into the can which was closed with a heavy lid and held in place by the crank. Then chopped ice, layered with lots of salt, was spread in the two-inch space between the outside of the can and the inside of the wooden ice cream maker. All the while the ice and salt were being added someone turned the crank at a steady pace.

When the crank could not be turned anymore the ice cream was frozen. Now the crank was removed and ice at the top of the can was moved away, kept to be put back in place. When the top was taken off, the yellowish ice cream stood in stiff curls and peaks around the wood and metal beater. But no one touched that ice cream. Not yet.

The beater was lifted out slowly as most of the ice cream was spooned back into the can. The beater was put into a long cake pan and what could still be spooned off it was eagerly eaten by all of the children. All of them had been given a spoon. Then the lid was put back with a cork in the hole where the beater had stuck into the crank, the ice was returned to its place on top of the lid and covered with newspapers and towels, and the whole thing was set aside to harden until the ice cream would be served on the pie for dessert.

A special treat for about two Sundays in June was strawberry shortcake. The strawberries had been picked from the carefully tended beds of Grandma, Mom, or one of the aunts. Some of the berries would have been crushed so that a lot of juice was included. The "shortcake" was a biscuit baked in a big pan, cut into pieces about four inches square and sliced once so that strawberries could be between the slices as well as on top and in the dish around the shortcake. It was called shortcake because it was baked with less shortening. Sometimes the whole confection would have whipped cream (made from real cream) on top. Then most of us added a little milk that would soak into the shortcake. Strawberry shortcake is still my favorite dessert.

When no fruit was in season, the pies would change to custard, banana cream, sour cream raisin, lemon meringue. Not many pies were beyond the reach of the Jacobs family women. None of the Jacobs men, nor any other Midwestern farmers that I knew of, ever showed any desire to become conversant with the wondrous workings women did in the kitchen. First, they didn't have the time.

Second, they didn't have the inclination. Third, their wives didn't want them to usurp their role and mess up their kitchen.

For most of those Sunday meals almost nothing had been bought from a grocery store except some of the fruits, the sweeteners, the seasonings, the condiments, and the flour. Even the milk was often fresh from one of the farms. If whipped cream was provided, it was made from fresh cream separated at our farm a few days before.

After dinner, the men would all go back to the living room where they would start at least one game of cards – usually Hearts or Pinochle. The women cleared the empty bowls and dirty dishes off the table and gathered in the kitchen to wash them and put them away. Automatic dishwashers would not arrive in our homes for decades. Sometimes older girls and boys were drafted to wash the dishes and wipe them dry, but that was never a regular thing.

When everything in the kitchen was clean and put away, some of the women might join the men to play cards. The party usually broke up about 3:30 or 4:00 in the afternoon, when our family had to leave to get home and milk the cows.

The next Sunday, we would do it all over again. Once in a while we would have Sunday dinner at Grandma and Grandpa Gonnerman's house, but that was rare. Grandpa's autocratic manner led him not to like all that company, and many in the Gonnerman family didn't like his. That was too bad, because Grandma Gonnerman was also a very good cook.

Grandma and Grandpa Gonnerman had a beautiful dining room with a large built-in china cabinet with glass paneled doors. But the thing in that dining room that I liked best was the large wooden planter with a sheet-metal liner that took up the whole nine-foot length of the south window that let us look out on the yard and the barn. The planter was always full of red geraniums that were carefully tended by Grandma Gonnerman. Part of that care included dumping all of Grandpa's cigar ashes around the plants. All that potash was probably why they always did so well.

Keeping the Sabbath

It took a really bad weather forecast in an already disastrous planting or harvesting season to convince Dad to work in the fields on a Sunday. Ordinary chores, of course, had to be done twice a day every day of the week to keep the livestock fed, watered, and comfortable. But I can count on one hand the times I remember him on a tractor on what we considered the Lord's Day. When Dad did work in the fields on Sunday it was because he had weighed the necessity of getting the crop planted or harvested against the probability that a half-inch rain on Monday might put him behind for a week – a week that was precious in the continuing cycles of planting, germination, and growth, or harvest and storage that would make feed available for the livestock throughout the winter.

But whenever Dad sat on the tractor seat and traveled back and forth across the acres on a Sunday, he struggled with the moral dilemma of laboring to keep up with the cycles of work that caused him to break the Third Commandment: "Remember the Sabbath Day, and keep it holy." The struggle was not that Dad (and Mom) did not like the commandments. They saw the Commandments as necessary guidance for the Christian life. They certainly emphasized them with their children. But neither of them liked even the remote possibility that they would intentionally break any of them.

What they saw as disobedience of God's law was not something they took lightly. In fact, sometimes they might have given more credence to God's law than to God's grace. They had no sympathy whatsoever for the "theology" of some folks who said, "I can worship God on the golf course – or any other recreational activity – just as well as in church." (Not many farmers ever found their way to a golf course during the thirties and forties.)

Families never missed Sunday church services, even when traveling conditions were difficult. Here the Jacobs family (l-r Grandpa, Mom, their dog, Grandma, and Mom's brother Clifford) traveled on Easter Sunday in their horse-drawn wagon to Brechon's corner where they had parked their car because the road to their farm was impassable. Notice the mud on the wheel. Then they drove six miles to Dixon where they went to church at Immanuel Lutheran.

Mom, I am sure, also struggled with the Third Commandment whenever she had to go to work as a nurse at the hospital in Dixon on Sundays. But I am also sure she was able to rationalize that as she was looking after the sick and the injured she was doing God's work, and therefore God would not only forgive, but bless, her professional caregiving – even on the Sabbath.

The Third Commandment meant a lot more to most of society in those days. Today's ubiquitous shopping centers, now open nearly round the clock, did not yet exist. Clothing stores were never open on Sundays. Grocery stores kept their doors closed. Even many gas stations didn't unlock their pumps on Sunday, a fact that made people remember to fill their automobile gas tanks on Saturday if they were planning a Sunday outing, and they had to calculate how far they could go and still get home on one tank of gas on one day. Farmers had a bit of an advantage here because they could back up to the tank of gas that was always on the farm to keep tractors moving.

That adherence to keeping the Sabbath holy still reaches into today's society in a few places. Even today, a Ben Franklin Five and Dime general store on a busy corner in Grand Marais, Minnesota, along the North Shore of Lake Superior in a popular tourist area, is never open on Sundays. It's interesting to watch tourists not familiar with the town nonchalantly walk up to the double doors of that store and try to open them. Some people obviously understand. Some simply walk away with disappointment written on their faces. Others who are a bit more aggressive give the doors a second and a third pull. They can hardly believe that any store owner would have the audacity to deny them access during these few hours on this one day they are in town. Some do not understand why those doors are closed and wonder at the strange business practices of the proprietor. Those who understand respect the policy.

Grand Marais' two biggest grocery stores, located along highway U.S. 61 about six blocks from the Ben Franklin Five and Dime, are also closed on Sunday. That sometimes can be more critical in a tourist town. Visitors who are camping and don't know groceries are unavailable in Grand Marais on Sunday, or simply forgot to get hot dogs or hamburger and some fresh buns on Saturday, have to adjust their menu the next day. The next closest sizable town is a long way to the east in Canada (and you have to have your passport to get back into the United States), and if you head west toward Duluth you have to drive about 20 miles to the small resort town of Lutsen.

Dealing with New Technologies

Swifter and clearer communication was coming into its own when Mom and Dad got married. Nearly everyone had a telephone as soon as lines had been strung into their part of the countryside. It was a long way from the cell phone or the internet, but it was effective for its day. The phones were fastened to the wall at about the height of an average adult's head when they were standing. They were in big wooden boxes with the tube you spoke into coming out of the middle of the front of the box. The device you listened to — the "receiver" — was a six-inch long piece of black Lucite (an early form of plastic) fastened to a cord that was about 30 inches long. You could listen at a short distance from the wooden box, but when you talked you had better be close enough to talk into the stationary mouthpiece.

If you lived in the country, perhaps the best part — or maybe the worst, depending on your point of view — was the party line. Private lines were available but costly, and I never knew any farmer who had one. Everyone on a party line had a distinctive ring. It was one long and two shorts, or two longs and three shorts, or three shorts, or any combination of long and short rings that could be used. Some party lines might include up to ten different phones. That's ten different locations, ten different farm houses, ten different rings.

If you were in the house and you were not particularly busy but you just wanted to keep up with what was going on in the neighborhood, and you heard the ring of a neighbor (everybody knew every neighbor's ring) you would wait until the ringing stopped, meaning that the person being called had answered (or wasn't home), and then you would pick up the receiver on your phone and listen in on the conversation. It was impossible to keep secrets with a party line. When you answered your phone you usually heard one or two or five soft clicks right away, and you knew that anything that was said was going to go all the way around the neighborhood in a flash.

It was community communication at its fastest, and it didn't slow down until phone service became affordable enough for nearly everyone to have a private line. The ubiquitous cell phones that nearly everyone carries today, and too many talk into too loudly and too frequently in the most crowded situations, or even while doing other things like driving, is not far removed from the farmer's party line phone on the wall. Add to that the ever present texting where the tester can become so involved in sending a message that all other personal social connections disappear. I'm convinced it's not an improvement.

Radio was nearly everyone's primary link to the wider world. We didn't have a television in the house until after I was in college. Most radios then were big wooden boxes with scroll work on the front backed by brocaded fabric that hid a speaker. Your radio usually had two knobs and a dial. You used one knob to turn the radio on and adjust the volume. You turned the second knob to find the station you wanted. The dial told you the call numbers of the station you were listening to. News reports coming out of that box put you in touch with nations that you could not even locate on a map or a globe.

The biggest thing I remember about radio is the entertainment it provided. Every evening, after the cows had been milked and the other livestock fed and bedded down and we had eaten supper, we would sit around the radio listening to "Bob Armstrong, the All-American Boy," "The Green Hornet," "The Shadow Knows," "Superman," "The Lone Ranger," "Fibber McGee and Molly," "Amos and Andy," "Rin Tin Tin," "The FBI in Peace and War," and other dramas, most of them adventurous, some of them comedic.

Each program was 15 minutes long. All of them had commercial sponsors that were always offering secret decoder rings, official badges that made you a member of some crime fighting group, special whistles, and other treasures. Every child wanted all of them. Some of them were free. Some of them required box tops or a quarter. All of them were nearly irresistible – and useless – but we thought they provided great, sophisticated fun.

The most important aspect of those programs was the way they fostered our creative imaginations. We visualized the action in every episode. We could see it happening in our minds eye. We felt the same adrenalin rush as our heroes. We didn't need television, in fact, when television began to dominate electronic communication it diminished our imaginations because everything was so vivid – first in black and white, then in color – that our imaginations, our creative personal involvement was no longer needed.

have focused again!!

The Ugly Face of Chauvinism

Unfortunately, the ordinary courtesies and civilities have a dark side. It's called chauvinism. According to Webster, that's "an unreasoning devotion to one's race, sex, etc. with contempt for other races, the opposite sex, etc." Even more unfortunately, the motivation for some people's chauvinism is nourished by biblical roots.

The Apostle Paul sets a shatteringly deep chauvinistic standard in his epistles:

> "Let a woman learn in silence with all submissiveness. I permit no woman to teach or to have authority over men; she is to keep silent" (1 Timothy 2:11-12).

> "As in all the churches of the saints, the women should keep silence in the churches. For they are not permitted to speak, but should be subordinate, even as the law says. If there is anything they desire to know, let them ask their husbands at home. For it is shameful for a woman to speak in church" (1 Corinthians 14:33b-35).

> "Be subject to one another out of reverence for Christ. Wives, be subject to your husbands, as to the Lord. For the husband is the head of the wife as Christ is the head of the church, his body, and is itself its Savior. As the church is subject to Christ, so let wives also be subject in everything to their husbands. Husbands, love your wives, as Christ loved the church and gave himself up for her" (Ephesians 5:21-25).

> "Wives, be subject to your husbands, as is fitting in the Lord. Husbands, love your wives, and do not be harsh with them. Children, obey your parents in everything, for this pleases the Lord. Fathers, do not provoke your children, lest they become discouraged. Slaves, obey in everything those who are your earthly masters, not in eye service, as men pleasers, but in singleness of heart, fearing the Lord ... Masters, treat your slaves justly and fairly, knowing that you also have a Master in heaven" (Colossians 3:18-4:1).

Other biblical texts in the Apostle Paul's epistles say similar things about the relationship of men, women, and children as well as the relationship of masters and slaves. They also include the connections to Christ and his relationship to the church, a foundational relationship that too often is left out of the biblical quotations when men use them to assert their dominance over women and children. And women use them to excuse their passiveness.

The church had been snail slow in addressing the problems that such passages motivate. In the first half of the twentieth century the pastor was often the most educated person in town. He was also expected to be the most forceful leader, and he usually was. Women had restricted roles: take care of the culinary duties by creating and bringing "hot dishes" to potluck dinners and other social functions, and being a persuasive force in making sure their husbands and children attended regularly with them. But the power and influence of women in the church and the rest of the community was always a subtle but forceful influence over the men in their families. A few congregations of conservative church bodies still do not allow women to vote in congregational matters.

Women were finally given a voice in church circles, but that happened largely because congregations could not find enough men to teach in their Sunday school programs. Ordination of women came only in the last half of the 20th century after huge battles regarding whether Scripture allowed it. The Roman Catholic Church continues its anti-women stance except for the promotion of nunneries.

In spite of the Apostle Paul's admonitions, the Gospels do not paint Jesus as someone who encouraged dominance over women. He never asserted such an attitude during his ministry.

Instead, he healed his disciple Simon's (Peter's) mother-in-law (Matthew 8:14-15; Luke 4:38-39); he healed the woman with a life-long, severe menstrual problem (Matthew 9:20-22); and he defended a woman when she anointed him with an expensive ointment (Matthew 26:6-13; Mark 14:3-9).

He challenged the Canaanite woman with a daughter "severely possessed by a demon" to express her faith, and then healed the girl because of the mother's confession (Matthew 15:22-28). He welcomed and blessed children who came to him even when his disciples tried to turn them away (Matthew 19:13-15).

His ministry had no boundaries or restrictions. When he ministered to a Samaritan woman at the well, he broke cultural norms by even talking to her. Yet he showed her the utmost understanding and respect (John 4:7-26). He healed the daughter of a Syrophoenician woman (Mark 7:25-30).

He took away the grief of Mary and Martha by raising their brother Lazarus from the dead (John 11:17-44). He honored his mother, even to the point of appointing his Apostle John as her "son" while being crucified (John 19:26). Jesus' first appearance after his resurrection was to Mary rather than to any of his male disciples (John 20:11-18).

No chauvinism or discrimination of any kind tarnishes the ministry of Jesus. Unfortunately, my dad, religious as he was, was chauvinistic. He was not unusual. Most relationships between men and women in those days had a chauvinistic pattern. Consider a mild example.

Our farm on the Lincoln Highway was only five miles from Immanuel Lutheran Church in Dixon where the whole family worshiped and went to Sunday school every Sunday. The trip usually took about ten minutes, but if we were really in a hurry it could be done in about seven. Even with that short distance, however, we were frequently late for church. That was one of Mom's biggest frustrations.

One Sunday morning, after we had been late for about four Sundays in a row, she announced at breakfast, "This morning the car is leaving at 9:15 whether anyone is ready or not." Mom could say things like that. I and my brother and sisters thought that was pretty funny when we pictured our driverless car pulling out of the driveway, but we didn't say anything. We just made sure we were ready to go on time.

Dad always seemed to be the problem. He and I would go out to finish chores after Sunday breakfast. I would think we had them all done in plenty of time to get back into the house, wash up, change our clothes and be on the way. But then Dad would always find just a couple of more things to do. Most of the time, the jobs were not essential. They could have waited for the next day, or even the next week. But Dad would decide to do them in what he thought were the couple of extra minutes he had between getting the chores done and getting in the house to get ready for church.

When I realized this happened regularly, I became sure that Dad delayed finishing chores on purpose just to aggravate Mom. Whenever it happened – and it happened a lot – the trip to church was less than pleasant. I'm convinced it was one of Dad's chauvinistic power plays.

Mom had some time and planning issues of her own. More than once, I remember, we would start off on a trip to visit relatives with a damp shirt hanging by the open back window so it would dry out and could be worn by the time we arrived. And either Donna or Mary Ann was having their hair combed on nearly every trip.

We were having supper one evening when I was either a junior or senior in high school. Everything was going along as usual and we were having an enjoyable family time until Dad wanted to use the saltshaker. He picked it up. It was empty. Dad's volatile anger kicked in immediately. He took the shaker and rolled it across the kitchen floor with force while telling Mom to fill it. I was furious. "Dad," I said. "You know where the salt is. Can't you see that Mom is busy? Why don't you fill it yourself?"

My vehemence caught Dad by surprise. He didn't answer, but he didn't fill the saltshaker. Unfortunately, I was so angry I didn't think fast enough to fill it myself either. I left the table.

Another time, when I was home from college for the summer, we were driving to Dixon. I can't remember why, but Mom was driving, a rarity when Dad was in the car. He was in the front passenger seat and I was in the back.

Shortly after we got started, he told Mom to keep her foot straight up and down on the accelerator rather than holding her foot at an angle with her toe pointed away from the brake the way she almost always did. She suggested quietly that she always drove that way and it was more comfortable for her. (Given the nature of her feet, already beginning to be deformed by the effects of serious osteoporosis which eventually kept her from walking, it undoubtedly was more comfortable for her to set her foot at an angle on the accelerator.)

Dad badgered her to change the position of her foot all the way to town. Mom never moved it, a show of independence that surprised me, but she never again drove if Dad were in the car. I never could figure out Dad's argument. I often let my foot work the accelerator at an angle, particularly when I wanted a little variety on long trips and before the invention of cruise control. But since Dad held his foot pointed straight up on the accelerator he thought everyone, particularly his wife, should hold her foot the same way. It was a silly supposition, and certainly not worth a ten-minute-long, demeaning argument.

Mom did not, however, go quietly into the darkness of chauvinistic abuse. One April Fools' Day she served pancakes for breakfast. Mom made delicious pancakes, and they were one of the family's favorite breakfasts. Sometimes we even ate them for supper.

On this particular day, however, she made Dad's pancakes more than memorable. She put a stack of three or four on his plate and went back to the stove to make more. Following his usual procedure, Dad buttered them and poured an ample amount of maple syrup (the artificial stuff, we couldn't afford real maple syrup) and began to cut them with the edge of his fork. But these were an unusually tough batch. He picked up his table knife and used that. Try as he might, he could not cut through those syrup-soaked delicacies.

After Dad had sawed away for a minute or two the truth was exposed. Mom had baked perfectly cut round rags into the pancakes. Dad did not find it funny, but Mom had a big smile on her face as she tended the cakes she was baking on the stove. Her shoulders might have even shaken a bit in quiet laughter as she stood at the stove with her back to the table. Dad was very quiet. He really didn't know how to respond. Then Mom, smiling, took that plate away and gave him a new plate with pancakes which she had not fooled with.

Church Matters

Churches and their members have had trouble with recognizing and alleviating a tendency toward chauvinism. Consider, for instance, the fact that women were not ordained in either the Lutheran Church in America or the American Lutheran Church until 1970. Both synods were part of the merger that eventually formed the Evangelical Lutheran Church in America (ELCA) in 1988. A few other Protestant churches and most certainly the Roman Catholic Church still insist that women will have no positions of power in their congregations.

Both Mom and Dad had died before our daughter, Joy, their granddaughter, decided to attend Luther Seminary in St. Paul to become a pastor. She worked hard, on the edge of financial deprivation for herself and her son, Carl, but she felt called by God and was committed to this momentous change in her life. She is an excellent theologian and a creative preacher. She is now pastor of a congregation of the ELCA in a town called Pocahontas in northwestern Iowa. Mom would have been proud. I'm not sure what Dad would have thought about such a development.

The discussion that made it possible for women to be ordained in some Lutheran Churches was almost as heated as the debate on the floor of the General Assembly of the ELCA in 2009. That decision, passed by the thinnest of margins, officially allowed gays and lesbians in committed relationships to serve as pastors. But no congregation could be forced to be served by a gay or lesbian pastor if they did not want one. I have no trouble with the totality of that decision. It was overdue.

Years earlier, when I was editor of the St. Olaf College alumni magazine, I received a letter from a young alumnus in Minneapolis asking me to put an announcement of a meeting of gay and lesbian alums living in the Twin Cities (Minneapolis and St. Paul) in the monthly alumni magazine. I wrote back and said that the alumni magazine could not publish such an announcement. I didn't say that I knew the substantial gifts of too many major donors would be at stake if they read that kind of article, but I did. My letter included an uninformed reference to the fact that I thought homosexuality was a choice – a choice that people made to live as either straight or gay. That started a substantial correspondence around the idea that homosexuality was not a choice. My correspondent insisted homosexuality was a given, a non-refutable condition at birth.

That initiated a personal re-examination of what, up to that point, I was sure was a fact. But the more I thought about it, the more I began to realize that homosexuality is a not a condition that anyone would choose. Why would they? If anyone had a choice between being straight or homosexual why would that person choose a stigmatized lifestyle that was deplored as abnormal by some and sinful by many? Why would they purposely make a choice that would quite possibly alienate their parents, other family members, and friends?

Then I began to think about God's creative process. The creation story in Genesis emphasizes that everything God creates is good. How could God back away from his loving creations by bringing to birth a gay or lesbian person who inherently would be bad? The

God I know would not do that. God creates people who are born as good creations no matter whether they are sighted or blind, hearing or deaf, right handed or left handed, blue eyed or brown eyed, short or tall, straight or homosexual. Human beings are not given the power of God to judge other people as God judges them. We are all born sinners. God will sort us out.

Scriptural references to homosexuality are few and far between. Jesus never speaks of it in the record of his ministry in the Gospels. He does, however, frequently admonish his followers to love one another, to refrain from judging one another, and to bear one another's burdens. People who fight so adamantly to make homosexuals second-class citizens, the worst kind of sinners and a little less than human, need to spend a little less time with the Law and a lot more time with the Gospel.

Consider the Apostle Paul's advice in 2 Timothy 3: 2: "For men will be lovers of self, lovers of money, proud, arrogant, abusive, disobedient to their parents, ungrateful, unholy, inhuman, implacable, slanderers, profligates, fierce, haters of good, treacherous, reckless, swollen with conceit, lovers of pleasure rather than lovers of God, holding the form of religion but denying the power of it. Avoid such people."

I find it interesting how many people who think of themselves as religious look at a list like that (Paul has several similar catalogs in his other epistles), and lock onto a word like "profligate." Then they make profligacy the most grievous of offences with definite sexual overtones and undertones and a reference that might include homosexuality. And all the remaining offences in that list are ignored, even though those are far more common and far more insidious in their own lives? It's a form of self-condemnation in the extreme.

Experiencing Bullying

Not many minorities lived in Dixon or anywhere else near us. Dixon High School had an enrollment of about 600 during the four years that I attended. In one sense, I was part of one of the minorities. About 30 of the students came from surrounding farms. We had gone to elementary schools on the periphery of the city. My first six years were in the one-room school in Nachusa, I was bussed five miles east to grades seven and eight in Franklin Grove. Apart from the farm kids, nearly everyone else in the high school had already been together for eight years attending the same schools in Dixon's elementary and middle school system. Most of them knew each other well.

The rural kids were a minority of their own. We were uncomfortable, not socially well adjusted strangers to the rest of the high school students as soon as we stepped through the door. We didn't even know most of the rest of the other kids who had grown up on farms unless we had met them through our associations in 4-H clubs. The rural girls and boys only came together and became acquainted in high school when their sex separated them into obvious groups. The girls attended classes in home economics with an emphasis on cooking, sewing, and home management. The boys took classes in vocational agriculture which included animal husbandry, horticulture, soil and water conservation, and pest control.

One girl – a couple of decades ahead of her time – braved substantial ridicule and bullying, not the least from the teacher, when she had the audacity to take vocational agriculture classes. Actually, that should not have been that unusual. Many rural girls were beginning to take agricultural projects in their 4-H activities. My sister, Mary Ann, had a dairy calf project. Others were involved in beef, sheep, chicken, and hog projects. In fact, I bought a gilt (a female pig) from a girl after we both showed in the same class at the Illinois State Fair in about 1949.

More than 80 girls were members of the Home Economics Club at Dixon High, perhaps evenly split between those from town and those from the country. Most of the boys who attended the vocational agriculture classes were also members of Future Farmers of America (FFA). Those of us who were 4-H club members – and most of us were – simply continued our animal husbandry projects as laboratories for our FFA membership. Those in FFA gained some cohesiveness and notoriety in school when they wore their deep blue corduroy jackets with their name on the front and the colorful FFA symbol covering the back. Almost no girls ever showed up in photos of FFA groups. That has changed dramatically. Members of an FFA group I saw in a photo in Iowa in 2013 were divided almost equally between boys and girls.

Back in the '40s and '50s, we did not recognize bullying as the problem it has become today, but it was there and, as a farm kid, I experienced my share of it. Before they received their driver's license and found the money to buy a car, farm kids rode school buses. And school bus rides frequently were terrible. Bus rides mixed kids of all ages. The older and bigger kids could be brutal. Those of us who wore glasses were tormented verbally with the nickname, "four-eyes." Maybe that doesn't sound serious, but it was one of many forms of disrespect and it hurt, particularly when we weren't that happy wearing classes anyway. They took our hats and played "keep away" with them. Even though the younger, smaller kid almost always got his or her hat back before being left off the bus, more often than not tears were running down the child's cheeks as he or she began the walk up the farm driveway. I don't remember a single bus driver, and they were all men back then, ever disciplining a bullying rider on his bus. That kind of behavior was simply tolerated as "normal." Sometimes the bullying was even more bothersome when homework was thrown out the window of the moving bus or a special project was destroyed on the way home. But I cannot remember the time an insensitive bus bully was even chastised, much less punished.

Unfortunately, even parents frequently did not take bullying seriously. It was just something to get used to until they got older and bigger. "Stop your crying and grow up," was the response heard by far too many bullied kids. Blaming the victim is never a compassionate or understanding response.

One experience in gym class during my freshman or sophomore year changed that for a while, but not for anywhere near long enough. One day, boxing was the featured gym class exercise. Most of us in the class — and surely me — had never boxed before. But I gave my glasses to the gym teacher to hold, was laced into the gloves as everyone had to be, and was matched up with another boy about my size (small) who I did not know. The rest of the class circled around the mat and started yelling as they did for every match. I was not aware of any of them cheering for either one of us.

We sparred around for a little bit, neither of us really knowing what we were supposed to do. Then I shot out my right hand and caught my opponent on the chin. His knees crumpled and he went down like a bag of seed corn, knocked out cold. Everyone, including the instructor, became very quiet. It was the first and only knockout in that class. I had a new reputation which seemed to spread quickly. I wasn't bullied on the bus for a few weeks.

Dixon High School enrolled 169 freshmen, 170 sophomores, 139 juniors, and 119 seniors during my freshman year, 1947-48. I was one of two boys wearing a tie in the class picture. I'm sure Mom, unaware of the way students usually dressed for school those days, mandated my wardrobe when I told her that class pictures were being taken. That tie was a primary encouragement for some serious teasing. But I never even considered taking it off.

Questions of Race and Politics

As far as I can tell from high school yearbook pictures, one African-American girl was in my class and one African-American boy was a junior. One Hispanic girl also might have been enrolled, but I'm not sure. That was the total enrollment of racial minorities. Sadly, I don't remember meeting any of those minority students, and I don't remember having any kind of social discourse with them. I probably avoided any opportunities I might have had to get to know them.

A small African-American community lived in Dixon, but I didn't know how big it was or where it was located. However, I do remember some language that occasionally floated around the house. Mom often referred to Negro infants and toddlers as "picaninnies." Maybe it was not meant to be derogatory, but I think it was. The most discriminatory term I heard with frequency was always around Christmastime when we would buy mixed nuts in the shell. Brazil nuts were in the mix, and Dad (and I think Mom) always called Brazil nuts niggertoes. That word is so ingrained in my memory that I still think it and have to catch myself from saying it when I'm cracking nuts at Christmastime and working on a big, dark Brazil nut. It's amazing how easy it is for some childhood memories to plague a person throughout his life.

Were Mom and Dad racist? I don't think so. But they were certainly racially uniformed, not knowing (or at least not talking about) the poverty, the violence, the lack of respect that African Americans as well as Native Americans put up with as daily occurrences not only in the deep south but in the industrial north as well. Were Mom and Dad racially insensitive? Without a doubt.

Wartburg College in Waverly, Iowa, my alma mater, was the subject of another perceived problem. Joseph R. McCarthy, republican senator from Wisconsin, was stirring up the country with his inflammatory anti-communist rhetoric and hearings in 1953 and 1954, my sophomore and junior years at Wartburg.

A few ultra-conservative Lutheran pastors jumped on the Mc-Carthy bandwagon by passing around the rumor that Wartburg College was teaching communism to its students. It was a blatant fiction. But when I came home for a brief vacation during one of those school years both Mom and Dad asked if Wartburg "was teaching us communism." Up until then I had been unaware of the insidious rumor mill at work against my college. I remember saying something like, "Of course not. But we are learning *about* communism, and if we don't know what communism is and what its leaders are trying to do, how can we fight it? My response caught both Mom and Dad by surprise, but it ended their concern about that question and it never came up again.

Preaching and Politics

A related thing happened when I was a student at Trinity Lutheran Seminary in Columbus, Ohio. I think it was during my second (middler) year. I had been invited to preach at Immanuel Lutheran Church in Dixon, Illinois, my home congregation. I was the first son of the congregation to go to seminary in preparation for the ministry.

The Saturday before I was to step into Immanuel's pulpit for the first time, Dad said to me, "I hope you aren't going to include any politics in your sermon." Again, I was caught by surprise. I responded, "Certainly not." And then I realized that Dad, as many laymen, did not have a clue about the study of homiletics dealing with the content and structure of a sermon. But then, why should he have?

Sermons in mainline Christian churches are based on assigned biblical texts, called pericopes. The preacher is expected to exegete that text, working with the original languages of Hebrew in the Old Testament and Greek in the New Testament as much as he or she is able, trying to figure out ways to communicate the original meaning of the scripture lesson. Then the pastor tries to relate the lesson of that scripture to contemporary life, offering hope to those who have lost it, faith to those who are searching for it, and salvation through Jesus Christ to everyone who is open to it.

Occasionally, that might drift into some politically tinged statements dealing with concern for and care of the hungry, the homeless, and the marginalized. After all, Jesus was very political, breaking with both the political and religious leaders of his day when he talked about feeding the poor, taking care of the sick, the crippled and the homeless, being sensitive to the needs of all people, understanding the Old Testament commandments and acting upon his new admonitions. But to fill a sermon with political dialogue treads on dangerous ground, not least of which is stepping across the line delineating the separation between church and state mandated by the United States Constitution in the First Amendment as well as putting congregations' tax exempt status as risk. That line has gotten muddied and is under duress today.

In recent national elections, far too many preachers were not only declaring their own political views, but urging their parishioners to take on those same views and vote accordingly.

Two proposals for constitutional amendments were on the ballot in Minnesota in the 2012 election. One would have made it illegal for gays and lesbians to marry, a proposition that was already stated in Minnesota law. The other would have required all voters to show a photo identification card at their polling place before they would be allowed to register and vote, a proposal that would have placed a major hardship on the elderly and those without transportation to an administrative office or easy access to a birth certificate.

Minnesota's Roman Catholic Bishop spent a lot of his diocese's money leaning on his priests and people with letters of admonition and threats of denying communion to those who voted against the gay/lesbian marriage amendment. That's a major erasing of the line separating church and state.

Thankfully, both proposals failed.

Politics did play a role in my seminary education, however. My roommate during our first two years of seminary was Joe K. Menn, probably the brightest man I have been privileged to know. Joe was a proud Texan, and a graduate of Texas Lutheran College in Sequin, another college of the ELCA. After earning his bachelor of divinity degree at the seminary, he went on to get his doctorate in history, became a member of the history department faculty at Augustana College in Sioux Falls, South Dakota, and then was named president of Texas Lutheran College, his alma mater. Unfortunately for Texas Lutheran and for the church at large, he died of cancer at the age of 44.

It took me awhile to adjust to Joe's mental superiority when we were roommates. I was not a bad student, but when a test was scheduled, I would study my eyeballs out and be satisfied with an A- or a B+. Joe would review his notes for 20 minutes and ace the exam. That took a little self-examination for my ego to get used to.

But the biggest thing Joe helped me with was my politics. Having grown up reading the always conservative *Chicago Tribune* and being the son of unrelenting Republicans, I generally walked unquestioningly along the Republican political path. But during the presidential campaign which pitted Dwight D. Eisenhower against Adlai E. Stevenson in 1956, Joe slowly but surely convinced me that the Democratic platform was much more sensitive than the platform of the Republicans to the plight of those with the greatest needs – particularly the unemployed, the homeless, and the hungry. I voted for Stevenson. He was soundly beaten, 442 to 89 electoral votes, but I never voted for a Republican again, and I've never been sorry.

Mom and Dad and the Mission Field

Mom and Dad announced to the family in 1967 that they were retiring from farming (that wasn't really a surprise) and were going to the mission field in Papua New Guinea for a year to serve as house-parents at the school for missionary children in Wau (that was a surprise to everyone). The family embraced their plans with excitement, as our parents began to think about tickets, itineraries, what to pack, and getting their first passports. (Actually, the church did much of that work after they learned what would work best for Mom and Dad.) They would be the first in the family to travel internationally since their ancestors had crossed the Atlantic to immigrate to America two generations earlier. The ancestors came by boat. Mom and Dad would fly.

Their plan was to spend the bulk of a full year in mission service in New Guinea, and then spend nearly a month coming home with stops in India (where another large Lutheran mission had been at work for many years), Israel (to visit biblical sites in the Holy Land), and Germany (where they would make connections with members of their ancestral family, at least on the Gonnerman side).

Dad took a book of sermons along and preached one to the congregation at Wau nearly every Sunday. When they returned the next year they were immediately in demand to tell the story of their experiences, and visited many churches in the area with their slides in hand.

One thing disturbed me, however, when we started getting letters from the mission field. Mom (she did all the letter writing) wrote about the climate, the flowers and other plants, the friendliness of the people, the geckos that lived in their house and lost their tails whenever they grabbed hold of them, and her and Dad's continuing good health and their enjoyment of their missionary assignment. She also made repeated references to their "boys," grown young men who helped them with work in and around the house where they lived.

I don't think that Mom or Dad knew that when white folks in the segregated South called African-American men "boy," it was strictly a racially pejorative term that was intended to demean them and put them down.

The use of the word "boy" to address men who were in subservient roles to the missionaries was endemic to the New Guinea mission field. Lutheran missionaries used and perpetuated what I considered to be demeaning terminology. Protestant missionaries historically followed similar patterns when they entered a new mission field to proclaim the Gospel. First, they dressed them to get rid of their near nakedness. Then they tried to teach the natives the language of the missionary, whether it was English, German, Swedish, Norwegian, or something else from another country.

Our oldest son, Mark, and his wife, Susan, spent two years as missionaries teaching English in Japan. Ruth, our youngest son David, and I visited them in Fukuyama one spring. Fukuyama was a city on the Inland Sea, three hours south of Tokyo by bullet train and close to Kyoto and Hiroshima. The cities and countryside were beautiful and fragrant with the perfume of cherry blossoms. Seasonal festivities under the flowering trees were everywhere, and involved everyone in Japan.

We attended the small Lutheran church in Fukuyama where Mark and Susan were members on Easter Sunday and witnessed the confirmation of one teenage girl. But the experience included some disappointments. No native music enhanced the service. The melodies of Bach and familiar American hymns floated out of the electronic organ. The paraments on the altar were from the liturgical supply house in the United States rather than having been designed and sewn by the people who made such elegant fabrics for their magnificent kimonos. The vases on the altar, purchased from the same supply house, were typical altar vases like those in the United States and held ordinary and not very creative bouquets in this land that specializes in exotic flower arrangements. Nothing in the service was indigenous to Japan. Thirty-two people were in attendance, and five of them were Gonnermans.

We learned, to our disappointment, that when Japanese converted to Christianity, they wanted "American Christianity" and could not be convinced to adapt their own culture to their new faith. It is a complicated conundrum.

In New Guinea, Dad and Mom unquestionably were products of their time and of the paternalistic philosophy of the mission department of the Lutheran church.

Mom and Dad returned to their farm house in Illinois from their mission service in New Guinea in 1968. The land was being farmed by Chuck Nusbaum, their neighbor across the road. His ancestry was Swiss, and he was one of the most organized and meticulous farmers I have ever known. When he started farming the 160 acres of the Gonnerman farm, he was working about 2,000 acres, planted almost entirely in corn and soybeans. Within a few years, his wife was using a computer in their home to keep track of their operation, weather forecasts, the time planting was done and harvests could be expected, their expenses for seed, fuel, new machinery and the return on those expenses. She also traced the rise and fall of grain prices so they could take advantage of the best times to either hold or sell their corn and beans.

Mom and Dad did not return to farming when they returned from the mission field, but they continued to live on the farm and found ways together for continuing acts of kindness while they also spread the word of their New Guinea experiences.

First, a pregnant teenager from Freeport, Illinois, was invited to live with them. She was the victim of an unfriendly and accusatory family life. Mom mentored her through her pregnancy. Her baby was born in the hospital in Dixon where Mom had been a nursing supervisor for many years. The teenager gave up her baby for adoption and returned to Freeport.

On another occasion, Immanuel Lutheran Church in Dixon sponsored an immigrant Laotian family. Mom helped with finding housing for the family, soliciting donations of furniture, and occasionally inviting the family's children to visit them for brief stays on the farm. She also helped the husband and father find a place to work.

Then Dad died in that horrible accident on April 10, 1972. With the help of her younger daughter Mary Ann, Mom found a small ranch-style house in Gilman, Illinois. It was conveniently across the street from Mary Ann and across town from her older daughter, Donna. She moved there in 1991 to live the rest of her life.

But even in her new house in Gilman she could not "settle down." She volunteered for the Vista program and served for a year as a nurse at the Rosebud Indian Reservation in South Dakota. A small trailer was provided for her to live in. She took her sewing machine and made clothes that could be worn by the Native American children. She provided the cloth for the clothes out of her own funds. The extent of the poverty, alcoholism and their related violence and abuse in the reservation families surprised Mom even though she knew that was a significant part of reservation life before she went to Rosebud.

One of her biggest disappointments was the conservatism of the only Lutheran Church in the area. It was located about 30 miles from her trailer, and she was excited when she found it. Then she learned that the congregation belonged to the Lutheran Church–Missouri Synod, one of the most conservative of Lutheran bodies, and the pastor would not serve her communion even though she had been a life-long Lutheran and had even served in a foreign mission field.

But she endured that slight, and came back after a year to tell anyone who would listen about the abominable living conditions and the hopelessness that plagued and still demoralized Native Americans on the Rosebud reservation.

Looking for Leisure

The culture of leisure was not a part of Dad's and Mom's existence. First, they were "married" to their cows. The cows had to be milked every night and every morning at regular times. It was almost impossible to hire a fill-in who could be trusted to keep up with that schedule, be adequately motivated to clean and sterilize the milking system (including its glass pipeline from the milking machines to the holding tank) both before and after every milking, and be observant enough to see if any cows were having any physical problems that needed attention. Mom and Dad were not even sure if they could trust their children to carry on in their absence even when we were old enough to do so. So they did not leave their cows to get away, even for a weekend.

When you grow up in that kind of work ethic it's hard to change, even when you don't have cows. It takes time and effort before "leisure" becomes part of your vocabulary. It took Ruth quite a while to get me to "relax" by simply sitting with her on the front porch of our flat during my internship in Detroit only months after we had been married. Occasionally, she still has to remind me that it won't hurt not to do anything for a little while, but that's becoming easier as I get older.

European countries have done an incredibly better job of mandating leisure for their workers, whether they are on an assembly line, in social services, or in administrative positions. Almost all the countries of Europe mandate a minimum of three weeks of vacation (and some countries, four weeks) when people *must* get away from work and enjoy a time of leisure to rest and re-create. Those countries have learned that rested and re-created people work more efficiently and productively when they come back to their jobs.

More farmers in the United States are beginning now to find a little time for that kind of break in their own lives to visit a state or national park for a few days and maybe even take a Caribbean cruise. Almost all factory workers in the United States have at least a two-week-long vacation – and sometimes three weeks – written into their contacts. But far too many still stay home, some because they cannot afford travel to someplace other than home, some because they are not interested in leaving home to do or see anything different from what they have known their whole life.

Some institutions, agencies, and businesses in three Upper Midwestern States – Michigan, Wisconsin, and Minnesota – all bordering on at least one of the five Great Lakes and all having lots of smaller lakes of their own, have arranged summer work schedules to help their people enjoy weekend leisure more easily.

It works something like this: people come to their jobs half an hour early (7:30 a.m. instead of 8:00), take a half hour for lunch instead of an hour, leave a half hour early (4:30 p.m. instead of 5:00) and then quit work and go home at noon on Friday. Both St. Olaf College and Luther Seminary had that kind of schedule.

Most Michiganders, Wisconsinites, and Minnesotans have an affinity for fishing and have lots of places to do it within one or two hundred miles or less. Their summer schedules let them get away at noon on Friday. Then they go – some to their cabin, some to a familiar resort, some to visit extended family, some to a campground. Many pull boats behind their vehicles, some pull pop-up tent trailers, some go in an RV (recreational vehicle), some go in a car or SUV (suburban utility vehicle) loaded with camping gear. They all end up on the shore of a favorite lake or stream. They arrive late on Friday afternoon in time to catch fish for dinner if they can, enjoy all day Saturday, and come home on Sunday, refreshed for the next week's work.

When our family was young and growing, Ruth and I bought a camping trailer. Our first one was heavy. It needed automated brakes, and we could pull it behind a station wagon. Then we got a smaller car and a lighter camper. Empty, the new camper weighed only 900 pounds. Once, in a rain, I set it up for occupancy in only four minutes. It slept six. All the clothes we needed were packed in bins in the camper which also included a cook stove, an icebox, and a heater for colder than usual mornings. Interior lights operated off the car battery.

One year we traveled to Yellowstone National Park with stops in the Black Hills, the Tetons, and Glacier National Park. We visited Washington, D.C., twice, New England, twice (once traveling there through Canada), the Atlantic Seaboard, Michigan (crossing the Mackinac Bridge and visiting Mackinaw Island), Illinois (Springfield and environs), Iowa (the Amana Colonies). Nearly every trip was filled with history, geography, geology, nature study, the arts, and a little fishing.

Some years we visited the campground of Itasca State Park, the headwaters of the Mississippi River, in Minnesota two or three times. A ranger there named Ben introduced us all to the geology, history, flora, fauna, and wildlife of the area. We often went to the North Shore of Lake Superior, camping first at Gooseberry Falls State Park, staying a few days, then moving on in order to Temperance River State Park (the river got its name from the fact that no sand or gravel bar was at its mouth), and then Cascade State Park. Once we camped all the way around Lake Superior, adding Canadian Provincial Parks to our experience.

The Gonnerman Cabin on the North Shore

One beautiful fall weekend we made a spur-of-the-moment decision to visit the North Shore of Lake Superior to see the autumn color. We – Ruth, Joy, David, and me – left on a beautiful Friday afternoon. When we got to the overlook park just outside Duluth we made a rest stop. I began to hear bits of conversation about where people were staying, and I got a little uneasy. I had not made any reservations anywhere.

But I knew where I wanted to stay. It was at the large Edgewater Motel on London Road on the east edge of Duluth. I walked casually into the office and asked for a room for six. They were full. I went out to the phone booth (they had those in the days that predated cell phones) at the edge of the parking lot. I called every motel and resort with cabins from Duluth to Grand Marais. No one had a vacancy. I walked back into the office and asked the woman behind the counter if she had any suggestions. "Well," she said, "I think there's probably something back in Minneapolis."

Our spur-of-the-moment visit to see fall color was turning into a disaster. Then I thought of Superior across the state line and St. Louis River in Wisconsin. The first motel I stopped at after driving off the bridge had just had a bus cancellation and I was fourth in line. We had a place to stay. The rest of the weekend was delightful.

But on the way home Ruth and I began to say, "Wouldn't it be great to have a place to stay on the North Shore whenever we wanted to come up?" The next fall Ruth and I made the trip back up to the "Shore" alone one weekend to look at available cabins. We didn't see anything we liked or could afford, but when we came home our name was on six realtors' lists. The week before Christmas we received a handwritten note in the mail from one of those realtors. "Something's coming on the market that I think is just what you want. Can you come up to see it?"

We're going to go to the North Shore to look at a piece of property during the week before Christmas? Right. But we did go to see the property the week after New Year's in 1983. The 1,000-foot-long

The Gonnerman cabin on the rocky North Shore of Lake Superior.

driveway south off Highway 61 had been plowed, but we saw the cabin under ten inches of snow. The realtor recommended that we not walk on the 224 feet of solid granite shore line because the snow would be hiding holes and drop offs that we couldn't see.

The cabin, painted blue, was old. The back entrance had a shack quality to it. It was locked with a padlock. Inside, was a two plate wood cooking stove and an old propane furnace. The building was L shaped. It had electricity that was turned on by throwing the levers on two fuse boxes. It had cold running water which came through a pipe which laid across the rock to the edge of the lake. The water was pumped into the cabin with a pump and pressure tank in a small pump house a little less than half-way between the cabin and the lake. The pipe had been taken out of the water and the pressure tank drained so they wouldn't freeze during the winter. The toilet was down a path about 50 feet from the back door.

The cabin had a long room that served as kitchen and dining room. The living room was on the lake side. The two bedrooms were both small, but the smallest had a double bed that left only about a foot of space on both sides and maybe three feet at the end.

The view was incredible. From the kitchen window you looked east out on the rocky shore of the lake about 250 yards to a point of land penetrating the view of the lake. From the living room you looked across the shore (the cabin was only about 70 feet from the water) and you could see all the way across about 20 miles of water to the south shore of the lake bordering Wisconsin. The cabin also came with a guest house which could sleep four.

Ruth and I went to lunch, talked it over, and decided to meet the sellers' asking price. We had joined the thousands of Minnesotans who have "a cabin on a lake."

The essential renovation started that spring. The first order of business was to get hot as well as cold (and Lake Superior water is very cold) running water. We also needed a new refrigerator.

Next, I wanted to improve the entry area and the access between the cabin, the guest house, the toilet, and the lake. I built an on-the-ground deck with a walkway so that people could walk easily to any destination. The main section had a railing with a small bench on the lake side. The south end of the deck ended in a four-step staircase so that people would not have to negotiate their way to lake access over grass and rocks that got slippery when wet.

It was the beginning of a series of renovations to the cabin that changed it dramatically. I realize that much of what I did was learned on the farm, working with Dad to repair or construct what needed attention. Dad gave me an education that would be hard to duplicate and which made it possible for me to change our cabin into a place that fits our lifestyle and provides a wonderful summer home.

Treated lumber, guaranteed to last for 30 years, had only recently come on the market. I used that for anything that either rested on or had close proximity to the ground. I had begun a relationship with the lumber yard in Two Harbors, about 20 miles from the cabin. Sometimes I could haul a small order of lumber in our car by putting down the back seat. Big loads, like the one I was getting for the deck, had to be delivered. In the early days, delivery was free.

When I was buying the deck lumber I asked the owner of the lumberyard, an older and occasionally crotchety man, whether I needed a building permit for my project. "Oh," he said, "We don't bother with things like that around here." I thought that was great and took him at his word.

Better access to the pump house was next, so I built a stairway down from the deck. I incorporated a bit of a relic in the stairway railing, a 25-foot-long section of a one-inch rope I had saved from the haymow of the big barn that had been built on our farm some-time in the '20s. It worked perfectly as a flexible railing and added what I thought was a bit of charm.

The staircase ended with a platform and railing along the east wall of the pump house. Then I extended that platform past the pump house and ended it with a three-step stairway down to the granite. That staircase got carried away by storm waves three times before I gave up and learned to negotiate the short drop from the platform to the rock without it.

I learned quickly about the power of water. The pipe from the pump house to the water's edge, with an additional four feet going down into the water, was about 60 feet long. When we first bought the property, that pipe was fastened to the rock with steel bands held by quarter inch toggle bolts. I soon learned that they were not big enough. Frequently, when we came to the cabin after a storm had riled up the lake, 30 feet or more of pipe had disappeared. The power of the storm-driven water would lift the pipe, tear out the first set of toggle bolts, lift the pipe some more, bend it over, break it off, and carry it away. Some summers we would lose about 60 feet of one-inch galvanized steel pipe together with the brass baffle that had been put in the line to keep the water from draining out of the pressure tank when the pipe was carried away by the water.

I invested in a three-eighths-inch hammer drill and sank three-eighths inch toggle bolts three inches into the rock to hold down the steel bands that held the pipe in place. They seemed immovable. The fastening system was better, but a major storm would also tear out that installation. Every time someone from the family would come to the cabin I would remind them that the first thing they had to do was look to make sure the pipe was still in the lake. If it wasn't, they were without water until the pipe was replaced.

The problem was exacerbated if the storm was recent or still in process. That would mean large waves – sometimes as much as five to ten feet high – would be rushing over the place where a person had to work to get the pipe back in place. I had a long rope available to tie myself to the pump house to make sure that I or anyone else would not get pulled into the lake by the waves. None-the-less, the cold waters of Lake Superior made the job miserable when they soaked you to the skin.

Next, I gave some attention to the guest house. It had a small and very old stairway and porch leading to the entrance. Both had seen better days and were now at the point of being dangerous. They also did not take advantage of the possibilities. Bugs were not a huge problem because of the almost constant gentle breezes coming off the lake. The biggest problem was not mosquitoes – squadrons of dragon flies took care of them – but small biting flies. Those flies could make being outside on a warm August day agony. So, I thought, it would be nice to have a screened-in porch.

The old staircase and porch came down easily. In fact, it frightened me when I saw how easily. Someone could have been hurt if they had been on that porch when it collapsed.

I started from scratch, using four by four posts at the corners and in the middle of the front. Then I used two by sixes for the stringers for the floor. One inch lumber was used for the floor. The posts extended high enough to be the primary support for a roof, something that had not been part of the original porch. Once the roof was in place I made the screen walls from floor to ceiling. We had the screened in porch that made being outside in the late summer enjoyable.

Storage of tools was beginning to be a problem. So we went to Duluth and bought a kit to build a utility shed. It's a modified "A" frame. Ruth and I put it together in one day and had the storage place we needed. One of the things stored there was an old lawn mower that was 30 years old when we bought it in the late '80s and, thanks to the talents of the owner of a small engine repair shop in Two Harbors, still runs.

I also have a good relationship with him. The last time I took the lawnmower to him for some work (the pull cord on the starter had broken), he told me that he almost replaced the sparkplug but decided not to because he thought it might be "original equipment." We only mow the lawn about two times a year. We leave it a bit on the wild side for a reason. Early in the summer the yard is full of Indian Paint Brush and Buttercups. A little later, Daisies and Queen Ann's Lace decorate the landscape. The fall gives us little blue flowers with yellow centers. A wild strawberry bed covers a south-facing slope. Why should we mow all that away?

The time had come to enlarge the cabin. But we needed a plan. We wanted an inside bathroom, and those small bedrooms had to be enlarged. Mark's wife, Susan, has a brother, Peter Pennypacker, who was a general contractor and did some architectural work in California. We asked him if he would be interested in doing an architectural drawing. He said, "Yes," and we sent him photos, a rough drawing of the layout, and very specific measurements. A few months later he had a drawing.

He had come up with the creative plan we wanted. Working from the foundation for a six-foot square room that was accessible only from outside the cabin and sometimes, before we owned the place, had been used for a bathroom with a chemical toilet, he enlarged the kitchen dining room area to the east and then used some of that space to enlarge both of the bedrooms to the west. The master bedroom was also extended to the north. He got rid of the shack-like entrance and replaced it with a new entry and extended that space west and north to provide the bathroom.

We had several meetings with the county planning board to request a variance. The old cabin was much closer to the water than any new cabin could now be built. Any addition could not go an inch closer to the lake than the original foundation, but any expansion that was away from the lake needed a variance to proceed. I provided multiple schematic drawings of the whole lot and shoreline, measuring exact distances from shore to foundation at critical points.

The county planning committee visited the site. They found a problem. When I had built the deck I did not know that anything more than three feet high needed a permit. The owner of the Two Harbors Lumber Yard was wrong. They *did* pay attention to "things like that." The railings I had put on the deck extended up about two feet beyond the regulation. The committee insisted that the only way they would grant the variance I needed was to saw off all the railings. Our lawyer from Duluth was outraged. He said, "That's the dumbest thing I've ever heard." I agreed. "Who's going to be at fault if someone falls off the edge of my deck?" The committee was not moved. After all, "Rules is rules." Finally, after much discussion and many promises, our plan was approved and we were able to purchase the permit to proceed. I sawed off the railings.

At first, I thought I would be able to do all the work on the renovated cabin myself – with a little help from family. Then one July Fourth weekend, when quite a bit of family person-power was on hand, we began to dig the trench for the footings. The deepest we could go before hitting bedrock was about 30 inches. Most of the time, we could only dig down a foot. I knew how to lay a foundation if I could pound in stakes. I didn't have a clue how to lay a foundation on solid rock. I needed help.

Ruth and I began to look for a contractor. We found the names of three that looked promising. Then we asked around at lumber yards and hardware stores to get a fix on their reputations. Jim Williams in Two Harbors rose to the top. Everyone we talked to said that Jim was a responsible man who would do a good job. Then one of them said, "He learned his trade from his father who made his living by propping up old cabins."

We contacted Jim. He had the time and was willing to take on the work. We had our contractor. I talked to him about a division of labor, wondering what I might be able to do to cut down on costs. He would do the new parts of the foundation, the framing for the outer and interior walls and make the exterior weatherproof. He would subcontract the plumbing. I would do the necessary deconstruction, do the wiring, and finish the interior walls. I agreed, and began taking much of the old cabin apart in the summer of 1995.

We had a huge dumpster brought in and began to fill it with the old interior of what would be our new cabin.

I was on a nine-foot stepladder, hard at work with crowbar and sledge hammer, on June 17, when the phone rang. Ruth had gone to do some grocery shopping so I climbed down, found the phone amidst the rubble and answered it. Our second grandson, Carl Norquist, had just been born to Joy, our youngest daughter, and her husband Jim. I knew Ruth would want all the details, but I couldn't see a piece of paper anywhere. Then I saw a scrap of cellutex, the material that had been used before wallboard to cover the inside of the walls. I pulled my carpenters pencil from the side pocket of my jeans and wrote the details of Carl's birth on the cellutex. We still have that memento of his birth.

With the addition of a bathroom we had to have a septic system installed. On the basis of Jim's recommendation we hired a firm that did that up and down the shore. They had to blast three times to make a big enough hole in the rock to hold the septic tank just west of the cabin. Then they had to build an above-ground leech field. Our cabin sits on only one acre of ground (rock), but the septic people saw a stand of spruce at the far northwest corner of the property, took down only the trees necessary, and left a rim of spruce to hide the pile of sand and stone that would hold the field. People who work on the North Shore have an appreciation for the ecology of the place and try not to disturb any more than they have to.

Two large windows had been put in the east wall, giving us a nearly unobstructed view of the lake. After Jim and his crew finished the superstructure he said he had never worked with such a precise and detailed set of architectural drawings. And the architect never saw the project, before the addition or after it was finished.

I began working on the electrical wiring as soon as the superstructure was finished. I had installed lots of switches and outlets before. But I had never taken on the wiring of an entire house. I bought the manual of rules and regulations for wiring in the state of Minnesota. I memorized much of it and had it handy for reference throughout the work. My son-in-law, Larry Koch, helped with the project. I had never realized before how much wire a wiring project takes, and I was going to make sure of two things: first, I would install plenty of outlets so we would always be able to easily plug in anything; second, I wanted all the switches to be in the logical places where a person might look for them to turn lights on or off.

The first thing I did was locate a twelve-breaker circuit box in the new entry space, easily accessible as someone came through the door. Then I figured out what would be included on each of the circuits. An electrician brought the electricity to the box. That was beyond my capabilities.

It seemed like we strung miles of wire. I learned a valuable purchasing technique. Everything for the electrical system was being purchased at Menards in Duluth. I estimated the number of electrical boxes I needed for outlets, switches, and junctions. Then I added a dozen more. Wire nuts came in big packages. I'd buy one big package, then several smaller packages. I bought wire in 100-foot rolls, then add several 25-foot rolls. That way, any package that was not opened could be returned for a full refund.

When the wiring was finished, I called the inspector. He complimented me on my work and passed it the first time he saw it.

I had begun to learn about the special culture that pervaded the North Shore.

First, people who lived there were conscious of environmental and ecological consequences. They knew that the Lake Superior environment was fragile in spite of the vast expanses of rock and the power of the water. They were concerned when they saw people moving in who seemed not to have that same understanding and consciousness.

Second, they were a gregarious lot. Almost every time I called in a specialist to do work that was beyond my capabilities they would finish the work in less than half an hour. And then they would stand around and become better acquainted. We would chat about the weather (of course), the fishing, road construction on Highway 61, new neighbors moving in, and they often commented on the really nice spot our cabin was sitting on. They didn't expect money on the spot and had no problem with sending their bill to our home. And they never charged for more time than the job took. The extra conversation was free – and a bonus.

Except for the small bedroom where we would use wallboard, all of the interior walls would be knotty pine. That's great lumber to work with and I learned how to use it from Jim and from studying other people's workmanship in public places. Five things were important: first, the ends of boards that butted against each other had to be cut square; second, ends that met looked better if they were beveled at the same angle as the bevel on the edges of the boards; third, care should be taken to make sure that joints between boards should not be in the same line, but should be staggered; fourth, the heads of the finishing nails should be buried in the grooves of the boards; fifth, you don't necessarily need a perfectly straight cut when you have to split a board if you use a finishing molding that hides the cut.

When the knotty pine was all up I built a rectangle out of one by fours on edge, put in a few cross pieces, and hung it from the ceiling on gold painted chains above the new electric stove and kitchen counter. Ruth hung her pots and pans from the grid, and that provided the visual divider that separated the kitchen from the dining area.

Now, all we had left was the living room area. I began deconstruction of that interior space. The first thing I learned when I tore off the cellutex that covered the walls was the age of the building. *Life*, *Look*, and a variety of movie and outdoor magazines, all dated 1947, were nailed in the wall to provide insulation.

As in the first section I dismantled, all of the structural lumber was full-cut two by fours. Nothing had been trimmed down as it is today. It was good to see the old lumber. It had not deteriorated in any way. But when I pulled the ceiling cellutex down I saw both a problem and a possibility.

The problem was the size and the number of nails that held the ceiling joists. The people who put this building together built it with the philosophy that if one size nail is adequate, use nails that are at least a third larger, and if one nail would be adequate, use three. The nails were spikes about six inches long. At least three held the ends of each strut that held the ceiling. Getting those struts out was a major undertaking that took a lot of sweat and muscle with a wrecking bar and a small sledge.

It was also quite apparent that the L-shaped old cabin had been made by putting two smaller cabins together.

A second look at the space above where the ceiling had been was big enough to hold a loft. What a gift! I extended the loft floor, which was the living room ceiling, to within about ten feet of the east wall, giving us the effect of a vaulted ceiling. Then I added a window in the peak for both light and ventilation, and built a decorative railing to keep people from falling off the edge. Finally, we ordered a circular staircase from a firm in a Chicago suburb, had them ship it to Two Harbors Lumber who delivered it to the cabin. Ruth and I put the staircase together. The height of the ceiling for the loft is a bit low for adults, but our grandsons could use it easily – and they did and still do even though they are now much taller. Four to six people can sleep there easily on futon mattresses.

Three big windows were installed in the living room wall, giving us an expansive view of the lake, including ore boat traffic and the south shore of Lake Superior in Wisconsin on a clear day.

We got rid of the old propane furnace that had been used earlier for heat, and had a propane fireplace with a blower installed in the east wall. I had anticipated this change and wired in a thermostat earlier. But the fireplace needed a surround. I had planned on simply using pine boards, but a woodcarving friend, Derick Melby, offered to carve the surround for us. His fee? Two weeks' stay at the cabin for him and his family.

The beautifully carved surround includes things we enjoy during different seasons at the cabin. Canadian geese flying across a setting sun under the mantle are bracketed by two pine cones. A leaping trout, a butterfly, a Luna Moth, a chickadee, a cedar waxwing, a hummingbird, columbine, bunch berry, and wild roses fill the vertical spaces on both sides.

The fireplace is raised off the floor about a foot and a half by four courses of bricks that had been in the old chimney. The elevation helps the blower circulate the heat better and make it easier to reach the pilot light and other controls.

Knotty pine covers the living room walls, and the west wall is a floor to ceiling book case with spaces for a TV and a DVD player. The book case is full, and includes a relatively large collection of short story and poetry anthologies, just the right kind of reading for anyone who is there for a short stay.

After the front entry was finished, I realized that we needed a new porch with a two-step staircase. One day as I was pondering

The west wall of the living room in the Gonnerman cabin.

this problem I realized that a larger deck would fit in the corner made by the cabin and the entry extension and the needed staircase could be part of that deck. That was the next thing I built, and it's a great place to sit anytime, but especially in the morning.

The only thing left to renovate was the guest house. It was not in real good shape, but it had possibilities. One major problem was the unevenness and "softness" of the floor. Jim and his crew took care of that.

The old door was a handmade thing that looked like it might have come off a barn. The windows were too small. The same cellu-tex covered the walls. I put in six new windows and a new, steel-clad door with a deadbolt – just like the front and back doors for the cabin. Two of the windows are four-foot-long horizontal windows, one above each of the bunk bed mattresses. I thought, "Those bunks are going to be used by grandsons, and they ought to be able to look out in the woods if they want."

On the end overlooking the lake I built a small desk with a bar of electrical outlets. It's at keyboard height and that's where I've written much of this memoir. When I look away from my laptop screen I look out at the lake through a few trees. It's as good a setting for writing as I can imagine.

The screened in porch had to be redone. Having floor to ceiling screen is not a good idea when dogs are visiting with our daughters. Now the porch has a short wall topped by a wide shelf. The new screen runs from that shelf to the top of the walls. The four-step staircase to the porch has been redesigned to include a landing at the porch door.

The final flourish that same summer was the building of a bell tower for a large iron bell that we had been storing in our garage since Ruth's dad died and we took the bell home as a part of her heritage. For years we had not known what to do with it. Then we decided it would be perfect at the cabin to call people, particularly our grandsons, up from the rocky shore when we were ready to eat.

The bell tower, the last thing I built at the cabin, is fastened to the back door deck, the first thing I did. It's a fitting, dramatic addition, and it rings loud and clear.

The renovation was finished just in time. Problems with balance and leg weakness will not let me to do anything but the most mundane of construction efforts anymore. Now Ruth and I will simply enjoy ourselves when we come to the cabin – she to knit, or quilt, or cross stich; me to read, or write, or carve.

And while we are there, we don't worry too much about the rest of the world. We just let it go right on by. After all, that's what leisure ought to be about. My parents did not experience the luxury of leisure, but we have been blessed to find the time and experience its joy.

HISTORICAL CONTEXT

*After Dad's death, Mom stumbled along in this
unstoppable era of progressive change
for another quarter of a century,
but, like most of her peers, she seldom embraced it.*

HISTORICAL CONTEXT

Few, if any, periods of time have been as loaded with historical people, events, and movements as the eight decades since Dad and Mom got married in 1932 in the middle of the Great Depression. Sociological, cultural, political, and technological events and concerns were braided together in a thick and sometimes fraying cable as Mom and Dad lived together and raised a family of four children into the second half of the twentieth century.

They were, in order:

1. World War II and its atomic aftermath;
2. The establishment of the United Nations;
3. The Berlin Wall and the Berlin Airlift;
4. The Korean Police Action;
5. The violence-prone response to the non-violent movement to improve the civil rights of the African-American minority (and other minority groups) of the United States population;
6. Six years of assassinations;
7. The fruitless long-term involvement and diminishing of international leadership related to the interminable Vietnam War;
8. The political insecurities resulting in Watergate and the resignation of President Nixon;
9. The attempt to pull away from mainstream cultural norms resulting in the Hippie Movement;
10. The militant dissatisfaction with a divided society that put cities in turmoil;
11. The leap into space that put citizens of the United States on the moon and returned them safely to earth, and then scattered satellites throughout the

skies making possible instant, live reporting of events around the world, Global Positioning Systems, more accurate and long-range weather reporting, and exploration of parts of space not even known before;

12. China's resurgence beginning with a visit from President Richard Nixon in 1972. That visit was the bud that blossomed into a much closer relationship, particularly in trade;

13. The technological explosion that brought the creativity of the computer and related technological marvels crashing into human existence, expanding possibilities for communication beyond imagination;

14. The nine/eleven attack on the World Trade Center towers and the Afghanistan and Iraq Wars and the "Arab Spring" that followed;

15. The expanding wealth of the one percent in the top financial circles with the correlation of a commensurate flattening and sometimes loss of income for the remaining 99 percent of U.S. citizens;

16. Global warming and its potential effect on climate, weather, and human existence;

17. The worldwide population explosion and what it might mean to future generations.

Brief expositions of each follow.

World War II

The news came on the radio on December 7, 1941, a Sunday, the "day that will live in infamy." Japan had attacked the United States by bombing the Pacific fleet in the harbor at Honolulu, Hawaii. The next day, speaking before a joint session of congress in a speech broadcast across the nation and around the world on radio, President Franklin Delano Roosevelt declared that, "since the unprovoked and dastardly attack by Japan on Sunday, December 7 . . . a state of war has existed between the United States and the Japanese empire."

The Japanese attack also brought the United States into the war Hitler and the Nazis had provoked in Europe.

Dad was 38. That, together with the fact that being a farmer deferred him from military service, kept him from having to serve in the armed forces. Since I was only nine, our family would escape service on either the European or the Pacific front. Newspapers kept us informed, and the rationing and blackout systems were daily reminders that as citizens we were a part of the conflict. Many families we knew were not so fortunate.

Small service banners with a white field and a red border and a blue star in the center began to show up in people's front windows when a husband or son or daughter was in one of the armed services. It was a practice revived from World War I. If a family had more than one person in the armed services, the banner would have a star for each. If any member of the family died in the war, his or her banner would be changed from one with a white star to one with a gold. Far too many gold stars decorated the banners in many neighborhoods.

Significantly, our family radio gave us an almost personal connection with the men and women fighting dictatorial expansionist oppression in Europe and the Pacific as we listened to reports of one battle after another during World War II. News of the war replaced some of the 15-minute dramatic adventure programs we had listened to in a more innocent time.

Names of men and women we came to know as war correspondents were legion and are still familiar. Edward R. Murrow broke new ground in his personal "You Are There" reporting. Ernie Pyle, Walter Cronkite, Andy Rooney, Christiane Amanpour, Morley Safer, Peter Arnett were among the people we trusted to tell us the truth about what was going on. And they did. Bill Mauldin's cartoons featuring disheveled GIs Willie and Joe provided a needed light touch not only for the soldiers but also for the folks back home.

The depravity of the Holocaust was discovered by advancing Allied troops in Germany and Poland only weeks before the end of fighting. The numbers – six million Jews murdered – forced most of the world into overwhelming anxiety as we wondered about the state of humanity that would initiate and countenance such horror. When victory in Europe was declared on May 8, 1945, the total war effort was focused on the Pacific theater.

Ruth and I visited Dachau on one of our earlier visits to Germany. It was an instructive, but not a pleasant experience. A sculpture just inside the gate depicts the pain, inhuman treatment, and hopelessness of inmates, and immediately sets the stage for the rest of your visit. Dachau was the first concentration camp in Germany, founded by the Nazis in March 1933. Built with accommodations for 5,000, it sometimes held four times that many inmates, primarily political prisoners, in abominable conditions. After 1939, thousands of ordinary people, most of them Germans, were enslaved as part of the German war effort and were often starved, tortured, and killed.

The people in the nearby town of Dachau (close to Munich) claimed not to know what was happening at the concentration camp in their own backyard, but when U.S. troops liberated Dachau, General Dwight D. Eisenhower did not believe them and ordered everyone in their town to go through the camp to see with their own eyes what had been happening there. It was a forced visit filled with remorse.

The Nazis made a distinction between *concentration* camps such as Dachau and *extermination* camps such as Auschwitz in Poland. Ruth and I also visited Auschwitz when we were visiting David, then teaching English in Poland in 1993. He had already seen Auschwitz; he did not want to see it again. The railroad that brought detainees in, the barbed wire fences that contained them, the "showers" where they were gassed, and the ovens where their bodies were burned are still there. It is a horrendous experience to walk those grounds and contemplate those inhuman instruments of oppression and death. But everyone should, particularly those who have any doubt that the Holocaust happened. The Soviets "liberated" Auschwitz on January 27, 1945.

World War II began with Japan's sneak attack on the U.S. fleet in Hawaii in 1941. It ended with the dropping of two atomic bombs, one on Hiroshima (August 6) and the other on Nagasaki (August 9) in 1945. Japan signed the terms of surrender on the deck of the battleship Missouri in the Tokyo harbor on September 2, 1945, three years and four months after the attack on Pearl Harbor.

Ruth and I and our son, David, visited our son Mark and his wife Susan, both teaching English in Fukuyama, Japan, in the spring of 1983. Two stops on that trip bracketed the beginning and the end of World War II. We visited Hiroshima while in Japan, and we visited Pearl Harbor in Honolulu on the way home.

The first city in the world to suffer a nuclear attack, Hiroshima has been rebuilt, and in the rebuilding it created Peace Memorial Park. One focal point at the edge of the park is the A-Bomb Dome, the skeletal ruins of the former Industrial Promotion Hall. The empty steel superstructure of the building's dome marks the iconic ruin. It and the windowless base of the building are all that is still standing of the closest building to the hypocenter. The ruin is an officially designated "site of memory for the nation's and humanity's collectively shared heritage of catastrophe."

In a park that oozes emotional recollection everywhere a visitor goes, the most emotional site in the park is the Children's Peace Monument dedicated to the memory of the children who died as a result of the bombing. Its focal point is the statue of a girl, Sadako Sasaki, who died from the bomb's radiation. She believed that if she folded 1,000 paper cranes she would be cured. She was not. In Sadako's memory, people around the world still fold cranes and send them to Hiroshima where they are placed near the statue. The Children's Peace Monument is always overflowing with thousands of multi-colored paper cranes.

The primary museum in the park is the Hiroshima Peace Memorial Museum dedicated to educating visitors about the bomb. Exhibits and information cover the build-up to the war, the role of Hiroshima in the war up to the dropping of the atomic bomb, and extensive information on the bombing and its effects. One unforgettable exhibit is a stone stair step dominated by the black shadow of a person who had been sitting there and was vaporized in the explosion. An estimated 140 thousand Japanese died as a result of the dropping of the first atomic bomb.

On the way home from Japan, Ruth, David, and I made our first visit to Hawaii, partly to ease the effects of jetlag when we would arrive back in Minnesota. While in Honolulu, we visited the USS Arizona Memorial in Pearl Harbor. We had toured the site of the end of the war in Hiroshima, Japan. Now we would see the site of the war's beginning for the United States at Pearl Harbor, Hawaii.

The USS Arizona Memorial is a national cemetery. In its massive hulk lie the remains of 1,777 sailors who went down with the ship when its forward magazine exploded from a direct hit by a Japanese bomb. All of the sailors' names are inscribed in the interior of the simple white superstructure built over the sunken Arizona's hull. Total American casualties in the Pearl Harbor attack were 2,386 dead (including those in the Arizona), and 1,139 wounded. Eighteen ships, including five battleships, were sunk or run aground.

Here's one more sobering statistic. Japanese people killed in the atomic bombing of Hiroshima (140,000) were nearly 60 times greater than the number of Americans who died (2,386) in the attack on Pearl Harbor.

irrelevant

Several veterans of World War II took advantage of the GI Bill and enrolled at Wartburg College when I was a student there. I became acquainted with more, some of whom had survived serious wounds, when I was in the national office of The American Lutheran Church.

One of the most ignominious episodes in United States history happened in 1942 less than three months after Pearl Harbor. President Roosevelt, with Executive Order 9066, authorized the interment in designated camps of 110,000 people with Japanese heritage living in California, Oregon, and Washington. Sixty-two percent of the internees were American citizens. About 1,500 residents of Hawaii were also interred. The internment ended in 1946. Many of the Japanese who had been victimized lost their homes, businesses, and much of their personal possessions.

The internment was not widely publicized. I do not remember Mom or Dad ever mentioning it or discussing its implications, and I don't recall that I had even heard about it before studying American history in college.

President Jimmy Carter conducted an investigation in 1980, appointing the Commission on Wartime Relocation and Internment of Civilians to investigate the camps. The commission's report, "Personal Justice Denied," found little evidence of Japanese disloyalty and recommended the government pay reparations to the survivors. Each internment survivor received a payment of $20,000. Congress passed and President Ronald Reagan signed legislation in 1988 that officially apologized for the internment on behalf of the United States government.

A little-noted development in 1939, the same year Hitler invaded Poland, was the first printing of paperback books by Simon & Schuster. They were called Pocket Books, measured four by six inches, and cost $.25 each. It was an innovation that in ensuing years encouraged thousands more people around the world to read books, primarily because they were so much easier to carry around than the larger and heavier hardbound copies.

The year after peace had been declared at the end of World War II, 1946, Sir Winston Churchill, speaking at Westminster College in Fulton, Missouri, acknowledged the division that was happening to the Allies with the belligerent isolationism and wanton denial of human rights by the Union of Soviet Socialist Republics (U.S.S.R). In a speech titled "The Sinews of Peace," Churchill declared, "From Stettin in the Baltic to Trieste in the Adriatic, an Iron Curtain has descended across the continent." That one declaration changed the way the democratic West viewed the Communist East for nearly the next half a century.

The Establishment of the United Nations

When the United Nations was founded in San Francisco in 1945 shortly after the end of World War II, it had bold and wide-ranging aims. They include: promoting and facilitating cooperation in international law, international security, economic development, social progress, human rights, civil rights, civil liberties, political freedoms, democracy, and the achievement of lasting peace.

It replaced the League of Nations which had fallen apart with the beginning of World War II. The United Nations was expected to stop wars between countries and provide a platform for dialogue. It included many subsidiary organizations to carry out its mission.

United Nations headquarters is in international territory in New York City. The International Court of Justice is in The Hague. Other offices are in Geneva, Nairobi, and Vienna. The organization had 51 member nations at its founding. Today that number has climbed to nearly 200.

It is organized into six principal divisions: the General Assembly (the main deliberative group); the Security Council (for approving resolutions dealing with peace and security); the Economic and Social Council (for assisting in promoting international economic and social cooperation and development); the Secretariat (for providing studies, information, and facilities needed by the United Nations); the International Court of Justice (the primary judicial organ); and the United Nations Trusteeship Council (currently inactive).

Other prominent United Nations agencies include: the World Health Organization (WHO); the World Food Programme (WFP); and the United Nations Children's Fund (UNICEF).

The General Assembly is the deliberative assembly of all United Nations member states (with each country having one vote). It might also resolve non-compulsory recommendations to states, decide on the admission of new members, adopt the budget, and elect non-permanent members of the Security Council. The Security Council has 15 members (five permanent with veto power, and ten elected) and is responsible for the maintenance of international peace and security. It is the most powerful part of the United Nations and may adopt compulsory resolutions. Its decisions include peacekeeping and peace enforcement missions as well as non-military pressure actions such as trade embargoes.

Six official languages – Arabic, Chinese, English, French, Russian, and Spanish – are spoken and printed in intergovernmental meetings and documents.

The top leadership position is Secretary General, currently held by Ban Ki-moon from South Korea. Former Secretaries General are: Trygve Lie, Norway, 1946-1952; Dag Hammarskjöld, Sweden, 1953-1961; U Thant, Burma, 1961-1971; Kurt Waldheim, Austria, 1972-1981; Javier Pérez de Cuéllar, Peru, 1982-1991; Boutros Boutros-Ghali, Egypt, 1992-1996; Kofi Annan, Ghana, 1997-2006.

The founders of the United Nations envisioned an organization that would act to avoid conflicts between nations and make future wars impossible. However, the Cold War divided the world into hostile camps and made peacekeeping agreements extremely difficult. When the Cold War ended, the United Nations had renewed calls to become the agency for achieving world peace. But too many new and continuing conflicts still disrupt peoples around the globe.

Disagreements in the Security Council about intervention and the use of military action made it impossible to prevent the atrocities in Bangladesh in 1971and the Rwandan Genocide in 1994. They precipitated the failures to deliver food to the starving people of Somalia or to intervene in the 1995 Srebrenica massacre or provide assistance in Darfur, as well as many other unresolved problems.

At the same time, the United Nations has had notable successes in encouraging disarmament. The pursuit of human rights around the world continues to be a central purpose. The United Nations charter calls on all member nations to promote "universal respect for, and observance of, human rights" and "take joint and separate action" to that end. The Universal Declaration of Human Rights, though not legally binding, was adopted by the General Assembly in 1948 as a common standard and the Assembly regularly takes up human rights issues. The United Nations Human Rights Council was established in 2006 to address violations.

In conjunction with other organizations such as the Red Cross, the United Nations provides food, drinking water, shelter and other humanitarian services to peoples suffering from famine, displaced by war, or afflicted by other disasters. The World Food Programme of the United Nations helps feed more than 100 million people in 80 countries every year.

The United Nations is not a perfect organization, but it accomplishes a lot when considering all the problems that plague people every day around the world.

Problems in Berlin

It was apparent by 1948 that the plans of the United States, Great Britain, and France for the rebuilding of Germany differed greatly from the plans of the Soviet Union. Stalin ordered all American military personnel maintaining communication equipment out of the Eastern Zone of Berlin on April 9, 1948. All land and water access to West Berlin was cut off by the Soviets on June 24. That forced responses to two questions: 1.) Where would necessary supplies come from for the occupation forces; and 2.) How would the more than two million Germans in Berlin get the necessities of life?

The need was incredible. The people of Berlin required supplies totaling 3,475 tons every day just for survival. The United States, together with Britain and France, decided on an amazing solution. Together they would do an airlift. Three 20-mile-wide air corridors, agreed upon with the Soviets in writing in 1945, provided access to Berlin. General Lucius Clay decided that the U.S. Air Force, using 102 Douglas C-47 Skytrains and two C-54 Skymasters would be the backbone of a daily, around the clock airlift. The C-47s could each carry three and a half tons; the C-54s, ten and a half.

But it had been determined that Berlin's *daily* food ration was 646 tons of flour and wheat, 125 tons of cereal, 64 tons of fat, 109 tons of meat and fish, 180 tons of dehydrated potatoes, 180 tons of sugar, 11 tons of coffee, 19 tons of powdered milk, five tons of whole milk for children, three tons of fresh yeast for baking, 144 tons of dehydrated vegetables, 38 tons of salt, and ten tons of cheese – a total of 1,534 tons needed every day to keep more than two million people alive. The C-47s would have the impossible task of making 1,000 flights a day.

General Clay and General Curt LeMay requested more C-54s. Fifty-two more C-54s were ordered to Berlin on June 27. By July 1 all of them were operating three minutes apart 24 hours a day on airlift flights. Major General William H. Tunner, "a transportation expert to end all transportation experts," was put in charge of the operation. Rheine-Main Air Base in Frankfort became the exclusive base for the C-54s, and Wiesbaden handled a mix of C-54s and C-47s. The British were flying Lancasters, Yorks, and Hastings aircraft.

Both of Berlin's airports, Tempelhof and Gatow were in continuous use.

The Soviets capitulated on May 12, 1949. The airlift ended on September 30 that same year, 15 months after it began. The U.S. had delivered almost two million tons of supplies and the British flew in more than a half million tons for the people of Berlin. Together they had flown 277,569 flights and traveled more than 92 million miles. The 101 fatalities during the operation, mostly from crashes, included 31 Americans.

A priceless story of one pilot's individual charity and concern for West German children has to be included here. One day First Lieutenant Gail S. Halvorsen noticed children standing at the end of a Tempelhof runway, watching the planes come in. He found a way to talk to them and decided they were in need of some treats. The day he met them he had only two sticks of gum in his pocket. He gave them what he had and watched them share it. Then he promised that if they watched for him the next day, he would drop them some candy. The children asked how they would know it was his plane. He said, "I'll wiggle my wings."

The children were there the next day on Halvorsen's approach. He rocked the airplane and dropped chocolate bars he had attached to a parachute improvised from a handkerchief. Every day more children were waiting at the end of the runway. Every day, Halvorsen would drop more chocolate.

He didn't tell anyone what he was doing. But mail addressed to "Uncle Wiggly Wings," "The Chocolate Uncle," and "The Chocolate Flier" started coming into Base Headquarters. His commander called him in and asked what he was doing. "Flying, sir," he replied. After answering the same question with the same response several times, Halvorsen was shown a newspaper by the commander. It had a picture of his plane with tiny parachutes trailing behind it.

General Tunner thought Halvorsen's candy drop should get more publicity. The candy drop was named "Operation Little Vittles," and many C-54 pilots participated. In the end, more than three tons of candy was dropped over Berlin, and Halvorsen became the most recognized pilot in the Berlin Airlift.

I was in high school during the Berlin airlift. I remember that Mom and Dad listened to its progress regularly on the radio and followed it carefully in the newspaper. But 11 years later Berlin would be back at the top of the newscasts. This time the news was about a wall.

The Berlin Wall was erected overnight on August 13, 1961, separating German citizens in democratic West Berlin from German citizens in communist East Berlin. It would stand as a testament to political subjugation until November 9, 1989 – 28 years. The wall stretched more than 100 miles, not only dividing Berlin at its center, but also wrapping around the western edge of the city, completely cutting it off from the rest of Germany.

At the end of World War II the Allied powers divided Germany into four zones, each occupied either by the United States, Great Britain, France, or the Soviet Union. Berlin, Germany's capitol, was divided the same way. The cooperative relationship between the Soviet Union and the other three Allies disintegrated. The intended reunification of Germany was in trouble. The organization of a divided Germany became official in 1949 when the zones occupied by the United States, Great Britain and France were combined to form the Federal Republic of Germany (West Germany), and the zone occupied by the Soviet Union became the German Democratic Republic (East Germany).

Living conditions in West Germany and East Germany, and the divided capital of Berlin, became drastically different soon after the war. West Germany experienced such rapid economic growth that it was called the "economic miracle." In East Germany and East Berlin individual freedoms were restricted as the Communist economy dragged. East Germany began to suffer a mass exodus as its citizens packed up and moved to West Germany. By 1961, East Germany had lost two-and-a-half million people. That's when East Germany's leaders decided to build the wall to keep their people in.

The first version of the wall was barbed wire with concrete posts, the same kind of construction the Nazis had built around their concentration camps. That was replaced soon with a concrete block wall topped by barbed wire. Next, a concrete block construction was supported by steel girders. The final version, built between 1975 and 1980, consisted of concrete slabs nearly 12 feet high topped by a smooth concrete pipe. The wall was further fortified by a 50-yard-wide "no-man's-land" on the eastern side. Parts of it were mined. Along some sections, the wall was further strengthened by East German soldiers manning machine guns at windows high up in buildings at the eastern edge of the no-man's-land. A small number of crossing points allowing a few people to go back and forth between east and west had random blockades that slowed down any vehicular traffic and were heavily manned by armed East German soldiers. The best known of these crossing points was called "Checkpoint Charlie."

Ruth and I saw the Berlin Wall twice. The first time was in 1970 when we were traveling with the St. Olaf Choir (I as photographer and publicist) on one of its European concert tours. The choir sang at the reconstructed Kaiser Wilhelm Memorial Cathedral. It also visited the wall where a seven-step staircase put people on a platform from which they could see across no-man's land. It took some time for all 70 members of the choir to get on the platform and have a look. Some of them were playing around with a Frisbee.

An Army Jeep was kicking up dust as it carried two soldiers into the area. They said, "You're being watched by East German soldiers with machine guns in the buildings on the others side of "no-man's-land." They are getting nervous. The choir members quieted down immediately, loaded up the busses, and we left.

The next day we crossed the wall at Checkpoint Charlie on our way to visit an Orthodox church. When the busses were just a little past half way through the checkpoint two security guards with pistols on their hips got in and came slowly down the aisle. They requested everyone's passport and spent what seemed to be an inordinate amount of time checking between your face and your picture to make sure they matched. The bus was deathly quiet. We knew that we had just crossed a border where it would not matter if we were "right" or "wrong." If either of those guards, both as young or younger than members of the choir, decided that we were "wrong" we would be "wrong." It was a horribly frightening feeling.

The second visit in 1991 was totally different. It was in connection with a visit to our son, David, in Poland. We flew into Berlin. The wall had been torn down by a huge number of West German dissidents only a short time before. Much of the space where the wall had been was marked only by a dark line about ten inches wide that snaked across the pavement. At the Brandenburg Gate, which had been just over the line on the east side, what had been no-man's-land had been turned into a free enterprise zone. Both sides of the street were lined with small booths – some under tents, some just a table – where we could buy pieces of the wall, parts of East German army uniforms, some East German guns, and all sorts of tourists' trinkets.

Ruth and I made our way to where Checkpoint Charlie had been. Little more than the sign was left. However, less than a block away we spotted a museum marked by a large, three-dimensional, red star. It was a museum honoring the people who had tried to cross the wall since it had gone up in 1961. We went in, expecting to spend half an hour. Three hours later we forced ourselves to leave. That museum holds records and newspaper accounts of all the attempts to escape East Berlin by going over or under the wall. Some of them were successful. Many ended in the death of the person desperate for freedom. It also has the cars with secret compartments where people hid, the hand-made "lighter than air" planes, the trunks with false bottoms where a small person could just fit. The whole museum was a mesmerizing historical account.

A correction to the popular historical record is needed here. President Reagan has gotten credit for the dismantling of the Berlin Wall after he said in a speech there, "Mr. Gorbachev, tear down this Wall!" (Mikhail Gorbachev was Secretary of the Communist Party of the Soviet Union from 1985 to 1991.) The Wall came down, but Gorbachev did not tear it down. Neither did Reagan. The Berlin Wall came down because of the courage and fortitude of dissident West

German young people who decided that enough was enough and tore it down themselves. They were joined by East German youth.

The Korean War

The world was not without war for long. The Cold War between western democracies and eastern totalitarian regimes was simmering. Then, on June 25, 1950, only five years after World War II ended, 75,000 North Korean soldiers crossed the 38th parallel, the boundary separating North and South Korea, in the Cold War's first military action. American troops entered the war as South Korea's ally.

The United States saw the war as a fight against the forces of international Communism, fearing that the Korean conflict might widen into war against the Soviet Union and China, possibly even the beginning of an unimaginable World War III.

Korea had been a part of the Japanese empire since the beginning of the twentieth century. At the end of World War II the Americans and the Soviets had to decide what to do with Japanese territories. The U.S. State Department divided Korea along the 38th parallel. The Soviets would occupy the territory north of that line with communist Kim Ll Sung as dictator, and the United States would be the occupying force in the south with anti-communist Syngman Rhee as dictator. It was not a comfortable situation. Border skirmishes were common and nearly 10,000 North and South Korean soldiers died in sporadic fighting before the Korean War began.

The war started as a defensive struggle to force the North Koreans back to their designated territory. That did not go well for United States forces. Harry S Truman was president and General Douglas MacArthur was commander in charge of the Asian theater. Chinese leader Mao Zedong sent troops to North Korean, warning the United States to keep away from the Yalu boundary unless it wanted full-scale war. Truman did not want to precipitate anything close to that kind of conflict. MacArthur, on the other hand, thought anything short of a wider war represented "appeasement." The two men did not particularly like each other to begin with. But this personal conflict heated up with the possibility that MacArthur might exceed his authority with an amphibious invasion of North Korea above the 38th parallel. Truman fired MacArthur and changed the Korean command.

Truman started peace talks in Panmunjom, North Korea. Negotiations stalled. Fighting continued. Finally, after more than two years of negotiations, an armistice was signed on July 27, 1953. The agreement, brokered by President Dwight D. Eisenhower, allowed prisoners of war on both sides to stay where they wanted, drew a new boundary near the 38th parallel that gave South Korea an extra 1,500 square miles of territory, and created a two-mile wide "demilitarized zone."

Nearly five million people died in the Korean conflict, more than half of them South Korean civilians. About 40,000 Americans died in action in Korea, and more than 100,000 were wounded. I knew one of those killed in action. He had lived in Nachusa, was a captain in the army, was about my age, and was killed the day before the Armistice was signed. Several Korean veterans were in my class at Trinity Lutheran Seminary.

The Armistice worked reasonably well until 2013, when Kim Jong Un, the new, 30-year-old leader, became increasingly belligerent, cancelled the terms of the armistice, and threatened South Korea, Japan, and the United States with atomic attacks.

The world we live in remains violent, volatile, and virulent.

Introduction to Civil Rights

The civil rights movement had been underway for only two decades when Mom and Dad flew to the New Guinea mission field in 1967. I never heard them talk about it, possibly because they had decided (correctly) that I had become much more liberal, both politically and socially.

President Harry S Truman had desegregated the U.S. armed forces by executive order in 1948. The Supreme Court announced its Brown vs. Board of Education of Topeka, Kansas, decision on May 17 that same year, unanimously agreeing that segregation in public schools was unconstitutional. That decision was a victory for NAACP (National Association for the Advancement of Colored People) attorney Thurgood Marshall who would later be named as the first African-American justice on the Supreme Court.

Rosa Parks refused to give up her seat to a white passenger and was arrested on December 1, 1955. (I had graduated from college that June and was then a seminary student.) The African-American community in Montgomery, Alabama, launched a bus boycott that lasted for more than a year until busses were desegregated on December 21, 1956.

In September, 1957, nine black students were blocked from entering formerly all-white Central High School in Little Rock, Arkansas, and President Dwight D. Eisenhower sent federal troops and the National Guard on behalf of the students.

Four black students from North Carolina Agricultural and Technical College began a sit-in at a segregated Woolworth's lunch counter on February 1, 1960. They were not served. But they were served at the same counter six months later.

James Meredith became the first black student to enroll at the University of Mississippi on October 1, 1961.

Martin Luther King, Jr., was arrested and jailed during anti-segregation protests in Birmingham, Alabama, on April 16, 1962, and wrote *Letters from Birmingham Jail.* King had been born on January 15, 1929. He attended segregated public schools in Georgia, and earned the B.A. degree from Morehouse College and the B.D. degree from Crozer Theological Seminary in 1951. He went on to graduate studies at Boston University and earned his doctorate there in 1955. He met his wife, Coretta Scott, in Boston, and they raised two sons and two daughters. When he became pastor of Dexter Avenue Baptist Church in Montgomery, Alabama, in 1954 he was already active in civil rights and a member of the executive committee of the NAACP. He accepted the leadership of the first great Negro nonviolent demonstration in Montgomery, Alabama, the first Negro nonviolent demonstration in contemporary times in the United States. The demonstration lasted 382 days. Elected president of the Southern Christian Leadership Conference in 1957, he traveled more than six million miles, spoke more than 2,500 times, wrote five books, and led the massive protest in Birmingham, Alabama that caught the attention of the entire world. His most famous address, "I Have a Dream," was the speech delivered from the steps of the Lincoln Memorial in Washington, D.C., on August 28, 1962, at the climax of the peaceful march of 250,000 people. He was honored with the Nobel Peace Prize at the age of 35.

Four little girls attending Sunday School were killed when a bomb exploded on September 15, 1963, at the Sixteenth Street Baptist Church in Birmingham, Alabama.

President Lyndon Johnson signed the Civil Rights Act of 1964 on July 2.

Congress passed the Voting Rights Act of 1965 on August 10.

President Johnson asserted that civil rights laws alone are not enough to remedy discrimination and issued an executive order on September 24, 1965, which enforced affirmative action for the first time.

In Loving vs. Virginia the Supreme Court ruled on June 12, 1967 that it is unconstitutional to prohibit interracial marriage.

Major race riots broke out in 1967 in Newark, New Jersey, (July 12-16) and Detroit, Michigan (July 23-30).

President Johnson signed the Civil Rights Act of 1968 (April 11) prohibiting discrimination in the sale, rental, and financing of housing.

In Swann vs. Charlotte-Mecklenburg Board of Education, the Supreme Court, on April 20, 1971, upheld busing as a legitimate means for achieving integration of public schools.

Congress voted to override the veto of the Civil Rights Restoration Act by President Ronald Reagan on March 22, 1988, expanding the reach of non-discrimination laws within private institutions receiving federal funds.

After two years of debates, vetoes, and threatened vetoes, President George H.W. Bush reversed himself on November 22, 1991, and signed the Civil Rights Restoration Act, strengthening existing civil rights laws and providing for damages in cases of intentional employment discrimination.

Civil rights movements were not limited to the United States.

When Nelson Mandela died on December 5, 2013, in Johannesburg, South Africa, tens of thousands attended an outdoor memorial service in FNB Stadium despite a pouring rain. Some said it was one of the largest gatherings of global leaders in history as representatives from around the world joined common laborers, entertainers, and religious figures to pay tribute. Barack Obama, president of the United States, said, "We will never see the likes of Nelson Mandela again." Calling him a "giant of history," Obama said to roaring cheers, "To the people of South Africa — people of every race and every walk of life — the world thanks you for sharing Nelson Mandela with us."

Civil rights and the fight against South Africa's policy of apartheid was the focus of the life and work of a man born Rolihlahla Mandela in Mvezo, Transkei, in 1918. His teacher at primary school, following the custom to give all school children "Christian" names, gave him the name Nelson. He became one of the world's most renowned agents for change early in life when he was expelled from his university studies for joining a student protest, but he completed his bachelor of arts degree by correspondence and graduated in 1943. He joined the African National Congress in1944 when he helped form the ANC Youth League. In 1952, after earning a two-year diploma in law, he and Oliver Tambo started the first black law firm in South Africa.

Arrested in a countrywide police sweep in 1955, which led to the 1956 Treason Trial, he was in the last group of 28 acquitted in 1961. The police killing of 69 unarmed protestors in 1960 led to the country's first state of emergency and the banning in April of the ANC and the Pan Africanist Congress. Mandela and ten others were put on trial for sabotage in the Rivonia Trial in 1963. He made his famous "Speech from the Dock" the next year: "I have fought against white domination, and I have fought against black domination. I have cherished the ideal of a democratic and free society in which all persons live together in harmony and with equal opportunities. It is an ideal which I hope to live for and to achieve. But if needs be, it is an ideal for which I am prepared to die."

He and seven others were convicted and sentenced to life imprisonment in 1964. After hospitalization for tuberculosis he was released from prison in 1990. Mandela and President F. W. de Klerk were awarded the Nobel Peace Prize jointly in 1993. The next year he was inaugurated South Africa's first democratically elected president. He stepped down from that post in 1999 after one term and continued to work with the Nelson Mandela Children's Fund he had set up in 1995 and established the Nelson Mandela Foundation and The Mandela Rhodes Foundation. Throughout his life, Mandela was continually devoted to democracy, equality and learning. He never answered racism with racism despite terrible provocation.

The example of Mandela's life continues as an inspiration to all the oppressed and deprived, and to all those who oppose oppression and deprivation.

Six Years of Assassinations

Six years in the sixties were, in one sense, six of the most violent years in the history of the United States. Four men were assassinated, all by gunshots.

The first was Medgar Evers, the 37-year-old field secretary for the NAACP in Mississippi. He was murdered on his driveway outside his home with a single rifle shot on June 12, 1962. Byron De La Lincoln, a member of the Ku Klux Clan, was convicted of the murder 30 years later in his third trial.

The second was President John F. Kennedy in Dallas, Texas, on November 22, 1963, another "day that will live in infamy" to borrow a phrase from President Franklin Delano Roosevelt. The president and his wife Jackie were riding in the back of an open car in a motorcade. The crowd was excited and jubilant over his presence in Dallas.

Just after they had turned onto Dealey Plaza at 12:30 p.m. three shots rang out from the Texas School Book Depository behind them. At least two of them hit the president in his neck and head. He was pronounced dead in Parkland Memorial Hospital at 1:00 p.m.

Lee Harvey Oswald was arrested as the assassin an hour later. He was shot and killed by Jack Ruby a short time later as he was being transferred from police headquarters to the county jail.

Third to die was Martin Luther King, Jr., shot down with one sniper's .30-caliber rifle bullet while standing on the balcony outside his room at the Lorraine Motel in Memphis, Tennessee, on the evening of April 4, 1968. African-Americans across the United States were outraged and took to the streets in a massive wave of riots.

James Earl Ray, an escaped convict, was arrested and pronounced guilty in his trial, but many people believed he was innocent.

On March 18 King had spoken to more than 15,000 people in Memphis in support of 1,300 African-American sanitation workers who had gone on strike. He returned to Memphis on April 3, and on that evening delivered his "I've Been to the Mountaintop" speech which included these words:

> "I don't know what will happen now; we've got some
> difficult days ahead. But it doesn't really matter with
> me now, because I've been to the mountaintop. And I

don't mind. Like anybody, I would like to live a long life - longevity has its place. But I'm not concerned about that now. I just want to do God's will. And He's allowed me to go up to the mountain. And I've looked over, and I've seen the Promised Land. I may not get there with you. But I want you to know tonight, that we, as a people will get to the Promised Land. And so I'm happy tonight; I'm not worried about anything; I'm not fearing any man. Mine eyes have seen the glory of the coming of the Lord."

Only two months later on June 6, 1968, Robert Kennedy, President Kennedy's brother, was killed by three bullets from a .22 caliber pistol while in a pantry corridor in the Ambassador Hotel in Los Angeles.

He had just given his victory speech to 1,800 supporters after learning that he won the Democratic primary naming him as their presidential candidate. He had ended his speech with, "Now on to Chicago, and let's win there!"

Kennedy's assassin, captured immediately, was Sirhan Sirhan, a Palestinian immigrant.

Many people remember exactly where they were when they first heard the news of one or more of these assassinations. I remember President Kennedy's. I was on the back stairway of The American Lutheran Church office building in Minneapolis, half-way between the third and second floors on my way down to the second floor lunchroom. Lester Heins, my boss in the public relations office was coming up the stairs and told me the awful news. The lunchroom that day was uncommonly quiet as we each, in a state of shock, thought about that news and its ramifications. I don't know where Dad and Mom were or how they reacted.

Ruth and I did not have a television when the president was assassinated, but we rented one so that we could watch the funeral in that awful aftermath.

Effects of the Vietnam War

Mom and Dad and their children had something else to worry about in the midst of the Civil Rights Movement. The Vietnam War had unintended consequences far beyond the deaths, the disabling wounds, and the dollars spent between 1959 and April 30, 1975.

Vietnam had been plagued by war for decades. The country had been under French colonial rule for more than half a century when Japan invaded the county in 1940. Ho Chi Minh, a communist Vietnamese revolutionary leader, returned after a 30-year absence in 1941. He established the Viet Minh. His subsequent announcement of the establishment of an independent Vietnam was followed by his establishment of a new government to be known as the Democratic Republic of Vietnam in 1945.

Despite Ho Chi Minh's hope that the United States would support him against the French and provide military intelligence about the Japanese during World War II, the U.S. maintained its foreign policy of containment (meaning preventing the spread of communism) and sent military aid to France. The French pulled out of Vietnam in 1954 after a decisive defeat at Dien Bien Phu. The Geneva Accords that same year called for a peaceful withdrawal of French forces and the temporary division of Vietnam at the 17th parallel into communist North Vietnam and non-communist South Vietnam. The Accords also called for a general democratic election in 1956 to unite the country under one government, but the United States, afraid the communists might win, did not agree to the election.

Ngo Dinh Diem was elected leader of South Vietnam, but was killed in a coup supported by the United States in 1963. The National Liberation Front, a group of communist sympathizers also known as the Viet Cong, was formed in 1960 to use guerrilla warfare against the South Vietnamese. The U.S. had been sending military advisers to South Vietnam. Congress, following President Lyndon Johnson's lead, passed the Gulf of Tonkin Resolution after U.S. ships reported they had been attacked by the North Vietnamese in international waters on August 2 and 4, 1964, escalating U.S. involvement when the president sent the first U.S. ground troops to Vietnam in March 1965.

The Vietnamese War lasted ten years. During that time, the United States introduced Agent Orange (a toxic substance that defoliated the jungle) and napalm bombs (a deadly fire accelerant) to the arsenal of modern warfare. Nearly 60,000 U.S. military personnel died in the conflict before it ended without victory on April 30, 1975.

Meanwhile, the populace back home in the U.S. became more and more disenchanted as the conflict dragged on. Demonstrations increased and became more prone to violence. The demonstration in Chicago against the war during the Democratic National Convention is thought to have played a major role in the presidential election of 1968. College campuses became breeding grounds for dissent.

Anti-ROTC (Reserve Officers Training Corps) sentiment gained impetus along with demonstrations against the Vietnamese War. The ROTC building on the campus of Kent State University was burned to the ground on May 2, 1970. Two days later, in the continuing anti-war demonstration in the town of Kent, Ohio, as well as the Kent State campus, four students were shot dead and nine were wounded by a few nervous Ohio National Guard soldiers among the 1,000 who were occupying the campus. That gave anti-war demonstrators across the country – especially on college and university campuses – another huge rallying cry.

Students and some faculty had also brought St. Olaf College into the anti-war fray. I had been director of information services on the administrative staff for eight years but this was a totally new experience, and I was conflicted. I was sympathetic to the anti-war views, but I was also concerned about what news of St. Olaf's involvement might mean for parents of students and the college's more conservative donors.

St. Olaf students, faculty, and staff were encouraged to participate in "Anti-War Week" on campus on April 13-17, 1970, only a couple of weeks before the Kent State shootings. St. Olaf students began an occupation of the administrative offices late in the afternoon of April 16 and continued the occupation all night until 5:00 p.m. the next day, announcing that they intended to remain in the building until the college agreed to end St. Olaf's Air Force ROTC program or until the demonstrators were forcibly removed. About 125 students (out of an enrollment of 3,000) participated, with about 40 or 50 staying in the building all night. The sit-in was exceptionally mannerly as such events sometimes go. No one was injured and no property was damaged.

As one of the administrators with an office in the building, I was among those who stayed with the students all night. Since my office was responsible for public information and all contacts with the media, I took notes and photographs throughout the night. I developed six 36 exposure rolls of black and white film the next morning, studied the negatives carefully, printed a proof-sheet for each film, and filed all the negatives and proofs in an unmarked folder at the back of a file drawer in my desk. It was not hard to decide that I would not use any of those pictures, although I wrote news and feature stories on anti-war week, the ROTC controversy on campus, and the overnight sit-in in the Administration Building for *The St. Olaf Alumnus*, the monthly magazine I edited for alumni and parents.

When I cleaned out my office before leaving St. Olaf in 1989 to begin a new chapter in my ministry as director of public relations at Luther Seminary in St. Paul, I looked at the photos I had taken of the sit-in one more time – and destroyed both the negatives and the proofs. No one else, not even the St. Olaf archives, needed to see them.

The sit-in ended when student representatives and President Sidney A. Rand reached an agreement that the review of ROTC at St. Olaf, already underway, would be speeded up and a decision would be reached by May 5 that spring. Of their own volition, the students swept and mopped the halls before they left the Administration Building.

Watergate

Another national disruption grabbed the headlines during the last years of the Vietnam War. The headquarters of the Democratic National Committee at the Watergate office complex in Washington, D.C., was broken into on June 17, 1972. At first it seemed to be nothing more than a "third-rate burglary." But the administration of President Richard M. Nixon began to try to cover up its involvement. Five men were arrested for the burglary. The Federal Bureau of Investigation connected cash found on the burglars to a slush fund used by the Committee for the Re-Election of the President (Nixon).

Two reporters with the *Washington Post*, Robert Woodward and Leonard Bernstein, began to cover the break-in and its aftermath, unpeeling one unsavory discrepancy and effort to hide information after another. Eventually, all of President Nixon's staff (including those who had participated in the Watergate break-in), either resigned from their positions or were imprisoned.

Nixon had a tape-recording system in his offices, and he had recorded many of the conversations that implicated him and his staff not only in the break-in but in their attempts to cover up the questionable acts that they had perpetrated after it. The U.S. Supreme Court unanimously ruled that the president had to hand over the tapes to investigating committees.

Facing near-certain impeachment in the House of Representatives and a strong possibility of conviction in the Senate, Nixon resigned his presidency on August 9, 1974.

The Hippie Movement

A new phenomenon intertwined with the Vietnam War fogged up the atmosphere for Mom and Dad and many of their contemporaries. Flowing out of the Beat Generation of the fifties, the hippie movement began in California in the sixties and spread across the country and into other parts of the world. Those in the hippie movement were young, most often between 15 and 25, and were frequently referred to as "Flower Children," not in a particularly positive way.

They often communicated through the arts, particularly folk music which they used to express their ideas about sexuality, drugs, authority, and political and social issues such as the Civil Rights Movement and the Vietnam War. (They favored the first, and were against the second.) The music festival at Woodstock in 1969 was attended by nearly 500,000 people.

Hippie clothing was casual at best. Sandals were big for both men and women. The women liked long, loose fitting shifts. Tie-dying was big as a pattern. Men wore casual pants and lots of slipover shirts without buttons. And bib overalls made a comeback. Many college students picked up the freedom of hippie fashion and brought it with them to college campuses. St. Olaf College was not immune.

I admit to having had real trouble with student styles in the '60s and '70s when, among other things, it became fashionable for young women to wear bib overalls. Why, I wondered, would anyone wear bib overalls on purpose?

I *had* to wear bib overalls on the farm before I became a teenager. I hated them. Most of the kids who weren't from the farm wore regular pants with belts. In my mind, bib overalls identified my status not only as a farm boy, but, worse, a *poor* farm boy.

But overalls were practical. The pockets in the bib in front of the chest could hold a large assortment of pencils, tools and other stuff.

The other pockets were deep and large. But bib overalls, I thought, marked me as someone who was not as smart, not as sophisticated, and definitely not as popular as the boys who didn't wear them.

I can still remember the day – I was about 13 – when I was able to wear blue jeans (with a belt) rather than overalls. I have not worn overalls since, but "carpenter pants," somewhat like overalls without the bib, are now among my favorite workpants. I like the pockets on the side of both legs and the hammer loop on the left. Those pockets hold nearly all the tools I need for most carpentry, mechanical, and gardening jobs. Now that I've retired and don't do much carpentry anymore, I've shifted to more casual pants. The hammer holder too often catches on some knob or other protrusion as I'm passing by. That stops a person in his tracks.

Dad and Mom, as many adults in their day, did not know what to do with all of the social and political upheavals. Facial hair began to gain popularity again among men. That's something that comes and goes in waves. Our problem is, we either don't know or we forget what the generations before us were like, and think that the current time we live in is the only norm. (A picture of the St. Olaf College Board of Trustees in 1886 depicts nine of the 11 men with beards, including the college's founder.)

I followed a fashion of the day during the mid-sixties and grew some rather impressive sideburns. The first time Dad saw them he said, "I hope you're going to shave them off." I didn't.

Ruth, our four children, Ruth's Dad, and I vacationed for a week in 1969 at Itasca State Park (the headwaters of the Mississippi River) in northern Minnesota. We rented a two-bedroom cabin in the park and had a great time fishing, hiking, and attending evening programs provided by a naturalist. St. Olaf faculty facial hair had graduated from sideburns to beards and I decided to grow a beard during our week at Itasca just to see what it would look like.

Back home in Northfield I told Ruth on Monday morning before going back to work, "Well, I guess it's time to shave off my beard." She responded with some surprise, "Don't do that. I like it." I've had the beard ever since, watching it turn from black to a salt and pepper blend to white.

I've learned that beards can elicit a lot of emotional reaction. I remember one Christmas at Mom's house in Gilman. All my siblings and their children were there. Sometime during the afternoon one of my nephews came up to me. He was about three or four and said, "My Dad and I are going to hold you down and cut that beard off." I looked him in the eye and asked, "Why would you want to do that?" He fled back to his Dad. Not too many years later he became a Marine and grew a beard himself.

Ruth and I visited the 50th wedding anniversary celebration of one of our neighbors. They were dear people ready to help anyone who needed it. I had known them since I was a small child. The party was held in a church in Dixon. We had already gotten our coats on to leave. I was near the door, but Ruth was still back by the cloak room where she overheard two women about Mom's age talking. She realized almost at once that they were talking about me, and it was obvious that my beard was the subject of their conversation.

"I certainly would never let my boy do that," one of them pronounced. The other agreed.

Ruth was laughing as she joined me to leave. I was nearly 40 years old at the time. We had been married for 15 years, had four children, and I hadn't lived with Mom and Dad at home for more than two decades. I doubt if either of those women had enough influence, even over one of their own sons, to stop him from growing a beard if he wanted one. Their knee-jerk emotional reaction to my beard was emblematic of an older generation's response to the cultures, the politics, the expressions of art, and the societal changes that were turning the world as they knew it upside down.

But far more serious concerns hung in the air than judgments about beards.

Cities in Turmoil

The unrest over the Vietnam War, deteriorating race relations, police brutality, segregated housing and schools, and underlying poverty were eating away at the social fabric of the country's urban centers.

It all came to a head in Detroit nine years after Ruth and I had lived there during my internship at Salem Lutheran Church in 1957-58. We enjoyed our life in Detroit, and our first son Mark was born there on April 3, 1958.

The simmering anger over ignored substandard living conditions came to a boil in 1967 when the police vice squad raided an after-hours, unlicensed bar in the center of Detroit's oldest and poorest black neighborhood. A party was in progress to honor two black servicemen who had returned from Vietnam. All 82 people attending the party were arrested. Rumors that the police had used excessive force raced through the streets.

Early in the morning a bottle was thrown through the rear window of a police car and a waste basket was thrown through a store window. Fires and looting spread throughout the northwest side of the city, then moved to the east side. The National Guard was mobilized and the 82nd airborne was brought in on the riot's fourth day. After five days of rioting, 43 people were dead, 1,189 were injured, and more than 700 had been arrested. Detroit has never returned to the city it had been.

A quarter century later, race riots erupted in Los Angeles on April 29, 1992, after a jury acquitted four policemen of the beating of African American Rodney King that had been videotaped and made public by a bystander. According to the web page libcom.org, "The rioting was the single most violent episode of social unrest in the United States in the twentieth century, far outstripping the urban revolts of the 1960s both in sheer destructiveness and in the fact that the riots were a multiracial revolt of the poor. In the initial phase of the Los Angeles riots, the police were rapidly overwhelmed and retreated, and the military did not appear until the rioting had abated."

The Race into Space

Much of the exploration of space ran parallel to the turmoil of the Civil Rights Movement and the bloodshed of the Vietnamese War. Whether they wanted to be or not, and whether they agreed with what was happening in both race and space, Dad and Mom were among thousands who could hardly avoid knowledge of the terrible inequities being addressed in race-related events, the war ostensibly to keep down the spread of communism on the other side of the world, nor the wondrous innovative explorations of parts of our universe never before imagined possible.

In the first case, battles driven by oppression and prejudice going back hundreds of years drove violent responses to multiple demonstrations of non-violence. In the second case, the war marked by "body counts," Agent Orange, and napalm could barely be comprehended as both generals and politicians fabricated facts to suit their own purposes. In the third case, technological wonders reserved earlier for comic books and science fiction novels suddenly became reality as science and technology teamed up to create one wonder of exploration after another.

The Union of Soviet Socialist Republics (U.S.S.R.) stunned the world on October 4, 1957, with the first successful launching of *Sputnik*, an object about twice the size of a basketball with antennas that would orbit the earth for a little more than a year. Just to make sure no one thought *Sputnik I* was a fluke, the U.S.S.R. launched a second one a month later. The exploration of space had begun, and the Soviets were the pioneers.

The United States countered with *Explorer I*, its first orbiting satellite, on January 31, 1958. It carried a scientific experiment that discovered the earth's radiation belt. Alan Shepard, Jr. became the first U.S. astronaut in space when he had a suborbital flight in *Mercury Freedom 7* in May 5, 1961.

Later that month, on May 26, 1961, President John F. Kennedy made a special address to a joint session of Congress challenging all of its members to commit the nation "to achieving the goal, before this decade is out, of landing a man on the Moon and returning him safely to the Earth." He continued, "No single space project in this period will be more impressive to mankind, or more important for the long-range exploration of space; and none will be so difficult or expensive to accomplish." Kennedy's pronouncement was met with awe, wonder, and not a small degree of excitement.

On February 20, 1962, John H. Glenn, Jr. rode *Mercury Friendship 7* and became the first American in orbit, orbiting Earth three times.

Edward White II makes the first United States spacewalk when he leaves *Gemini 4* for 22 minutes on June 3, 1965. On June 2, 1966, *Surveyor 1* was the first space craft to make a soft landing on the Moon. On October 11, 1968, the crew of Walter M. Schirra, Jr., Donn F. Eisele, and Walter Cunningham orbited Earth once in *Apollo 7*, the first manned Apollo mission. That same year, on December 21, *Apollo 8* became the first manned spacecraft to orbit the moon. The crew of Frank Borman, James A. Lovell, Jr., and William A. Anders rode their spaceship on ten lunar orbits in six days.

Then, on July 20, 1969, eight years and two months after President Kennedy's "Man on the Moon" speech, Neil Armstrong and Edwin Aldrin, Jr., flying in *Apollo 11*, made the first manned soft landing on the Moon, bounced around in the first moonwalk, planted the United States flag, and returned safely to Earth. When Armstrong's feet first touched the Moon's surface, he said the words that will remain immortal: "That's one small step for man; one giant leap for mankind." It was an amazing moment, witnessed on live television by everyone in the world who wanted to watch – and most Americans did.

A little less than a year later, on April 11, 1970, James A. Lovell, Jr., John L. Swigert, Jr., and Fred W. Haise, Jr., blasted off in *Apollo 13* for a second mission to the moon. But it was not to be. An oxygen tank explosion nearly destroyed the space ship. The crew jettisoned the moon lander, and ingenious people on the ground figured out ways for the men to survive and land safely back on earth in the face of horribly bad odds.

On January 31, 1971, the *Apollo 14* moon mission was launched by the United States with Alan Shepard, Stuart Roosa, and Edgar Mitchell on board. They landed in the Fra Mauro highlands, the site that had been planned for Apollo 13. The landing area was explored with the help of a two-wheeled cart, allowing the collection and transport of a large amount of lunar material back to the United States. Before leaving the Moon's surface, Shepard became the first person to hit a golf ball on the Moon.

Apollo 15 astronauts David Scott and James Irwin drove the first "rover" on the moon on July 30, 1971. The next year, Harrison Schmitt, arriving on the Moon in *Apollo 17*, drove a similar rover over the Moon's surface. The cart and both rovers are still on the moon. All the astronauts returned home safely.

The space program began to change its purposes and its vehicles. The first space shuttle, *Columbia,* was launched for the first time on April 12, 1981. The Russians launched their space station, *Salyut 7* a year later on April 19, 1982. Sally K. Ride became the first woman to travel in space when she was part of the crew of the shuttle *Challenger* on June 19, 1983.

New tasks were added to the space program, and on April 24, 1990, the shuttle *Discovery* deployed the Edwin P. Hubble Space

Telescope astronomical observatory. Unfortunately, the telescope did not function as anticipated, and on December 2, 1993, the shuttle *Endeavor* made the first in-orbit service of the Hubble. The repairs worked perfectly, and the astronomical observatory began to send back spectacular pictures of areas of space that no one had ever seen before.

Nearly 200 space flights were made by astronauts from the United States and Russia by the end of 2001. Interest waned in more manned travel to the moon. But other interests took its place. The Soviet *Salyut 7* was launched by the Russians. The planets of Venus, Jupiter, Mercury, and Mars were explored by orbiting satellites as well as by landers that traveled the surface, taking photographs, digging up soil samples, checking for water, and sending all of the information back to Earth through more and more sophisticated cameras and computers.

The biggest space project was the designing and assembling of the International Space Station. The mission of the station continues to be to "enable long-term exploration of space and provide benefits to people on earth." The International Space Station creates a permanent orbiting science institute in space. It provides a long-duration platform for research in areas of life science, including medical research, in a nearly gravity-free environment. Construction began on November 20, 1998, with the launching of a U.S.-owned, Russian-built *Zarya* control module. That was followed two weeks later on December 4 when the U.S. shuttle *Endeavor* carried the U.S. built *Unity* connecting module, and the shuttle's crew connected the two modules during a 12-day mission.

The shuttle *Discovery* delivered supplies on May 27, 1999, and members of the crew struggled through a space-walk of nearly eight hours to install two exterior cranes along with a variety of tools and equipment for future use. The living quarters and control center module, *Zvezda* (Russian for star), arrived from Russia in July. The automated docking of this unit with the initial pair of linked modules allowed the U.S. to start a series of shuttle missions to add American-built components. Laboratory modules from Europe and Japan followed. The five-member crew of the shuttle *Endeavor* installed a set of solar arrays on December 1, 2000 to close out the century.

In the first U.S. space mission of the twenty-first century on February 7, 2001, the shuttle *Atlantis* delivered a laboratory module called *Destiny*. In three space-walks the astronauts installed a grappler for the station's robotic arm as well as a radio antenna. Additional modules that have been added include two multi-purpose logistics modules known as *Leonardo* and *Raffaello*, a joint airlock, and the Russian docking compartment. When the space station is completed, an international crew of seven will live and work there for terms of three to six months. Vehicles for return of the crew are always attached to the space station to ensure the men's and women's safe return to earth in the event of any emergency.

At the end of 2012, 1,046 operating satellites were orbiting Earth. The United States put 455 of them in place; Russia added 110; and China sent 107 aloft. The American satellites have changed our lives in ways unimagined a half century ago.

Global Positioning Systems (GPS) map the globe and show every river, lake, field, forest, city, street, factory, school, and house. Our vehicles can be tracked and farm machinery can almost be put on automatic pilot as they go back and forth across a field. Other satellites make it possible to hear events around the world on our radios and see them on our televisions instantaneously. Still others make the prediction of weather a much more precise task than it has ever been before, showing developing storms days before they reach the populations where they might be disruptive. One satellite counts and records every lightning strike in the world. One focuses only on the periodic changes on the sun. Others mark the continuing melt of glaciers and polar ice, and other significant signs of accelerating climate change.

China's Ascendancy

President Richard Nixon, corrupt as he was when dealing with the ramifications of Watergate, must be credited with opening China to the western world and particularly to the United States. It might not have been "the week that changed the world" as Nixon claimed after he returned from his historic visit to China in February 21-28, 1972. But that trip unquestionably was a critically important moment in the beginnings of Sino-American rapprochement.

Nixon, always aware of the power of television images, made it a point to leave Air Force One alone to shake the hand of Chou En-lai, the first premiere of the People's Republic of China when he stepped on the ground at the Beijing airport. Later he also met with Mao Tse-tung, the leader of the Chinese "cultural revolution."

Nixon was accompanied by Secretary of State William Rogers and his predecessor, Henry Kissinger. Rogers is not heard from much during the China visit. Kissinger handled almost all of the diplomatic conversation including talks on the independence of Taiwan.

Most importantly, Nixon's visit established channels of communication regarding trade. Today, it is sometimes hard for shoppers in the United States to find clothing and other items that are not labeled "Made in China" and recurring problems develop regarding the illegal copying of artistic material such as music and movies generated in the United States as well as concerns with Chinese hacking into sensitive computerized information.

Democratization has come to China slowly and with great difficulty. Mao Zedong called for a "cultural revolution" in 1966 to purge the nation of old customs, old culture, old habits, and old ideas. A core of "Red Guards" was established to punish party officials and any others who showed "bourgeois tendencies." The Guards also went after religious organizations – Christians, Muslims, Buddhists, and Confucians – as well as the educated. Within a year, China was in chaos. Hardly anyone was beyond being purged.

A co-conspirator with Mao was Zhou Enlai, China's premier, foreign minister, and a leading figure in the Chinese Communist Party. As Mao's health failed his wife, Jiang Qing, began to take over with three compatriots. Called the Gang of Four, they controlled the media. But the Chinese people were getting tired of the movement.

Zhou died in January 1976 and two million people filled Tiananmen Square for his memorial service. Mao died in September that same year, and the "cultural revolution" was over.

Tiananmen Square encompasses more than 525,000 square yards and is the world's largest central square. The square is at the entrance to what is known as "The Forbidden City" constructed beginning in 1417. It includes the imperial palaces of the Ming and Qing Dynasties. A huge portrait of Mao decorates the wall above the main gate

Almost a quarter century has passed since the event remembered as Tiananmen Square, one of the most traumatic episodes in Chinese history, when nearly a million Chinese, most of them students, crowded into the Square to protest for a greater democracy for nearly three weeks. On June 4, 1989, troops and police stormed the

Square, firing indiscriminately into the crowd of protesters. Reports indicated that thousands might have been killed, and 10,000 were arrested. Countries from both the East and the West denounced the massacre. The United States Congress voted to impose economic sanctions against the People's Republic of China in response.

But China has been a mixed bag as it has tried to move into the twenty-first century. When I visited China in 1986, the country was trying hard to move past its traditions into the modern world. I never saw a parking lot for automobiles then. But I saw hundreds of parking lots for bicycles in all of the major cities I visited, all holding hundreds of bicycles. Few cars were on the streets. But all of the streets were rivers of bicycles. And when I walked down the sidewalks I soon learned that when I heard that little bell behind me it meant "don't move sideways and I won't hit you – just keep walking straight ahead."

Bicycles are still important for personal transportation in China. But the country's industrialization since Nixon's visit has now filled the streets with automobiles. And the automobiles, together with emissions from house chimneys and factory smokestacks, have filled the atmosphere with fumes that create smog so thick it is dangerous for both vision and health. The United States embassy monitor on air quality in China classified the quality of air in Beijing as "hazardous" in January 2013.

In an age when most of the countries of the world are trying (with varying degrees of success) to cut back on pollution and its greenhouse gases, China has become one of the world's biggest polluters. According to Earth Policy Institute, China ranked number one as the most polluting country in the world in 2013 when its $CO2$ emissions totaled 2,395 tons, an increase of 44 percent in the last five years.

China – and consequently the world – is paying the price of growing too fast with a heavy reliance on fossil fuels.

Learning to Live in a Computerized World

It didn't always look like a turn for the better, but the coming of the computer was also changing everyone's life in the last half of the 20th century. Dad's introduction to this whole new world was cut short by his death in 1972. After Dad's death, Mom stumbled along in this unstoppable era of progressive change for another quarter of a century, but, like most of her peers, she seldom embraced it.

One Christmas Ruth and I gave her a new radio. It operated with push buttons rather than knobs, and it could play tape recordings. I'm not sure she ever got used to the new technology. A few years later, we gave her a small calculator, thinking it would help her with her personal bookkeeping which she was doing all by herself after Dad died. If she used that calculator at all, her use was minimal. She continued to prefer doing her "sums" with a not-too-sharp stub of a pencil and a well-worn eraser. She had a lot of company among other people of her age.

But the computerized world had been born, and its growth would not be stopped. In fact, it would accelerate even beyond the imaginations of its creators. The following brief catalog of significant events in the technological advances has been culled from a 21-page, single spaced, "Timeline of Silicon Valley" (www.scaruffi. com/politics/silicon). It describes not only what happened and who were the major players, but also demonstrates how fast it happened.

Some start the history of computing with the development of an adding machine by William Burroughs in 1885. Five years later, Hermann Hollerith's "tabulator" was chosen to record the national census. Hollerith's Tabulating Machine Company was acquired by a new company in 1911. That company changed its name to International Business Machines (IBM) in 1924. Burroughs made his adding machine portable in 1925.

An electronic digital computer was developed by John Atanasoff at Iowa State College in 1928. Tommy Flowers is credited with building the world's first programmable digital electronic computer, called Colossus, in 1943. One year later, Howard Aiken of IBM introduced the first computer programmed by punched paper tape. He called it the Harvard Mark I.

AT&T Bell Telephone Laboratory's John Bardeen, William Shockley, and Walter Brattain demonstrate the principal of amplifying an electrical current by using a solid semiconducting material they called a "transistor."

The first commercial computer, called UNIVAC I (Universal Automatic Computer), was built by J. Presper Eckert and John Mauchly in 1951 and delivered to the census bureau. The UNIVAC handled numbers and the alphabet equally well and separated the complex problems of input and output from the computation facility. But it wasn't going to fit in anyone's briefcase. It was 25 feet wide and 50 feet long and contained 5,600 tubes, 18,000 crystal diodes, and 300 relays, but it had an internal storage capacity of only 1,000 words and 12,000 characters.

The first conference on artificial intelligence was organized by John McCarthy and held at Dartmouth College in 1955 (the year I graduated from college). After that, improvements in computer technology went to warp speed. Shockley founded the Shockley Transistor Corporation in Mountain View, California, in 1956 and hired Robert Noyce, Gordon Moore, and others. A year later Noyce and Moore quit Shockley Transistor and formed Fairchild Semiconductor. Jack Kilby invented the integrated circuit at Texas Instruments in 1958. (The integrated circuit is a micro-sized silicon device containing a large number of electronic switches.) The next year, two things happen at Fairchild: Jean Hoerni invented the planar process that enables great precision in silicon components; and Noyce designed a planar integrated circuit.

IBM introduced both the first "mainframe" computer and the first "operating system" in 1964, and the next year Moore predicted that the processing power of computers would double every 18 months, a prediction that was to become known as "Moore's Law." Making the first proof of that "Law," Digital Equipment Corporation used integrated circuits and unveiled the first successful mini-computer in 1965. That same year, Olivetti, a European computer manufacture, introduced the first affordable programmable electronic desktop computer.

Hewlett-Packard entered the business of general purpose computers in 1966. That same year the United States had 2,623 computers; 1,967 of them were at work for the Defense Department.

Kilby, still at Texas Instruments, developed the first hand-held calculator in 1967. The year 1968 was big: Noyce, Moore, and Andy Grove founded Intel (Integrated Electronics) to build memory chips; Barclays Bank installed the first networked "automated teller machines" (ATM); and Doug Engelbart of the Stanford Research Institute demonstrated the first system to use a device called a "mouse."

By 1972, at least 60 semiconductor companies had been founded in what was now known as Silicon Valley in California.

Japan jumped into the action when the Sharp Company developed the LCD (Liquid Crystal Display) technology in 1973. Ed

Roberts invented the first personal computer, the Altair 8800 in 1974. The touch-screen user interface was invented by Sam Hurst the same year.

Bill Gates and Paul Allen founded Microsoft and developed a version of BASIC for the Altair personal computer in 1975. The next year Steve Wozniak and Steve Jobs formed Apple Computer and built the first microcomputer in Jobs' garage. Two years later Jobs and Wozniak developed the Apple II. By 1980 integrated circuits incorporated one hundred thousand discrete components. IBM's PC (personal computer), launched in 1981, incorporated an operating system that had been developed by Gates' Microsoft. Two years later Compaq introduced the portable PC, compatible with the IBM PC.

Apple introduced the Macintosh in 1984, revolutionizing desktop publishing. Hewlett-Packard introduced the first ink-jet printer in that same year and came back the next year with the LaserJet, a printer for the home market. Also in 1985, Microsoft shipped the "Windows" operating system to customers. Later that same year Arpanet is renamed Internet. The World-Wide Web debuts on the Internet in 1991. The next year the first text message is sent from a phone.

By 1994, Silicon Valley has mushroomed to 315 companies. Amazon.com is launched on the web in 1995. That website became known as the "world's largest bookstore."

Between 1998 and 1999 venture capital investments in Silicon Valley increased from $3.2 billion to $6.1 billion, a jump of more than 90 percent. In 2000, nearly one-third of Silicon Valley's skilled workforce is foreign-born, mostly from Asia.

Mark Zuckerberg founded Facebook, a social networking service, at Harvard University in 2004. Notebook computers accounted for 53 percent of the computer market in 2005, the same year that Yahoo, Google, America OnLine (AOL) and Microsoft's Network (MSN), the four big Internet portals, have a combined worldwide audience of more one billion people. Jack Dorsey creates Twitter, another social networking service, in 2006, the same year that the World-Wide Web has one hundred million websites.

In 2010, Apple introduced the tablet computer, iPad, that sold one million units in less than a month, and Facebook has 500M users. The smartphone market grows 55 percent, with 269M units sold worldwide.

Changes happened so rapidly in the computer industry that obsolete, was no longer an adequate word to describe how quickly something new on the market would replace that thing you bought less than six months ago. The computer has revolutionized nearly everything -- writing, research, study, farm records, business records, medical records and technology, ecological awareness, filing, personal communication, radio, television, music, photography, even recreation.

I am continually amazed at what my grandsons have been able to do since they entered middle school. I never did a research paper until I was a junior in high school, the same year I learned to type. Some of my college classmates had never done a research paper nor learned to type until they were in college. Now students from sixth grade on know how to research their subjects of interest on the web, type their papers beautifully (using spell-check as needed), and even include illustrations in their finished presentation. Furthermore, they write well, with a creative use of language and an expanded vocabulary. They also create power point programs they use to supplement their oral presentations.

Dad died while the computer age was still in its adolescence. That's unfortunate, since his early study of radio and television would have given him a platform of interest to really enjoy a computer. He also had learned to type, so he would have been familiar with the keyboard.

Mom was never proficient technologically (except in nursing), and she never learned to type. I doubt whether she could ever have been persuaded to use a computer even if she had one available. She was not unlike many in her generation. On the other hand, looking at the sampling at Kildahl Park Pointe in Northfield, Minnesota, the cooperative for seniors where Ruth and I live, only ten out of 51 living units (five percent) do not have a computer. Four couples have a computer system for each spouse. Currently, 53 percent of all American adults age 65 or older say they use the internet or e-mail.

But whether Mom or Dad and other seniors used (or use) the computer at all, they cannot escape being influenced by it. Computers have become an undeniably ubiquitous part of all society.

Introduction to the Middle East

The whole world changed dramatically within a few hours on September 11, 2001, when 19 militant Muslim extremists hijacked four airliners and were successful in three out of four suicide attacks on targets in the United States. Two of the airliners were flown into the twin towers of the World Trade Center in New York City, one hit the Pentagon in Washington, D.C., and one – due to the bravery of U.S. citizens on board who attacked the hijackers – crashed in Pennsylvania. (It was thought that the ultimate target of the fourth airliner was either the White House of the United States Capital.)

Ruth and I were at our cabin. I was preparing to do some work on our ongoing renovation project there when Ruth called me inside. She had heard a report on the radio about an airliner crashing into one of the World Trade Center towers and turned on the TV. I came inside. We were both mesmerized by the scene of the burning tower with the plane sticking out of the 80th floor. Then we watched as a second airliner flew into the 60th floor of the second tower. A third plane flew into the west side of the Pentagon a short time later.

Then the even more unthinkable happened as both trade center towers collapsed on themselves leaving only a pile of ash and a few twisted pieces of construction steel while incinerating most of the people who had not gotten out. The towers, built to withstand 200 miles-per-hour winds and any conventional fire, could not withstand the horrible heat generated by jet fuel. The nearly 3,000 people who died in the trade center attacks included almost 400 first responders who were trying to get people out of the buildings. At the Pentagon another 189 military personnel, civilians, and the passengers on the plane also died.

The carnage was created by an unbelievable attack on the United States, the worst by a foreign entity since the Revolutionary War. The perpetrators were Islamic terrorists from Saudi Arabia and several other Arab nations, allegedly acting in retaliation for the United States' support of Israel, involvement in the Persian Gulf War, and continued military presence in the Middle East. The attack was financed by Saudi fugitive Osama bin Laden's Al Qaeda terrorist organization, a group few Americans had heard of before the attack.

Mom and Dad had both died – Dad in 1972, two years short of three decades before the beginning of the 21st century, and Mom in 1998, three years before the tragedy of nine/eleven. It's probably just as well. The world changed forever on that disastrous day. Relationships between Christians and Muslims had not been good since the Crusades of the Middle Ages. Now those relationships had deteriorated into charges and countercharges going in both directions with little hope of peaceful resolution.

The first response by President George W. Bush to the terrorists who perpetrated the World Trade Center and Pentagon bombings was to draw together a coalition of armed forces to launch Operation Enduring Freedom, an attack on Afghanistan, considered to be Al Qaeda's home base, on October 7, 2001, less than a month after the attacks. The coalition included the United States, the United Kingdom, Australia, France, Canada, and the Afghan United Front.

The original objective in the invasion of Afghanistan was to capture Osama bin Laden and dismantle Al Qaeda. The U.S. also had another target – remove the ultra-conservative Muslim fundamentalist Taliban regime from power. At first, the coalition was successful against the Taliban but many members escaped across the border into Pakistan.

The United Nations Security Council established the International Security Assistance Force (ISAF) including troops from 42 countries at the end of December 2001, and the North Atlantic Treaty Organization (NATO) assumed control of ISAF in 2003. Members of NATO provided the bulk of the force. A new Afghan government, the Islamic Republic of Afghanistan, was established. Hamid Karzai was elected president in 2004.

The Taliban began to return in 2003, gained strength, and established a campaign of insurgency against the Afghan government and ISAF troops. The conflict expanded into Northwest Pakistan. A team of U.S. Navy Seals, in a night-time raid by helicopter on May 2, 2011, killed Osama bin Laden in his compound in Abbotabad, Pakistan. Leaders of NATO plan to remove all troops from Afghanistan by the end of 2014.

In 2010, the Afghanistan War rivaled the Vietnam War as the longest in U.S. history, and American deaths stood at more than 1,000. President Barrack Obama promised that the U.S. and all other coalition troops would be out of Afghanistan by the end of 2014 and that the country's security would be turned over to its own military forces.

In 2013, of the 8.2 million Afghan students in school 3.2 million were girls, a tremendous accomplishment since the Taliban fought against having any girls at all enrolled in school.

Unfortunately, a year and a half after the invasion of Afghanistan, President Bush, encouraged by Vice President Dick Cheney and Secretary of Defense Donald Rumsfeld, pulled back from the encouraging campaign in Afghanistan to invade Iraq. Secretary of State General Colin Powell had made an emotional appeal for backing from the United Nations, assuring that assembly that Iraq was dangerous to world peace and stability because, among other concerns: 1) it had a stockpile of "weapons of mass destruction;" and 2) Iraqi President Saddam Hussein was harboring and supporting Al Qaeda. Neither assertion proved to be true.

On March 16, 2003, the United States advised U.N. inspectors to leave Iraq. The next day President Bush issued an ultimatum that Hussein and his sons should go into exile within 48 hours. On March 20, an American-led coalition conducted a surprise invasion of Iraq without declaring war. (The Senate had, however, approved a Joint Resolution with large bipartisan majorities on October 11, 2002, providing the Bush administration with a legal basis for the invasion.) The plan for financial support of the war was that it would be paid for by a share of Iraqi oil wealth. That did not happen either, one of the reasons that the U.S. deficit ballooned out of control.

Baghdad fell on April 9, 2003, ending Hussein's 24-year rule. Much of the populace celebrated, and a large statue of Hussein was torn down. But massive disorder followed, including the looting of the National Museum and other public and government buildings.

President Bush staged a theatrical visit to the aircraft carrier *USS Abraham Lincoln* at sea near San Diego. In an attempt to remind people of his experience as a National Guard pilot, he was flown to the deck in a fighter plane and then made a victory speech to the sailors and airmen on board under a banner reading "Mission Accomplished." That wasn't quite true. Hussein and his sons were still at large, and battles with insurgents continued to take a heavy toll of U.S. and other military forces.

Hussein's sons were shot and killed by U.S. troops. Hussein was captured by U.S troops and turned over to the newly formed Iraqi judicial system. He was hung on December 30, 2006, after being convicted of crimes against humanity by the Iraqi Special Tribunal for the murder of 148 Iraqi Shi'ite men, women, and children in the town of Dujail in 1982 in retaliation for an assassination attempt against him.

The ages-old sectarian violence between the Shia and Sunni factions of the Muslim faith continues with large numbers of casualties among both militants and civilians.

President Barack Obama announced an 18-month withdrawal window for combat forces in February 2009 with about 50,000 troops remaining in the country "to advise and train Iraqi security forces and to provide intelligence." Iraqi Prime Minister Nouri al-Maliki supported the pullout. Obama declared on August 31, 2010, "The American combat mission in Iraq has ended. Operation Iraqi Freedom is over and the Iraqi people now have responsibility for the security of their country."

The Iraq war was expensive in both cash and blood. It's almost impossible to determine the total number of dollars spent. But estimates of Iraqi civilian and combatant deaths total more than 190,000. U.S. losses total 4,488 military personnel and 3,400 security contractors killed. Deaths of coalition forces add up to 319. None of those numbers counts the number of casualties who lost limbs or came home with post-traumatic stress disorder (PTSD).

1% vs. 99%

The changing distribution of wealth has become an increasingly disturbing problem, particularly to the 99 percent who don't have much. Even though the proportions were not as bad then and the middle class was relatively strong, Dad and Mom dealt with that horrendous distribution inequality for their entire lives. They were definitely in the "don't have much" category. Their children and grandchildren as a group are better off than they were. But financial disparities, always present in history to some degree, have grown decidedly worse in the last quarter century.

Some of that disparity exists even in the top one percent where the lower half of those admittedly rich people have far less than those in the upper half. Of course, when you are talking in billions at the top half and hundreds of thousands at the bottom half none of the one percent has to worry about whether they can pay the rent or where their next meal is coming from.

In the United States in 2010 the top one percent of households held 35.4 percent of all privately held wealth and the next 19 percent held 53.5 percent, leaving only 11.1 percent of wealth for the bottom 80 percent.

A study by Norton and Ariely in 2010 revealed that most Americans are oblivious to the disparities. Of the bottom 40 percent of the population financially, the lowest two quintiles hold just 0.3 percent of the wealth in the United States. That's a picture of poverty so extreme it does not even allow for subsistence. Most alarming, wealth equals power. Those in the upper one percent financially wield substantially more than one percent of the political, economic, industrial, agricultural, and social power. If the top one percent of households have 30-35 percent of the wealth, that's 30 to 35 times more wealth than they would have if wealth were equally distributed. And we can infer that they must be more powerful.

Note that the incomes of the richest of the rich, the top 400 income earners in the United States, tripled during the administration of President Bill Clinton and doubled during the first seven years of the administration of President George W. Bush. Also note that in 1960 the annual pay of the average CEO was 42 times larger than annual pay of the average factory worker. Forty years later, in 2000, the average CEO was taking home 531 times the annual pay of the average factory worker. Those figures backed down to 411 to 1 in 2005 and 344 to 1 in 2007. The same ratio is only about 25 to 1 in Europe.

It's no wonder that in 2011 groups of disenchanted people who had played by the rules, did what they were told, and now had nothing to show for it, or even worse were thousands of dollars in debt, tried to mount a protest. They announced their identity as "The 99 Percent." Their movement was called "Occupy Wall Street," and showed up in most metropolitan areas. Their stories of poverty and hopelessness were legion and filled newspaper reports around the country.

Ezra Klein, a reporter for the *Washington Post*, wrote regarding "Occupy Wall Street": "There are a lot of people who are getting an unusually raw deal right now. There is a small group of people who are getting an unusually good deal right now. That doesn't sound to me like a stable equilibrium."

Klein continues, "The organizers of Occupy Wall Street are fighting to upend the system. But what gives their movement the potential for power and potency is the masses who just want the system to work the way they were promised it would work. It's not that 99 percent of Americans are really struggling. It's not that 99 percent of Americans want a revolution. It's that 99 percent of Americans sense that the fundamental bargain of our economy – work hard, play by the rules, get ahead – has been broken, and they want to see it restored.

Occupy Wall Street ran out of energy after a few months. It called attention to a major problem of the lack of equity in the country's financial imbalance. But nothing changed.

Global Warming

Mom and Dad didn't worry much about climate except for the occasional tornado, hail, and rains that created infrequent flash floods. Their children spent the first half of their lives without much additional worry. But times and the climate have changed. Global warming is a reality that grows increasingly threatening with every passing decade.

A series of reports were published by the Intergovernmental Panel on Climate Change (IPCC) in 2007 drew on the work of 2,500 of the world's leading climate scientists. The reports confirmed consensus of scientific opinion on key questions related to global warming. They were endorsed by 130 nations.

A summary report in 2007 confirms that global warming is now "unequivocal" and states with 90 percent certainty that human activity "very likely" has been the primary cause of rising temperatures worldwide since 1950. The report also says the global warming is likely to continue for centuries, and that it is already too late to stop some of its serious consequences. It also says, however, that if we act quickly we still have time to slow global warming and lessen many of its anticipated problems.

A subsequent IPCC report shows that the cost of controlling greenhouse gas emissions worldwide and avoiding the most serious aspects of global warming is affordable and would be partially offset by economic gains and other benefits. That conclusion refutes the argument of many industry and government leaders who say that taking serious action to reduce greenhouse gas emissions would lead to economic ruin.

Climate change increases the risk of many types of record-breaking extreme threatening weather events across the country. In 2012, some 3,527 monthly weather records for heat, rain, and snow were broken in the United States, more than the 3,251 records smashed in 2011. Some of those newly-broken records had stood for 30 years or more.

Extreme record-breaking events occurred in all 50 states in 2012. The contiguous states recorded the hottest March on record. July was the hottest month ever recorded. Extreme weather events inflict tremendous costs on people and property. Other events in the United States in 2012 include: the worst drought in 50 years across the nation's breadbasket with more than 1,300 counties across 29 states declared drought disaster areas; wildfires burned more than 9.2 million acres and destroyed hundreds of homes; hurricane Sandy generated a 13.88 foot storm surge (breaking the all-time record in New York Harbor) and ravaged communities across New Jersey and New York with floodwaters and winds in which 131 people died. The cost of Hurricane Sandy is estimated at $71 billion.

Climate scientists say that these and similar events represent a climate-induced trend. International insurance giant MunichRe recently concluded that from 1980 through 2011 the frequency of weather-related extreme events in North America nearly quintupled. A recent analysis by the International Panel on Climate Change, the world's most respected scientific body on the subject, concluded that climate change will likely amplify heat, drought, heavy precipitation, and the highest wind speeds of tropical storms. The list of dramatic record-breaking changes goes on and on.

People are advised to do several things to protect their families from extreme weather. First, stay informed. Subscribe to local extreme weather or emergency alerts, and make sure all battery-powered communication devices are functional. Second, check on relatives, friends, and neighbors who might be vulnerable to climate-health risks. Third, be prepared with an evacuation plan and emergency supplies.

Population Explosion

While all that history has been happening, the population of Earth tripled. That's more than a little scary, and is becoming a major issue as we move into the future. In October, 2011, a child was born (probably in India) that lifted the population of the Earth to seven billion. That would not be a particularly troubling concern except for a few facts:

The world reached a population of six billion people only 12 years before the seven billion mark. And 100 years ago the world's human population was only 1.6 billion.

Reporter Leo Hickman wrote in *The Guardian* in January 2011, "With rising greenhouse gas emissions and resource depletion ever-growing concerns, the approach of this year's population landmark has become an awkward, even unwelcome presence in the environmental debate. No one likes to talk about it, for there are no easy answers."

Scholars have made the case that population growth alone is only half the problem. The United Nations predicts that population growth will plateau at nine billion around the mid-twenty-first century before starting to fall.

The bigger problem is the rapid rise in consumption. Some say inequities in consumption, where the average American has the same carbon footprint as 250 Ethiopians, is our most pressing environmental issue. The solution to the expanding population problem is for "the rich to stop consuming so much." Food output around the globe must be vastly improved through biotechnology, mechanization, food processing, and irrigation. Reducing consumption is a much easier task than tackling population growth.

Paul Ehrlich, Bing Professor of Population Studies at Stanford University, says, "What many of my colleagues share with me is the view that we would like to see a *gradual* decline in population but a *rapid* decline in consumption habits."

Every region requires its own solution, says Ehrlich. "In the U.S., where the population has risen by 10 percent in a decade, largely due to immigration, it is super critical that we tackle the population rise because we are super consumers. But, in general, in the rich countries where population growth has stopped or fallen, we should now be concentrating on reducing per capita consumption levels."

Dr. Tim Jones, the British author of *Future Agenda*, believes that by 2050, 75 percent of us will be living in cities. "The major trend we need to grasp is rural-urban migration," he says. Our greatest challenge, says Jones, is to build cities that address the realities of rapid growth: "Sprawl is already being rejected as a deeply inefficient model for growing cities."

Carl Haub, the Conrad Taeuber Chair of Population Information at the Population Reference Bureau in Washington, D.C. and author of the *World Population Data Sheet*, an internationally respected annual report providing population, health, and environmental indicators for more than 200 countries, has been counting the world's peoples for the last three decades. He says, "In terms of future growth, everything depends on the birth rates in developing nations. There is a presumption that the global average will come down to less than two children per woman after 2050, but there are big question marks about this. For example, everyone is pessimistic about sub-Saharan Africa where birth rates overall are not coming down at all. The political situation is key. Both Zimbabwe and Cote d'Ivoire were seen as bright spots by demographers, but now things are much bleaker. Sub-Saharan Africa will double in size by 2050. Nigeria is 158 million now, but will be 326 million by 2050 and will continue rising. Starvation is actually quite rare at the moment in sub-Saharan Africa, but standards of living will continue to fall."

Haub is already thinking ahead to the eighth billion person being born sometime around 2025. He concludes, "The twentieth century saw many things happen that greatly helped to reduce the death rate, such as public health campaigns, immunization, and provision of clean water. The challenge for the twenty-first century is different: it's all about managing birth rates."

Mom and Dad didn't worry much about the one percent vs. the 99 percent, global warming, or the population explosion. They left that to their progeny.

THE ETHNIC DIVIDE

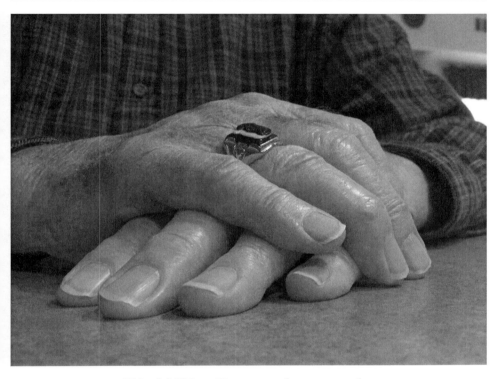

*World War II opened eyes to the
great diversity of people and their origination.
For most it engendered a sense of appreciation of
the differences as well as of the similarities.*

THE ETHNIC DIVIDE

Poverty at home and the promise of a better life on the other side of the Atlantic Ocean during the last quarter of the nineteenth century brought a flood of immigrants to the United States from all over Europe – Austrians, Danes, Dutch, Finlanders, French, Germans, Irish, Italians, Poles, Norwegians, Swedes, Swiss. Many became acquainted with Ellis Island, entrance to the home of plenty.

Those who had been farmers began immediately to sink down roots in the massive Midwest. Interestingly, they sometimes passed by the fertile land of parts of the rolling prairies for land that reminded them more of the places from which they had come. Or some just got tired of traveling any farther west. The area around the town that was to become New Glarus in central Wisconsin, for example, became the new home of many Swiss dairy farmers. The outcroppings of rock that interrupt the rolling flow of fertile land must have made them feel more at home in these new surroundings where mountains were nowhere to be seen.

The ground of southern Minnesota was fertile, but much of it was also filled with rocks, and winter's freezes would push new stones to the surface of the fields every year. "Picking rocks" had to be done every spring before plowing if the farmer did not want to risk breaking his plow on an obstacle that had been there for centuries but was buried just a few inches deeper the year before. Piles of rocks of all sizes are still part of many of the few fencerows that still exist. Rocky land was familiar to Scandinavian farmers, so even though prairie without rocks could be found only a couple of hundred miles farther west or south, they stopped where the rocks gave them a feeling of what they had left back home. And they had never before had so much land that was so fertile.

The house we moved into in Northfield in 1967 had a sloping back yard that made it almost useless. But if it were terraced, not only would the slope be diminished, but we would also have great places for flowers. I hired a man with a small caterpillar tractor to do the work and staked out where I wanted the terraced elevations to be. After he finished, the yard was a mess. But I began to structure the space as I had imagined it would be. Railroad ties came first to form a base. I got those free from the railroad. At that point in my life I was strong enough to handle them by myself. (Loading 80-pound bales of hay when I was a young teen-ager must have helped.)

After the base was set, two or three railroad ties high, depending on the location, I needed lots of rocks. I drove the nearby country roads, looking for rock piles. When I saw a pile that looked promising I determined which farm the pile belonged to and visited the farmer to get permission to take some of his rocks. I was never turned down. The farmer was glad to get rid of them. All the rocks were free. I carried the rocks home in my utility trailer, dumped them out, and began the fun of placement above the railroad ties.

After I had been doing this for a few evenings and weekends, I noticed that my neighbor to the back was standing in the corner watching my progress. Many times, I saw him shaking his head. I went over to explain what my grand plan was for the terraces. He was a little incredulous. A retired farmer, he had spent most of his life trying to get rid of the rocks in his fields. Now I was hauling them into my yard on purpose. To him, that exchange didn't make much sense.

The terraces shaped up well, and the next spring the tulips and other perennials I had planted in the fall – including three kinds of sedum to fill the spaces between the rocks – made the terraces and the rest of the yard bright with color. My idea was a success. I expanded the garden with perimeter beds, some elevated, most not. Most of those beds were filled with tulip bulbs every fall and produced massive color the next spring. When we moved from that house in 2009 about 3,000 tulip bulbs were in the ground, and I had been inviting the neighborhood in to see the spring splendor every year. My four years of classes in vocational agriculture in high school paid dividends I had never expected.

Back to the immigrants.

Not all the people who came from Europe were farmers. Many who came from Norway and Sweden had been fishermen and boat builders. They found a home on the North Shore of Lake Superior and Isle Royal where they could continue in the trade they knew, catching mackerel and lake trout with hook lines and nets until the invasion of the lamprey – brought over by Atlantic shipping that docked in Duluth in the early part of the twentieth century – also an immigrant of sorts, almost wiped out the lake trout population.

Ruth's Åland Island Heritage

When Ruth and I traveled to Europe in 1974 with all four children, one of our stops was the Åland Islands, a huge archipelago half way between Stockholm and Helsinki. The islands are the home of Ruth's grandparents who settled near Midland, Michigan.

The 6,500 islands that make up the Åland archipelago are divided into 15 parishes, each with its own church. Before we left on the trip, Ruth's genealogical research through offices in Helsinki confirmed that her grandparents had lived in the Föglö parish. We found the church. Hundreds of years old, it was built with thick stone walls, and had an ornate steeple. As most European churches, it was located in the middle of a cemetery. As in most Scandinavian churches, a large model boat hung from the ceiling.

The pastor, a retired seaman, took us into a kind of historical depository where he showed us handwritten church records dating back to the seventeenth century. He found listings for both Ruth's grandmother and grandfather. They had both lived in the Föglö parish, in opposite directions from the church. We learned from the pastor that Martin Janssen, a relative of Ruth's grandmother, lived on a farm several islands away. We got into our rented car and headed for the island where Martin Janssen lived. All of the islands were connected by bridges until we got to the last one before the one where Martin Janssen lived. That was connected by a cable ferry.

The wedding of Ruth's mom and dad. Anna Carlson Harper, a school teacher, is seated in front of her husband, Frank Harper.

When we got to the end of the road, the ferry was at the dock of the other island and had to come and get us. It was a small ferry, holding two cars. After our car was loaded and we were on our way, I asked the ferry captain if he spoke English. He said, "No." I took his picture but did not attempt any more conversation. He had a teenage son along with him, but, in typical Scandinavian shyness, he never offered any comment. Undoubtedly, because of the Scandinavian emphasis on languages in their school system, he would have spoken some English.

We drove off the ferry when we reached the island, asked a resident near the road where the home of Martin Janssen was, and found it. No one was home. We walked around and took a few pictures. But we could tell we were under observation from neighbors so we didn't stay long and went back to the dock for the ferry.

A few weeks later after we had returned to Northfield, Ruth received a letter from a relative in Wisconsin who had heard from Martin Janssen, the ferry captain. A small picture was included with the letter. It was a picture of a cable ferry in the Åland Islands, the same cable ferry we had ridden on to get to Martin Janssen's home. Thinking back, we realized too late that the captain certainly would have known Martin Janssen. It never occurred to us that the ferry captain might have been Martin Janssen. But he was. We never asked. He never offered. We had been standing within three feet of Martin Janssen and did not know it. Ruth now carries on a Christmas correspondence with his family. He died a few years ago, but correspondence continues with his widow.

One of the things we learned in our stop at the Åland Islands was why her ancestors immigrated. We saw five-acre "fields" that had been created by scraping soil together from small patches between large rocks surrounding that field. Her grandfather had been a seaman who farmed such fields when he was not on the ocean. It was an extremely hard life that barely kept body and soul together.

When he moved to Midland, Michigan, he settled on 160 acres of sandy soil northeast of town where he and the woman he married – who also happened to come from the Åland Islands – made what would be called a "decent living." Neighbors admired his abilities as a "good farmer." They said, "If he had settled on a good piece of land, he would have been rich."

Of course, not all European immigrants were farmers or fishermen. Many settled in industrial cities where they formed their own communities in places such as New York, Detroit, Chicago, and smaller towns such as St. Paul, Minnesota, and Rockford, Illinois.

Getting to Know Germans

The German psyche was brought home to us with a couple of experiences when we traveled through much of Germany with the children on the same trip that took us to the Åland Islands.

We decided one day to have lunch at a rest stop on one of the autobahns. The first thing we saw when we entered the building was a wall full of automated vending machines. What a challenge! First, find out what the younger children, Joy and David, wanted (the two older ones, Mark and Gay, could fend for themselves). Then we had to figure out the instructions in German for how the machines worked. With a little coaxing from enough coins in differing denominations called Marks, the machines pushed out sandwiches, chips, coffee, and soda pop. Everyone in the family loaded up with at least two, and some, three, parts of our lunch and headed for the dining room.

Ruth and I looked around. The place was crowded and all we could see were small tables about two feet in diameter, each with two chairs. A tall man who in a fancier restaurant would have been a maître de came over and greeted us in German. I asked, *"Sprecken sie English?"* He gave the standard response to that question in many countries where English is not the primary language: "A little." "We need a table for six," I said. He went to one of the little tables that was not being used, took two chairs each from two other little tables, jammed them around the small table he had selected, and said, "Table for six." We sat down. Our food containers were stacked two and three deep. But as far as the tall German man was concerned, our problem had been solved. We ate.

A few days later we were ordering breakfast in a little restaurant across the street from the cathedral in Cologne. By this time we had learned that when you order a pastry it comes with coffee. A waitress came. I was ready. *"Sprecken sie English?"* "A little." "We want *zwie* (two) *kaffee, fier* (four) *applesapt, sechs* (six) pastries." Sure enough, the first thing that came was six coffees. Ruth and I sighed, and accepted the coffees. The four apple juices and six pastries followed. All of it was very good, but we couldn't drink all the coffee.

Now, let's go half way around the globe. I ran into the same kind of mentality in China when I was traveling with the St. Olaf Choir as photographer and publicist on its first concert tour in Asia in 1986. Throughout the tour I took pictures of all the members of the choir either singly (or in small groups if they lived in the same location) and sent the film back to my office in special mailers I was carrying with me. My office would develop the film, make prints, and send the pictures with a brief news story of the tour in the Orient to each choir member's home town paper. Most of them – particularly if they went to small town papers – were used. The system was working fine until I got to a memorable city.

Since our group seldom stayed in any hotel more than one or two nights before moving on, I always filled out the return address with my office address. But that was not going to work at the central post office in this Chinese city. Amazingly, the woman behind the counter spoke passable English. She insisted that the return address had to be the hotel where I was staying in her city. "That would be useless," I tried to explain. "I'm only staying there tonight. Besides, I don't even know the name of the hotel, and I certainly can't write the name in Chinese."

Then she did the unbelievable. She reached under the counter and pulled out the book of Chinese postal regulations, in Chinese, of course. The book was at least four inches thick. I could not suppress a laugh. Except for the difference in languages, it looked just like the book of postal regulations I had to deal with quite often back in Northfield, Minnesota. I found the St. Olaf professor of Chinese who was traveling with the choir and had him write the name of the hotel in Chinese on my special envelope. Now my valuable little package of film could be mailed. It arrived in the usual three days, and the photos were sent to the appropriate newspapers.

It's amazing how much photo technology has changed since that trip to the Orient in 1986. I carried 120 36 exposure rolls of 35 mm film on that trip. My camera bag, the film packed in lead-lined bags to protect it from airport X-rays, two cameras, three lenses, and a small typewriter, weighed more than my luggage. In today's digital age, two cameras with lenses, two or three ten-gigabyte memory cards, and a small laptop computer could have handled the job, and photos and news stories could have been sent back to the office by e-mail. Furthermore, I would not have had to worry about airport X-rays fogging the film. When our son David spent a month in South Africa in January 2013 he carried one camera that fit in his pocket, a ten gigabyte memory card, an extra battery, and a battery charger.

Several other experiences on that trip to the Orient testify to ethnic differences and differing stages of technology as well as social concerns and development as a person moves from one country to another.

Press conferences were often part of the St. Olaf Choir's Chinese itinerary. Since I often conducted college-related press conferences back in the states, I paid close attention. One conference was being covered by three television stations. As the cameramen were setting up their lights and cameras, I realized that the electric cords did not have any plugs to connect them to outlets. They only had two bare wires. When they found an electrical outlet, they simply pushed the two bare wires into the slots and turned on the equipment. That's a long ways from acceptable procedure in the United States. But everything worked. No smoke came out of the outlets, the cameras rolled at their correct speeds, and the press conference went off without a hitch.

I had noticed when we checked into our hotel rooms that my TV had a cord without a plug at the end, only two bare wires, just like those TV cameras and lights. I could not understand Chinese TV, of course, but I liked to turn it on to see what kind of programming they had. I looked at the bare wires where the plug should have been, thought, "Why not?" and gently pushed those wires into the holes in the outlet in the wall. The TV came on. I was amazed, and still am.

One of the things I found in a few unaccompanied forays around the places where the choir stayed in China was gardens full of Bonsai trees, some with a hundred or more of these little trees. I have always been intrigued by the gardening art of Bonsai, nurturing alive and growing trees that would normally grow 20 or 30 feet tall, pruned back elaborately from the beginning of their life, with the branches shaped into graceful patterns. Most of them are never allowed to get bigger than two (or maybe three) feet tall even though they are growing vigorously in flat dishes with only two or three inches of moss covered soil. Some Bonsai are 30, 50, even 100 years old and have been passed from one gardener to another for generations.

I wanted to do that. So I bought some books on Bonsai culture. The first page of the first book I started to read began, "First, you have to find the perfect rock." I kept reading to find out how I might know a perfect rock when I found one. I read it to the end, and while it talked about containers and the kinds of trees that adapt well to Bonsai gardening, and the daily watering necessary to keep them alive, and pruning and training the branches by bending heavy wires around them, the book never bothered to explain how I would know the perfect rock. I guess Oriental people just know a perfect rock when they see it.

I had acquired a couple of Bonsai trees over the years. I tried to follow the directions that came with them, but they always died. I dug up some spruce seedlings in the woods behind our cabin and tried them. They died. Apparently those little trees wanted me to find them the perfect rock. But I could not. Reluctantly, I stopped trying to grow Bonsai.

One thing caught me completely by surprise in China. A "national" guide was with the choir all the time. Every time we came into a city we would also be joined by a "local" guide. One time, when the local guide had finished his assignment with us, he was saying goodbye. As he concluded his remarks he added, "And God bless you." Some of us looked up in surprise. We had not heard that before in China. He noted our surprise, and said, "I can say that. I'm a Christian."

A couple of cities later I was investigating a bookstore. I always had time to browse around when the choir was rehearsing for that night's concert. As expected, everything in the bookstore was in Chinese except for one small bookcase filled with paperbacks with English titles. As I was looking that over, a young man came up to me and greeted me in passable English. (Many times when a citizen who speaks English in a country where that is not the principal language sees someone they think speaks English they are likely to try to start a conversation for "practice.") His English was limited but pretty good. We had a brief conversation – I don't remember what we talked about – then I realized I had to get back to the choir or I would miss the bus. I excused myself and hurried away. Half a block later the same young man was beside me. He said, "I'm a Christian. Do you believe in God?" I assured him that I did. Then I excused myself again and got on my bus.

On another stop, our hotel was near the edge of the city. Farmland was just across the street. It was the wheat harvesting season. I had seen some self-propelled combines harvesting in other areas, but here the Chinese "technology" was ancient, going back centuries. The wheat was cut by scythes and sickles and carried from the fields and laid on the streets and roads. There, it would be trampled by the vehicular and animal traffic for a few days until the grain had come loose from the straw. The straw would be picked up and put in storage to be used as bedding in the winter.

Using ancient methods, the grain would be scraped together into piles and thrown into the air where the breeze would blow away the chaff and let the grain fall in a relatively clean pile on the road. That worked fine when they had a breeze. But if they didn't have a breeze they would have to wait until one came along. Except here, they had come up with an ingenious solution to a lack of moving air. A fan powered by a small gasoline engine had been mounted on the back of a bicycle. They backed the bicycle up to the pile of grain, started the engine, and began throwing shovels full of grain into the air. The fan did the work it was supposed to do, blowing the chaff away as the grain fell into a neat pile beneath it. The ancient and the somewhat more modern methods had been married perfectly to solve a major harvesting problem.

Other problems were not so easily solved. Our national guide offered to accompany me on my little hike into the countryside. She told me that if anyone knocks on a farmhouse door, it didn't matter whether they were friend or stranger the person who answered the door was obliged to invite the visitor in. The guide picked a farm at random and knocked on the door. A woman answered. She invited us in.

The house consisted of three rooms, a kitchen-dining-living room and two bedrooms. The rooms were connected only on the outside by a four-foot wide sidewalk that ran the length of the building. It had been raining hard a few days earlier. If I stepped off the sidewalk I would be stepping into about six inches of really slimy mud. It was obvious that the mud did not support any kind of lawn. When the ground dried out, it would turn to dust.

The first two rooms we passed were bedrooms. The "beds" were made of clay and were about six feet long, four feet wide, and three feet high and were covered with handmade quilts. They did not look comfortable. However, they had one modern touch. Two deep indentations had been pushed into the side about ten inches from the top. When the cold of winter came, burning charcoal was pushed into those indentations to warm the bed. All the rooms were the grey color of dried clay. A few pictures on paper were taped to the walls to break up the monotony. They were not particularly effective.

The kitchen had a cook stove, a table with several chairs, and a few cupboards. I saw no evidence of running water. As I was coming down the sidewalk along the side of the house I saw a small pen made of interwoven sticks that held about a dozen pigs, each weighing about 60 pounds. Another pen, also made of sticks, was about 20 feet farther along. It held about 20 chickens. Both pens were on a slope, with the chickens below the pigs. But the thing that really got my attention was the well. It was lower on the slope in a straight line with the pig and chicken pens about 20 feet farther down the slope. I knew that if I drank any water from that well I would be sick within hours.

But, as I feared, the woman, fulfilling her role as a hospitable hostess, offered the guide and me a cup of tea. It was a moment of truth. But I decided quickly that even if I were to break traditional Chinese rules of etiquette regarding being a good and grateful guest I dared not drink any water that came from that well, even if it were boiled. I waved away the offer as graciously as possible and munched on a small home-baked cookie the woman offered me instead. I was not aware of any undue strain I had put on the offered hospitality. With effusive gestures of thanks we left the farmhouse after the guide had finished her tea and I had finished the cookie.

To see the conditions under which Chinese farmers and their families lived was a priceless experience. I was relieved when the guide assured me that I had not made an unforgivable social blunder. She really hadn't wanted to drink that tea herself, but thought that as a native Chinese she had probably built up some immunity against whatever multitude of microbes inhabited that water.

Introduced to Diversity

When I was born in the United States, the ethnicity of immigrants generally was not a concern since everybody in the neighborhood had come from the same country, and maybe even from the same community in Europe. But World War II changed all that. It opened eyes to the great diversity of people and their origination. For most it engendered a sense of appreciation of the differences as well as of the similarities.

But being of German background in the United States during both World Wars put them in a different class. Immanuel Lutheran Church in Dixon where both Mom's and Dad's families were members, and where Mom and Dad were married, was known primarily as the German Lutheran Church. That became a questionable association toward the end of World War I, but it morphed into a derogatory concern during World War II. The ethnic designation was dropped and never used again.

Another irony needs attention. Some 425,000 German prisoners of war were sent to 686 prison camps across the United States during World War II. Most of the camps were in the south because the housing provided did not have to be substantial enough there to hold out the severe winters of the states farther north. But only three states – Nevada, North Dakota, and Vermont – among the contiguous 48 did not have at least one prisoner of war camp. Many were in the farm land of Illinois, Iowa, Minnesota, and Wisconsin.

The German prisoners included both high-ranking Nazi officers as well as foot soldiers. They were put to work helping farmers, lumberjacks, and apple pickers. A few had been captured at sea as U-Boat sailors. Many were shipped from Normandy. Some were from General Rommel's African Tank Corps. At first, the camps included a mix of soldiers, some only conscripted from the German population, others maintaining their allegiance to Hitler and the Nazis. After fights broke out between these groups, however, they were separated in different facilities.

Many in the first group made friends with Americans and celebrated their holidays with them. Some married American women. Some simply did not want to return to the devastation that had been rained down on most of the urban places in the Fatherland. What would they find? They did not know if any living relatives survived or, if they had, how they might be found. They had no job and no prospects to have one. They liked the comparative serenity of small town and rural America. They had the option to stay, and many of them did.

Getting to Know Swedes

A new awareness of diversity started in the Gonnerman family when Fred, totally German, married Ruth, mostly Swedish. His introduction to her family was a revelation. Ruth took Fred home with her to Midland, Michigan, to meet her family. Fred had already become well acquainted with her Dad, Frank Harper, and had asked him for Ruth's hand in marriage. He had said an emotional, "Yes."

I was more than a little nervous about this meeting. Ruth assured me that everything would be fine. We entered the living room where most of Ruth's relatives in the Harper clan — uncles, aunts, cousins — were seated around the perimeter. I expected a barrage of questions delving into my life, my interests, and my relationship with Ruth. There was a kind of mumbled greeting. Then, silence. No questions. No comments. Nothing.

After a few minutes, I could not handle the quiet. I asked a question. I don't remember what the question was, but I know I tried to make it open ended to begin a conversation. I heard a couple of, "Yups." Then silence. I waited awhile. Then I asked another question on a different subject. "Nope." That's the way the evening went.

An hour or so later — it seemed much longer — someone said, "Well, it's time to get home." Everyone got up, told me it was nice to meet me, and left.

I had just spent one of the longest evenings of my life. I asked Ruth what was wrong. She said, "Oh. I thought they were quite talkative. That's the way conversations always go here."

The loquacious German had just met the quiet Swedes. It was a totally new experience for me. My own family was used to conversational sparring which was usually loud, sometimes contentious, and filled with non-stop overlapping. Often, the talking was too loud. I had just been introduced personally for the first time to one of the identifying differences between nationalities and ethnicities.

Those differences were brought home again when I became director of information services at St. Olaf College, and my family, then with only two children, moved to Northfield, Minnesota.

Most people who hear the name, St. Olaf, know that there has to be a Norwegian connection. The tightness of that connection was announced with a lion's roar the first year I was at the college.

A National Guard helicopter landed on the football field one bright fall day and deposited His Majesty Olav the Fifth, King of Norway, on campus.

It wasn't as though we didn't know he was coming. The Secret Service had been on campus for two weeks to ensure the tightest of security. The king was also not a stranger to St. Olaf College. He, or another member of Norway's royal family, had been there several times. The college had even gotten permission to fly the Norwegian flag on Old Main during his visit.

People lined the walk-way to Boe Memorial Chapel, where the king would speak. Nearly all of them waved small Norwegian flags. Many – particularly women – were dressed in the native costumes of the areas in Norway their ancestors had immigrated from when they came to the United States toward the end of the last century. It was a totally festive occasion, and it included a grand lunch and a receiving line where everyone who wanted could meet the king.

My office had been involved for weeks with all the publicity and all the printed programs for each of the events. I and my staff knew all the protocols. But in my first reflections on all the hoop-la for the king's visit I thought it bordered a bit on the silly side. Then I began to reflect on what events immigrants from Germany might have that would be comparable. The best I could come up with was Oktoberfest, a beer and brats party held in many German communities every fall. After two world wars in which Germany was an aggressor, German heritage was not a particular admirable thing to flaunt in the United States.

Children Broaden International Awareness

The world the Gonnermans knew widened even more when our children, who had all been on international programs, graduated from college and began to literally "make their way in the world."

Mark was the first. He and his wife Susan Pennypacker spent two years teaching English in Fukuyama, Japan, on the Inland Sea. That gave Ruth, our son David, and me a chance to visit Japan during the cherry blossom festival and the Easter season in 1983. It was an amazing experience to travel in a country where the English language was nearly non-existent. Thankfully, Mark and Susan spoke Japanese and served as guides or we would surely have been lost almost all of the time.

One example: Our flight arrived in Tokyo. We knew we would be lost immediately. But Mark had sent us a train schedule, highlighting the Bullet Trains that we would most likely be using. Then he marked the stop for Fukuyama and wrote, "Check your watches, when you get a few minutes from Fukuyama, get your luggage to the door and be ready to get off. When the train stops at the time on the schedule for Fukuyama, get off."

We did, the door opened exactly on schedule, and there in front of us on the platform were Mark and Susan. That's how dependable Japanese trains are. Would that schedules in the United States could be anywhere close to that.

Joy was next. She also taught English in Japan. She was in Nagoya for three years. I was able to visit her, and she served as a translator when the St. Olaf Choir made its first tour in the Orient in 1986 and I accompanied them as photographer and publicist. The tour spent a week in Japan, a week split between Taiwan and Hong Kong, and two weeks in China.

In Taiwan, I had my first and only taste of shark's fin soup. I don't know if I was not impressed because it seemed to me to be tasteless or because I kept thinking of the shark population being decimated by the inhumane harvest of their fins. But shark's fin soup once is enough. I will never order it on my own.

David spent one semester in Poland while he was a student at St. Olaf. He was a history major with an overriding interest in World War II, so the place was a perfect fit. Early in the summer after he graduated from St. Olaf in 1990, he received a hand-written letter offering him a teaching position in Poland as professor of English and American Culture. He accepted and moved to Poznan, Poland, that fall.

He stayed for five years. That gave Ruth and me a chance to visit him in Poland twice. The first visit in 1991 we saw a gray country, still not healed from the scars of World War II. The pockmarks of bullet holes still decorated many buildings. Road sides were not mowed. Yards were in disarray. A palpable sadness seemed to cover the people.

We returned two years later. The difference was astounding. Road sides were clean. Front yards were verdant flower gardens. Infrastructure was being rebuilt in nearly every city. Most importantly, we met David's fiancée Kasia. We hoped to be there for their wedding. But the appropriate documents could not be received in time, so the wedding could not take place until after we had returned home.

When David came home from Poland, Kasia was by his side as his wife. She is a delightful addition to our family. She already had a master's degree in linguistics and American literature. She had never driven a car before. In fact, when we were traveling together in Sweden, David drove our rented car one afternoon. Kasia giggled and exclaimed, "You really can drive!" She hadn't known whether to believe him or not when he had told her that he could. Private cars were highly unusual in post-war Poland. Everyone learned early how to use public transportation, and public transportation could get any person who knew the language just about everywhere they might want to go. But one of the first things Kasia did when she got to Minnesota was to study the driver's manual and get her driver's license, passing the road test on her first attempt.

Once she had her driver's license she got a job as a salesperson for health insurance for labor unions that required a lot of driving, often at night.

Within a few months she had a position in the Rolvaag Memorial Library at St. Olaf College. A year or so later she enrolled at St. Catherine's College in St. Paul in a master of library and information science degree program. She received that degree in a year and a half and has been reference librarian at the St. Olaf library ever since.

Jump a generation. Our grandson, Christopher, son of Mark and Susan, took a "gap year" following his graduation from high school in 2008 and moved to Spain to study Spanish. He's now fluent enough to read novels in Spanish. After completing two years of college in San Francisco, he studied Portuguese and spent a half a year in Brazil.

One of Ruth's and my favorite trips was a two-month stay in Tromsö, Norway, when we exchanged houses and cars with a family while the wife taught a course in linguistics at St. Olaf College. Tromsö is above the Arctic Circle, so we never saw the sun set during the entire two months we were there, June and July.

Language is not a problem for visitors to Norway from the United States. Anyone who is 35 or younger has been studying English from third grade to the completion of what we would call high school. One experience: I needed a haircut while in Tromsö so I made an appointment at a barbershop in a little shopping center Ruth and I often frequented. When I went, I saw two barber chairs and two young women. After I sat down and one of the women came over, I asked her if she spoke English. She said, "Yes, but I get my tenses mixed up." I laughed. "Lady," I said. "In the United States, lots of people don't even know what tenses are." We had a delightful conversation.

I can remember when my home congregation, Immanuel Lutheran Church in Dixon, Illinois, tried to get past its unofficial name, German Lutheran Church, because of the German reputation for belligerence and anti-Semitism during the wars. The congregation learned that it could change its name, but it was a lot harder to change the negative attitudes that had built up over several generations. Pejorative words such as Hun, Kraut, and Nazi are hard for some people to forget, even sometimes when they are of that ethnic background themselves. More positive things associated with Germany such as the Reformation, Christmas trees, "Silent Night," Johann Sebastian Bach, good beer and wine, fantastic woodcarving, Gutenberg and his printing press, Martin Luther and the first edition of the Bible translated into the people's language seem to have been shoveled out of ethnic memories.

I began to appreciate Norwegian identity. In fact, I began to identify myself as "German by heritage, Swedish by marriage, and Norwegian by occupation." A Swenska Klub was formed in Northfield – partly so that the Swedish folk would not be swallowed up by the Norwegians – and the Gonnerman family was an active participant. The two meetings a year celebrating the festivals of Santa Lucia (both Gay and Joy served as Lucia in the candle-lit pageant) and Midsummer consistently featured the best pot-luck dinner in town. We also participated regularly in Norwegian Syttenda Mai festivities every May.

One of the things we've learned as we've travelled internationally is that national customs and arts blend together.

When we traveled to Italy about two decades ago we learned about what we thought was a strange practice whenever we went into a small restaurant or a coffee shop, particularly those along a major highway. We learned to go to the glassed-in counter where foods were displayed, pick out what we wanted, write it down if we thought we couldn't remember the Italian, go to the cashier, tell that person what we wanted, pay for it, and take the receipt back to the counter and give it to the person behind it. That person would hand us what we had paid for and we would take it to a table to enjoy it. We also learned that whatever delicacies we selected tasted even better with cappuccino.

When we got home, Ruth bought our own cappuccino maker. Ever since that trip to Italy Ruth and I enjoy a cappuccino with a cookie or a bar or a biscotti every afternoon at 3:00. That little routine is now the Italy in our life.

One result of several trips to Scandinavian countries was that Ruth and I began to really like open-faced sandwiches, especially for lunch. We brought that nicety home, and until 2013 I made up to a half dozen trays of open faced sandwiches for every Christmas Eve. The main ingredient of each sandwich ranges for salmon to sardines to pickled herring to anchovies to tiny shrimp to sliced eggs to scrambled eggs to sliced pork to sliced roast beef. Those ingredients are placed on French bread, rye, or pumpernickel, each slathered with cream cheese or butter. Embellishments include fresh dill, lettuce, parsley, thin sliced cucumbers, sliced or small wedges of tomato or lemon. Two or three of those are a meal for anyone, especially when you know that they will be followed by rice pudding, fruit soup, fruit cake, and at least half a dozen varieties of Christmas cookies. In more recent years, with David, Kasia, and their sons here, Polish dishes such as borscht, red cabbage, and pierogies (little pasta-like envelopes filled with meat) have been added to the holiday menu.

Ruth and I have also developed a taste for crystal. Our curio cabinets are overflowing. Mementos include a four-inch-high, six-and-one-half-inch wide flat vase with a girl cut into one side looking at the moon and stars on the other that Ruth purchased in Stockholm; a four-inch-tall crystal pear with a quarter cut out and a yellow and blue center that Fred bought in Prague; crystal star candle holders were picked up in Bacharach, Germany, along the Rhine River; and a blue and green vase was carried home after Fred bought it in Mürano, an island near Venice where crystal and glass are specialties. A crate of crystal from the Orrefors "seconds" showroom was purchased and shipped home from Sweden. Much of that was given away. One prize piece is a six-inch high crystal leaping trout. A variety of crystal and glass candle holders were bought at department stores in Oslo and Stockholm when those cities (plus Copenhagen) were on the itinerary for a study program in Nineteenth and Twentieth Century Scandinavian Art in January 1978 with Reidar Dittmann, a good friend who was St. Olaf professor of Norwegian and Art History.

Dishes have also played an international role in our house. A 12-place set of Rosenthal dishes, distinctive for their pedestal cups, was purchased in a department store in Frankfurt, Germany, with money that had been given to Ruth by her Dad. That purchase was a bit rushed since we were on our first trip abroad and traveling with the St. Olaf Choir on a concert tour. Those dishes now belong to David and Kasia.

Another set of dishes began with a purchase of Rörstrand cups and saucers with a distinctive pattern of blue flowers on white porcelain called Bon Ami in a store in Mariehamn, the largest city in the Åland Islands, between Stockholm and Helsinki. Gay bought plates and had them shipped home when she visited Molde on the north coast of Norway while on a concert tour with the St. Olaf Choir. Joy added another beautiful piece when she bought the coffee server in San Francisco while on a concert tour with the Augustana College (Sioux Falls, South Dakota) Choir. We still have that set.

Another kind of dishes are wooden plates hand carved in Poland. Two large wooden plates and a couple of small ones hang in our living room. We purchased the large ones on one of our visits to David when he lived there. The others are gifts.

Ruth encouraged me seven years ago to try woodcarving in classes being given at the American-Swedish Institute in Minneapolis. We've enjoyed membership there for many years. The classes are taught by Bill Jaeger, who announces in one of the first classes that, "You can't make a mistake that I can't correct," to instill a bit of confidence. He's right. I was sure in the first year that I had made a mistake beyond redemption. With half a dozen cuts, he saved the piece, and I was back in business.

I've been hooked on carving. I had noticed in my first class that only one other person was a first-time carver. But the class had about a dozen people in it. Then I realized that all the others had been carving for many years. They just keep coming back to class to enjoy the camaraderie and pick up a few new tricks with each passing class.

A year after my first class I began giving carvings to my children, siblings, and grandsons for Christmas. The carvings have included small Scandinavian people, ornamental spoons, dogs carved from egg-shaped blanks, and stylized pine trees. Ruth has received a new, hand-carved Santa Claus for each of the past six years. Two carvings were displayed at the Minnesota State Fair the last two years. Most significant, I sold 20 to retailers two summers ago.

Ruth has added many Scandinavian folk arts to our life. She has knitted Norwegian sweaters for everyone in our extended family and supplemented those treasures with mittens and hats. She has made and collected countless quilts. She made three quilts with fabric from her mother's dresses. Seven of her "twist stitch" bell pulls hang in our home, together with eight of her needlepoint creations. (Some with a Christmas theme are rotated with the seasons.) Three tapestries – two purchased in Scandinavia and one in Poland – decorate our walls. We also had art from Japan, China, and Taiwan that we didn't have room for when we moved to Kildahl Park Pointe, a cooperative for seniors, a few years ago.

The ramifications of ethnic influences have become significant in the Gonnerman family, and although I can't travel internationally anymore it's an influence that continues to expand.

THE GONNERMAN GENEALOGY

The known Gonnerman genealogy begins with the birth of Johann Henrich Gonnerman in Wommen, Germany, in 1615. Johann was a farmer, the preponderant occupation of every generation that followed him. Immigration to America began in the 1870s. In addition to the farmers, a few of the Gonnermans were teachers, one was a farming landlord, and one was a musketeer.

Some 200 years later, Johannes II Gonnerman (born in Heinebach, Germany, in 1811) and Magdalene Elizabeth Döll (born in Heinebach in 1816) were married in 1833. They had seven children. Five of them immigrated to America where Katherine Elizabeth, Magnus (Marcus), and Henrich settled in the community of Ashton, Illinois, Konrad went to Dixon, Illinois, and Johannes went to Hartley, Iowa. All of them were farmers.

Heinebach (on the Fulda River), Wommen, and Berneburg, all birthplaces of Gonnermans in Germany, are a cluster of small towns about 120 kilometers (75 miles) northeast of Frankfurt and about 50 kilometers (31 miles) southeast of Kassel. Eisenach, the home of the Wartburg Castle, Luther's place of hiding and retreat during the Reformation, is only about 25 kilometers (15 miles) to the east.

Ruth and I took our four children on a trip to Scandinavia, Germany, and England in 1974 to introduce them to international travel and visit our ancestral homes. Mark was 15 and David was five. Ruth's grandparents came from the Åland Islands, an archipelago of 6,500 islands between Stockholm and Helsinki. We came away knowing where both her grandparents had lived and the conditions of their lives before immigrating to America and settling near Midland, Michigan.

Shortly after we arrived in Germany we visited the little town of Wommen. It was a dicey stop. First, the town is very near what used to be the East German (communist) border, and I was afraid the road might take us unknowingly across that border and we would have a hard time getting back into West Germany. When we arrived in Wommen I found the home of the Lutheran pastor. Unfortunately, his English was a little worse than my German. (I had already learned that I might be able to ask some rudimentary questions, but I couldn't understand the answers, so I had stopped trying.)

The pastor did, however, understand enough of what I was trying to say to direct me toward a house where the people living there had the Gonnerman name. We headed that way. Then I thought, "If the pastor can't speak English, what hope do I have that this unknown person with the Gonnerman name might be able to?" I chickened out.

We drove around the town until we found the cemetery, and all of us got out to look at the tombstones where we discovered a few names that were somewhat familiar because those same last names were on the membership roll of Immanuel Lutheran Church back in Dixon, Illinois. As far as I was concerned that verified that we were visiting a Gonnerman ancestral town.

Somewhat frustrated, we drove out of Wommen and headed southwest toward Heidelberg where we had our "splurge night" reservation to stay overnight in a castle high above the Neckar River. That was a delightful stop. Our family had seen the place of our German ancestry, but had not filled in any of blanks regarding the people, the personalities, and the reasons for their immigration to the central United States. The visit had not been a complete failure, but it was weighted with disappointment.

Dad's and Mom's parents were all first generation children of German immigrants.

Fred Gonnerman (originally Alfred), Dad's father, was born on February 14, 1870 in Ashton in northern Illinois. His mother, Anna E. Shafer, was born on December 27, 1873 in Franklin Grove, about ten miles west of Ashton.

Fred and Anna were married on April 19, 1900 and lived and worked on a farm near Ashton until 1922, when they moved to the 160-acre farm they had bought that wrapped around Nachusa on the little town's southern and western edges. Ashton, Franklin Grove, Nachusa, and Dixon were all located in an almost straight east-west line along the road that was to be named the Lincoln Highway.

The move of between 15 and 20 miles took place almost a quarter century after they were married, and it put them into the new house they had built the same year. The new house sat like a lonely sentinel on a treeless acreage on the southeast corner of the farm. A variety of trees, including a spruce windbreak on the west and north, an orchard, and a formal garden with an arborvitae hedge would all come later.

The house was an expansive, two-story, four-bedroom home with a full basement and a full attic. It had electricity with push button switches for the lights, running hot and cold water, and central heating provided by a coal-burning furnace in the basement. Cooking and baking, however, were still done on a wood-burning stove.

A garage, a barn, a corncrib, a machine shed, a hog house, and a chicken house would all be added to the homestead as needed.

Grandpa Gonnerman, as he was known by the children of Marcus and Marie, is remembered for the cigars he smoked in a big black chair in a corner of the dining room next to the box where Grandma Gonnerman grew bright red geraniums. Grandpa always put his cigar ashes directly into the geranium planter and Grandma moved them along the entire length of the elevated box under the long dining room windows. Everyone knew the ashes were the secret of the geraniums outstanding growth. The room always had the strange combined aroma of cigar smoke and geranium blossoms.

Coffee was a continuing delight for Grandpa. He intensified that delight by pouring his coffee, whitened with milk, into a saucer and sipping from it, moistening the ends of the hairs of his mustache and wiping them off on his sleeve (he almost always wore long- sleeved shirts).

Grandpa Gonnerman farmed with horses. I remember seeing three teams in their stalls in the east end of the barn. I don't remember ever seeing Grandpa Gonnerman drive a tractor, even after Dad had moved from steel-wheeled to rubber tired and much more comfortable machines.

Fred Gonnerman died on November 1, 1955. He had broken his hip in a fall, an ingrown toenail became infected, gangrene set in, and his leg had to be amputated above the knee. He was not an easy patient to take care of, but Dad's sister Margaret provided his needed nursing services in her small house in Dixon until his death. He is buried next to Anna in the cemetery in Franklin Grove.

Grandma Gonnerman was a short, thin woman who overflowed with energy. She is remembered by her grandchildren as creative and refined, words not always attributed to farm wives on the north central prairie.

Of all the delicacies she baked in her kitchen, *kuchen* was the best. It started with sweet bread dough laid flat in a nine by 12 inch pan. Depressions pressed into the dough were filled with sour cream and fruit. Peaches, cherries, and raspberries were the best when they were in season. When they were not, Grandma searched the shelves of canned fruit in the basement until she found the delicacy for that day. Then she coated the whole confection with granulated sugar before putting it in the wood-fired oven. The result, hot out of the oven, cut into pieces about four inches long and two inches wide, was absolutely delectable. It would not have lasted an hour without Grandma's close monitoring, but she always held back a portion big enough for her and Grandpa's Sunday breakfast from whatever siblings, cousins, and me were in the kitchen. Grandpa liked *kuchen*, too.

Somehow Grandma Gonnerman also found time to design and care for a formal garden reminiscent of smaller gardens in Germany. A cement pond, lined at the edge with stones, was the focal point, and goldfish and water lilies lived there. The garden included an impressive bed of tea roses, an astounding collection of perennials of all sizes and colors, and annuals to fill any spaces that were left over.

A blue spruce tree was planted near the pond. The bottom branches were pruned to resemble a square box, then the next one-and-a-half to two feet of branches were cut off next to the trunk, creating the illusion of a tree in a box. A large cherry tree was another focal point in the garden, and a family of wrens used an old teapot hanging on the stub of a branch as their annual home for years. The west border of the garden was a low grape arbor where black raspberries thrived.

I spent many hours as an adolescent hunkered down among the grape vines and raspberry bushes, staying out of sight while I enjoyed all the berries I could reach. I was sure that Grandma Gonnerman knew I was there, but she never gave away my hiding place when somebody in the family wanted me to do something else.

Grandma was sick with cancer when she and Grandpa celebrated their 50th wedding anniversary in 1950. Her bed had been moved into the first-floor parlor that housed the piano. Bed-ridden and in pain, she still insisted that everyone in the family celebrate their anniversary. They did.

Anna Schafer Gonnerman died three weeks later on May 1, 1950. She is buried next to Fred in Franklin Grove.

Mom's lineage started with her immigrant German grandparents, Wilhelm and Marie Dirks Hoppe. Wilhelm was born in Jeer, Dukedom of Oldenburg, Germany, on May 17, 1835. He immigrated to Oxford, Ohio, where he continued his blacksmithing trade. Marie was born in Tettens, Dukedom of Odenburg, Germany, on October 15, 1850. She came to America in 1869 and married Wilhelm in Hamilton, Ohio, on October 7, 1870.

Mom's grandparents relocated in Bellingville, Indiana, where they lived until 1873, when they moved to Danforth, Illinois. Eight years later they moved again to Charlotte, Illinois, where Wilhelm continued his trade as a blacksmith until 1890 when he gave up blacksmithing and purchased what was to be the Hoppe homestead west of town. They raised nine children there, one of whom was Gesena M. Hoppe, born on April 6, 1877. Gesena was Mom's mother.

Gesena's brother Herman's cabin, built on Pleasant Hill Road in Kingston Township northwest of Sycamore, Illinois, and now known as the Ellwood-Miller cabin, was moved to a five-acre site in Hoppe Park in the DeKalb County Forest Preserve District in 2012. The DeKalb County Board is restoring and preserving wetlands contiguous to the new site for the historic cabin which has been transformed into the focal point of an educational and cultural center.

Henry Jacobs, Mom's father, was born on October 9, 1876. Gesena M. Hoppe, Mom's mother, was born April 6, 1877. They were married on February 22, 1905.

As I remember, Grandpa Jacobs and Grandpa Gonnerman were on opposite ends of the personality spectrum. Grandpa Gonnerman was loud, overbearing, and abrasive. Grandpa Jacobs was quiet, shy, and completely non-assuming. I never heard him raise his voice. He went about his farming with quiet competence together with totally committed neighborliness.

Grandpa and Grandma Jacobs moved 120 miles from a farm near Charlotte, Illinois, to a new 160 acre farm south of Dixon, Illinois, in 1914. The move was dramatic. It was made in three railroad cars and included everything – livestock, machinery, household goods, and their three children, one an infant.

By the late thirties, when I first remember visiting Grandpa and Grandpa Jacobs on their farm south of Dixon, always with siblings and sometimes with cousins, Grandpa had a pony. It was a big pony, and it was brown, and all of the grandchildren rode him whenever they visited Grandpa and Grandma Jacobs.

I remember only one warning: "Don't get on the pony before you're out of the barn because you'll bump your head and get knocked off when you come out the barn door." Otherwise, our rides on Grandpa's pony were without limits. We took turns riding him bareback all over the farm. If Grandpa had a saddle, we never saw it.

Grandpa Jacobs lived with us after a stroke, and Mom provided all the nursing he needed. Henry Jacobs died quietly on December 9, 1956. My sister, Mary Ann, found him sitting in a chair in the living room when the family came home from church.

Grandma Gonnerman was a small woman and Grandma Jacobs was on the large side. Otherwise, they were similar in many ways. Both were great cooks and bakers. My sister, Mary Ann, has special praise for the raisin-filled cookies that often came out of Grandma Jacobs' oven. Grandma Jacobs is also remembered as an excellent seamstress, an art she passed on to her daughters, including Mom.

Her gardening was not as creative as Grandma Gonnerman's, but she enjoyed working with her flowers and had some plants that were unusual for gardens in northern Illinois. Both also had large vegetable gardens that not only provided fresh produce in season, but also provided an abundance of both fruits and vegetables for canning that would sustain their families through the winter.

Grandpa and Grandma Jacobs were both relatively healthy when they celebrated their 50th wedding anniversary with many friends and neighbors on February 22, 1955 in the basement of Immanuel Lutheran Church in Dixon.

Although 50th anniversaries are almost common and 60th anniversaries are not unusual today at the beginning of the twenty-first century, back in the fifties the 50th anniversary was a notable benchmark that called for elaborate celebration. It's astounding to have had all four of our grandparents alive for their 50th wedding anniversaries.

Gesena Hoppe Jacobs died of cancer on October 30, 1955, eight months after her 50th wedding anniversary. She and Henry are buried side by side in a cemetery in Dixon.

Marcus Frederick Gonnerman, Dad, was born to Alfred (Fred) and Annie Schafer Gonnerman on August 8, 1903. He was the only son and second oldest child of four children. All were born in Ashton, Illinois, where Fred and Annie farmed. Margret was born on November 19, 1901; Dorothy was born on November 20, 1906; and Marion was born on November 30, 1909.

Marie Antoniette Jacobs, Mom, was born to Henry and Gesena Hoppe Jacobs near Charlotte, Illinois, on November 18, 1905. Her two sisters and brother were also born in Charlotte. Welma Gesena was born on June 20, 1909, and died in 1991; Grace Cecelia was born on February 13, 1912, and died in 1968; and their brother, Clifford Henry, was born on October 5, 1914, just before the family moved to another farm south of Dixon, Ill. Two other boys died in infancy, Giske in 1905, and Claus in 1909.

Marcus Gonnerman and Marie Jacobs were married in Charlotte, Illinois, on June 28, 1932. Dad died on April 10, 1972, and Mom died on December 11, 1998. They are buried side by side in Dixon, Illinois.

Mom and Dad produced four children, all four years apart except for the last daughter who broke the pattern by being half a year early. The relatively long spaces between children stretched out the care and parental support needed for any child at any given time. Unfortunately, that same family planning had the unintended consequence that the children had difficulty in developing attachments or friendship until we had grown up and began to have our own families. Even half a year closer makes a difference. Paul and Mary Ann, the last two of the children (with only three and a half instead of four years between their births), remember being close friends growing up.

The firstborn was me, Frederick Henry, born on June 4, 1933 almost a year after Mom and Dad were married.

Second was Donna Marie, born on April 4, 1937.

Third was Marcus Paul (he was known as Paul from the very beginning to keep him from getting confused with Dad), born on May 29, 1941.

Finally, Mary Ann joined her siblings on November 11, 1944, one week before Mom's 36th birthday.

All four Gonnerman children were born at Katherine Shaw Bethea Hospital in Dixon, about five miles west of the family farm in Nachusa.

My wife, Ruth, the daughter of Francis (Frank) William Harper and Anna Clara Carlson, was born October 16, 1932. Her father had been born on February 2, 1899 in Mercer County, Ohio. He died in May, 1971. Her mother had been born on February 12, 1907, in Midland, Michigan. She died in childbirth in August, 1935.

Frank was the son of Thomas Webster Harper, born December 17, 1848 in Mercer County, Ohio, and Anna Wagner, born May 28, 1866, in Toulon, Illinois. Frank's father was the son of William McKendry Harper, born March 27, 1824, in Pennsylvania, and Sarah Young, born December 29, 1822 in Indiana.

Gonnerman siblings with spouses at Christmas 2002 (l-r): Karen and Paul Gonnerman, Donna Schuler (Ernie could not be there), Russell and Mary Ann Schuler, Fred and Ruth Gonnerman.

Ruth's maternal grandmother Anna was the daughter of Jacob Wagner, born May 12, 1881 in Germany, and Gertrude Kartz, born November 17, 1890, also in Germany. Ruth's paternal grandparents were Carl John Carlson, born March 18, 1872 and Clara Julanda Thorsberg, born September 9, 1873. Both Carl and Clara emigrated from Föglö Parish in the Åland Islands between Stockholm, Sweden, and Helsinki, Finland.

Somewhere in that heritage Ruth also has a connection to Johnny Appleseed, the pioneer who planted apple trees throughout the Midwest.

Ruth and I were married on June 16, 1957, two months before Fred began his internship at Salem Lutheran Church in Detroit. That schedule had become the standard at that time for many seminarians who were married during their theological study.

We have been fortunate to travel abroad frequently, with visits to Norway, Sweden, Denmark, the Åland Islands (Ruth's ancestral home), Germany (my ancestral home), Austria, Switzerland, Holland, Belgium, France, Italy, Poland, Czechoslovakia, and Japan. Fred also accompanied the St. Olaf Choir as photographer and publicist on its first tour in the Orient, spending a week in Japan, a week split between Taiwan and Hong Kong, and two weeks in China.

We both retired in 1998. Fred finished a book on parish publications and public relations that he had been working on for several years in connection with workshops on the subject around the country. *Getting the Word Out: The Alban Guide to Church Communications* was published by Alban Publishing Company in 2003. It includes a foreword by Martin Marty, a noted theologian and church historian who is a friend. The book was well received ecumenically.

We have four children, Mark, Gay, Joy, and David.

Mark William Gonnerman was born April 3, 1958 in Detroit, Michigan. He holds a bachelor of arts degree with a major in history and philosophy from the Paracollege of St. Olaf College, where he graduated Phi Beta Kappa in 1980. He earned a master of divinity degree at Harvard Divinity School in 1987, taught pre-modern Japanese history at Harvard College as a teaching fellow for two years (1985–87), was awarded a master of arts degree in religious studies (1989) at Stanford University where he completed a Ph.D. degree in religious studies with a concentration in modern religious thought in 2004.

At Stanford he was founding director of the Aurora Forum, a public lecture series that frequently aired on KQED Public Radio in San Francisco (2003–2010). He served on the religious studies faculty at Stanford as a lecturer before he became professor and chair of the doctoral program in spirituality and psychology at the Institute of Transpersonal Psychology in Palo Alto, California in 2011.

He married Susan Pennypacker (born April 21, 1955), also a St. Olaf Paracollege graduate, on June 21, 1980 before they went to Fukuyama, Japan (near Hiroshima) as missionaries to teach English and engage in peace education work for three years with the Japanese Evangelical Lutheran Church.

Their son, Christopher, was born August 21, 1990. He became fluent in Spanish when he took a gap year in Spain after graduating from Palo Alto High School, then spent two years at San Francisco State University before going to Brazil to study Portuguese in 2012.

Mark and Susan divorced in 1999. Mark married Meri Mitsuyoshi on October 27, 2001. Meri, a native of San José, California, who was born November 3, 1961 graduated with a bachelor of science degree in electrical engineering from the University of California, Berkeley in 1984. She performed with San Jose Taiko (1986–2000) while working in Silicon Valley firms such as Hewlett-Packard, Agilent, and Avago Technologies (2005–present). In 2011, she began studies toward an M.A. degree in counseling psychology at the California Institute of Integral Studies in anticipation of an encore career as a therapist.

Gay Suzette Gonnerman was born November 6, 1959 in Columbus, Ohio. She earned a bachelor of arts degree *cum laude* with majors in religion and Norwegian from St. Olaf College in 1981. She sang second alto in the St. Olaf Choir for two years (including the 1980 tour of Norway) and went on the St. Olaf Global Semester in 1980-81, visiting Rome, Egypt, Jerusalem, India, Nepal, Taiwan and Japan over a five-month period.

The choir tour in Norway gave Gay a chance to use her Norwegian major. Due in part to jet lag, she and her roommate, Melissa Flynn, overslept in Oslo on the first morning of the tour and missed the choir busses. Packing quickly, they took a cab to the train station, bought tickets, and caught up with the choir in time for lunch. Director Kenneth Jennings and the members of the choir were both surprised and pleased to see them. Up until that moment of reunion, they had not even been missed. After that, the choir did a passenger count before the busses left to make sure everyone was on board.

One summer, when Gay and a large contingent of students from other colleges worked for a popular resort in northern Minnesota, she was presented with a large nametag during an orientation meeting. It said, "Hi, I'm Gay." When her parents named her, Gay was a perfectly fine name. Within the first two decades after her birth the word had taken on connotations that were a shade less than positive for some people. Gay asked the resort for a different nametag, one that said, "Hi, My Name Is Gay." She got it right away.

She served as Director of Children's Education at Grace Lutheran Church in Eau Claire, Wisconsin, from 1981 to 1983. She married Roy Forsstrom in 1983; they were later divorced. Gay earned a master of divinity degree at Yale Divinity School in 1986, and moved back to Minnesota.

Gay began a career in non-profit fundraising in 1988. She married Larry Koch on June 7, 1992. They have one son, Nathaniel, born July 19, 1995. Larry has three other children, Elizabeth, Paul, and Naomi, from a previous marriage. Gay is senior development officer at Dunwoody College of Technology in Minneapolis, and Larry is a vendor operation specialist with Target Corporation, also in Minneapolis.

Joy Marie Gonnerman was born February 4, 1963, in Minneapolis. She received a bachelor of arts degree with majors in art and religion from Augustana College, Sioux Falls, South Dakota, in 1985. She sang alto, and sometimes tenor, in the Augustana Choir.

Joy spent three years as a missionary teaching English in Nagoya, Japan. When she came home, she worked for the Minneapolis Humane Society before she began her own business called "All Creatures Great and Small" in which she presented programs for schools, non-profit organizations, and birthday parties, using animals from her extensive menagerie. Every birthday party was tailor-made to the whims of the child whose birthday was being celebrated. Joy gave the celebrant a list of what was available in her collection of creatures, and their wishes always overrode what the parents might suggest.

Joy's list was expansive. It included a goat, dogs, cats, a rabbit, and chickens for openers. Then the list went on to a couple of kinds of snakes (none venomous, of course), rats, a hedgehog, a tarantula and a scorpion, hermit crabs, a parrot, a variety of birds, hissing cockroaches from Madagascar, giant millipedes, a prehensile-tailed skink, a blue-tailed skink, salamanders, a bearded dragon, turtles and a tortoise, and frogs and toads.

Everyone at the parties was encouraged to hold and handle any creature Joy introduced if they wanted. And Joy had a way of taking away whatever fear and squeamishness there might have been so that children of all ages found the courage to be totally involved in her programs. Her parties and appearances in classrooms were always a success.

Her soft-coated Wheaten Terrier Ryli posed for some advertisements and won National Therapy Dog of the Year Award in 1993.

She and James Norquist were married in Minneapolis on August 25, 1990. They had one son, Carl, before they were divorced in 1999. Joy went back to school and graduated from Luther Seminary in St. Paul with a master of theology degree in 2008. Joy is now pastor of St. Peter Lutheran Church in Pocahontas, Iowa.

David Frederick Gonnerman was born September 24, 1967, in Minneapolis.

An incident when David was about six years old has to be reported here. In a drive through the countryside one summer when Joy and David were in the car, we saw field after field of soybeans that had an abundance of what is called "volunteer" corn growing among the beans. Showing off my agricultural background, I explained that the misplaced corn was called "volunteer" corn because it was growing where it wasn't wanted from seed that had survived from the corn that had been harvested there the previous year.

A couple of weeks later we were again driving on the same road. This time only David was with us. He saw a soybean field infested with corn and announced, "Look, there's some unorganized corn."

Both Ruth and I laughed at David's comment. Anyone who has worked with volunteers knows that disorganization is almost always the hallmark of the beginning of volunteer efforts. The anecdote falls in line with a 4-H T-shirt I used to wear: "Don't blame me. I'm a volunteer."

David received the bachelor of arts degree with a major in history from St. Olaf College in 1990. He plays the bass clarinet and was a member of both the St. Olaf Band and the St. Olaf College Orchestra.

The fall following graduation David traveled to Poland where he taught English for five years. While there, he met Katazyna (Kasia) Joanna Zimnicka, a native of Poland who was also teaching English. They were married in Olsztyn, Poland, on October 30, 1995, and David returned to the United States with Kasia the following summer.

Both are on the St. Olaf staff. David is associate director of marketing and communications for media relations, a department in the office that I established, and Kasia is research librarian at the Rolvaag Memorial Library. She took evening and weekend classes to earn her master of library science degree from St. Katherine's University in St. Paul in 2000.

They have two boys, both born in Northfield. Nicholas was born on October 20, 1996, and Jacob was born on October 14, 1999.

Donna, my first sibling, was born blind in her right eye. Before she started school a specialist fitted her with a hand-painted glass shield that looked exactly like her good eye. She has worn a shield in that eye ever since. After graduating from Dixon High School in 1955 she attended Wartburg College for a two-year program and graduated in 1957 with a concentration in parish work.

She worked for the Children's Home in Muscatine, Iowa, for five years, and met Ernest (Ernie) Schuler whom she married on May 19, 1963. They moved to Waverly, Iowa, and opened a small restaurant. Their restaurant closed after a year, and they moved to a brick farmhouse near Franklin Grove, Illinois. Ernie took care of cattle there for two years.

Then they moved to the vacated farmstead on the Lincoln Highway where Dad and Mom had lived and worked for almost two decades where Donna had grown up. The house was now electrified, but the bathroom was still outside. Donna and Ernie added an indoor bathroom while they lived there.

Donna and Ernie also renovated the old corn crib and expanded the egg production to include about 1,000 laying hens. Dozens of eggs a week were sold to wholesalers in the Dixon area. They had an arrangement with the Campbell's Soup Company to buy all their hens each year. Then the soup company replaced them with new ones. The first four of their five children were born in Dixon, only five miles west of the Gonnerman homestead.

After Barbara was born in 1970, they moved to Gilman, Illinois, Ernie's hometown. Now the Schuler brothers, Ernie and Russ, both once again lived in the same town.

Donna served as supervisor for the custodial staff at Prairieview Lutheran Home, a home for the aged in Danforth, Illinois, until she retired in 2009. Taking after her mother, Donna taught Sunday School at St. Paul Lutheran Church in Gilman for 15 years as well as handling janitorial services at the church. After retirement, she started a small business making doll clothes. Ernie held several jobs before settling as cook in one of the town's truck stops.

She and Ernie have five children, Matthew, Christine, Gloria, Barbara, and Mark.

Matthew was born on December 15, 1965 in Dixon, Illinois. He served in the Marine Corps for four years before returning to Gilman where he works at Prairie View Lutheran Home as a cook for 155 residents.

He married Michelle Crum, a nurse, on October 26, 1991. She already had one child from a previous marriage. They added three children to their family: Alicia, born September 22, 1987; Rachel, born April 20, 1992; and Benjamin, born April 30, 1994. Matthew and Michelle were divorced in 2000.

> **Readers' Alert:** *The Gonnerman children and their progeny are unquestionably all "above average" as Garrison Keillor claims for the people of Lake Wobegon on his long running radio program, "A Prairie Home Companion." The material that follows includes some expansive detail and episodes of human interest for each of the children. The children of the children are all identified with basic genealogical information. The children of the children of the children are identified with similar but truncated genealogical information. Accolades regarding honor rolls, special interests, and outstanding accomplishments (which almost all of them demonstrated) have been left out since all of those things are still very much in flux.*

Christine was born on February 27, 1966, in Dixon, Illinois. She became a nurse after study at Olivet University in Kankakee, Illinois. She married Ken Clark on July 20, 1995. They had one son, Kristopher, born February 1, 1989, and were divorced in 1993.

She married Brad Wetzel on August 30, 1997. Abby was born on June 19, 1999. Christine now works as a nurse at Carle Hospital in Urbana, Illinois, and Brad is employed as a mechanic by Caterpillar Company. They live in Champaign, Illinois.

Gloria was born on July 27, 1969. She was employed at Farmers State Bank in Danforth, Illinois. She married Jay Kuipers on June 27, 1998. Jay works at NAPA Auto Parts in Gilman. They have two sons, Justin, born on May 8, 2000, and Jacob, born on August 7, 2003, and live in Gilman.

Barbara was born on October 21, 1970 in Dixon, Illinois. She earned a degree in social work from Indiana University and works for social service in Indiana. She married Mark Brewer on May 4, 1991. Mark was in the U.S. Air Force Reserves for 22 years, serving in Kansas for four years. He now works for Grissom Air Force Base in Peru, Indiana. They have three sons, Colton, born April 25, 1995, Connor, born May 2, 2001, and Corbin, born March 8, 2005. They live in Monticello, Indiana.

Mark was born on January 17, 1979 in Watseka, Illinois, 14 miles east of Gilman. Mark is a mechanic with K.C. Summers Automobile Dealership in Matoon, Illinois. He married Jennifer Zerrusen, a special education teacher for the Charleston (Illinois) School District, on June 5, 2004. They have a daughter, Lillian (Lilly), born September 8, 2010, and live in Matton, Illinois.

Paul, my brother, was a jet engine technician specialist in the U.S. Air Force in Puerto Rico and Michigan from 1959 to 1963 before being honorably discharged in 1963. He married Karen E. Spencer in Dixon on September 20, 1964. They have two children, Gregory and Debra.

Karen graduated from Swedish American School of Nursing in Rockford, Illinois. She took nursing positions over the past 48 years in medical-surgical nursing, orthopedics, allergy, and dermatology. She retired in 2013 from Triune H.G. (Health Group) of Rockford where she had been a nurse case manager working with insurance companies and employers to get insured employees back to work. She was listed in the 1995 edition of *Who's Who in Nursing*.

After his stint in the Air Force, Paul was assistant manager for the F.W. Woolworth store in Dixon for three years before beginning work with Commonwealth Edison in 1966. Promotions moved him and his family from Dixon to DeKalb to Rockford to Freeport (all in northern Illinois). The northern Illinois utility company changed its name to Exelon Corporation before Paul took early retirement in 1996 as dispatch manager at the age of 55 after 30 years with the company. Since retirement he has expanded his prowess as a photographer and enjoys varieties of volunteer work with seniors who are members of his church.

Paul and Karen built a new home in 2002 in 13 acres of virgin timber near the village of Ridott, Illinois, close to Freeport. Paul was hospitalized in 2011 with a life-threatening case of West Nile disease contracted from a mosquito bite, but was blessed with a complete recovery.

Paul and Karen are experienced antique collectors, always on the lookout for another piece of Americana to add to their collections of food containers, toys, knick knacks, and small furniture pieces. Paul has made a profitable hobby out of reconditioning antique pedal cars, buying the little vehicles in various states of disrepair and turning them back into their original condition.

They have taken numerous Caribbean and Alaskan cruises, sometimes alone, sometimes with family and friends. They have also traveled through most of the lower 48 states.

Greg was born on October 26, 1966 in Dixon, Illinois. Grandmother Gonnerman helped with his delivery. Greg graduated from Hawkeye Institute of Technology in Waterloo, Iowa, in 1989. He graduated from William Penn University in Des Moines, Iowa, with honors in 2002.

He married Rebecca (Becky) Maring in Ankeny, Iowa, on September 27, 1997. Greg works for Century Link in West Des Moines, where he is general manager of consumer technological support. Becky works in Des Moines for the State of Iowa as a pre-sentence investigator.

They have two children, Grant, born on April 15, 2001, and Alyssa, born on May 7, 2005, both in Ankeny.

Debra was born on November 8, 1969 in DeKalb, Illinois. She earned a bachelor's degree in business with a major in marketing from Western Illinois University in 1991.

Debra (Debbie) Gonnerman married James (Jim) Schuler (not related to Donna's husband Ernie, or Mary Ann's husband Russ) in Freeport, Illinois, on May 16, 1992.

Jim earned a liberal arts degree from Western Illinois University in Macomb in 1991 with a major in political science, a minor in history, and teaching certificates in both. Jim's business promotions moved them to Lexington, Kentucky, before they moved to Pecotonica, Illinois, a small community between Freeport and Rockford. A couple of years after moving to Pecotonica, Jim and Debbie built a new home on six acres of virgin timber next to Debbie's Mom and Dad. Since 2001 Jim has been territory sales manager for Semblex Company in Elmhurst, Illinois, a position that takes him abroad frequently to Brazil, England, and Italy.

Debbie has held a number of positions in banking. She was operating supervisor at Kent Bank in Freeport from 1991 to 1993. In Lexington she was customer service specialist with Central Bank and Trust from 1993 to 1995, and now works as a teacher's assistant at Carl Sandburg Middle School in Freeport.

Jim and Debbie have two children, Alex, born May 19, 1995 in Lexington, and Hannah, born November 25, 2002 in Rockford.

Mary Ann followed her Mom into nursing, graduating from the same nursing school in Milwaukee in 1965. She met her husband, Russell Schuler, at Donna's and Ernie's wedding. Russ and Ernie are brothers. Mary Ann and Russ were married on April 17, 1966, and they moved to their home in Gilman that same year. They have two children, Susanne and James.

Mary Ann was on the nursing staff at Riverside Hospital in Kankakee, Illinois, from 1966 to 1969. She worked at Iroquois Memorial Hospital in Watseka from 1969 to 1978, then worked for a private physician from 1978 to 1992 when she returned to Iroquois Memorial Hospital and a satellite clinic until retiring in 2007. She still keeps busy with nursing as a volunteer parish nurse at St. Paul Lutheran Church where she and Russ have been members since moving to Gilman.

Russ worked for 33 years for the Illinois Bell Telephone Company which became Ameritech Telephone Company. He retired in 1999, but still does telephone repair work. Russ has always enjoyed working with machinery. He restores antique tractors and uses his backhoe service to dig graves in the local cemetery and help area farmers with their field tiling.

They enjoy traveling, particularly in the west, and hope to visit many more places in the United States. They also love to cruise in the Caribbean and took an Alaskan cruise in 2006. But their biggest joy is fishing. Russ has had a succession of fishing boats that he used from Northern Minnesota to Arkansas, and they have caught more than their share of fish from walleye to bass to lake trout and lots of others in between.

One year they brought Mom with them to visit us at our cabin on the north shore of Lake Superior. I chartered a fishing boat out of Beaver Bay. Much of the fishing we did during the two hours we were on the water was done only about 150 yards from the shore of the Gonnerman cabin. We caught five lake trout and one salmon. Later, Russ and I caught a few more lake trout from the shore.

On an excursion up the shore we stopped at Lutsen Lodge to take a coffee break in the restaurant. Everyone had a piece of fresh blueberry pie and a cup of coffee, and we all agreed it was the best blueberry pie they had ever tasted. Mom, in particular, was impressed.

As we headed back to the cabin, I said, "Now, if we can just see a deer and a bear, your trip will be complete." Several deer cooperated within a few miles as they either crossed the road ahead of us or were seen grazing along the side. Then, just as we were driving out of Taconite Harbor, a big black bear ambled across the road about 200 feet in front of the car. I looked at the rear view mirror just in time to see Mary Ann with both her mouth and her eyes wide open in surprise. The day was complete.

Mary Ann and Russ have two children, Susanne, born on November 18, 1967, and James (Jim), born on June 9, 1970.

Susanne took her nurses training at Aurora University in Aurora, Illinois, earning a bachelor of science in nursing degree, and has worked in a variety of hospitals throughout her career. She is now a school nurse with Unity School District at Tolono, Illinois. She married Timothy Gateley, a good athlete who was her high school sweetheart, on June 29, 1991, in Gilman.

Tim, a graduate of Eastern Illinois University in 1989, is a high school administrator where they live in Tolono. He earned the master of education degree from Governor's State University in University Park, Illinois, in 1998.

They have two children, Kyle, born on January 1, 1996, and Leah, born on December 23, 1999.

After graduation from Gilman High School, Jim Schuler graduated from Spartan School of Aeronautics in Tulsa, Oklahoma, in 1990, becoming a master aircraft mechanic. He worked for Frasca Air Services until 1994, when he moved his skills to Eagle Creek Airport in Indianapolis, Indiana, where he stayed until 1998. Then he moved back to Frasca until 2005. He now works for the University of Illinois Aviation Department in Champaign, Illinois, where he helps maintain a fleet of 35 planes.

Jim married Debra Konkel on April 30, 1994; they were divorced four years later.

He married Kris Talbert on August 7, 2000. They live in Paxton, Illinois, and have two children, Aaron, born on May 29, 1997, and Emma, born on January 5, 2002.

Kris received the bachelor of science degree in social work in 1993 and a master's degree in social work in 2003, both from the University of Illinois. She is the social worker for P-B-L School District in Paxton.

APPENDIX TWO

BIBLIOGRAPHY

Assassinations
http://newsone.com/2583396/medgar-evers-death/
www.jfklibrary.orgJFKJFK-in-History/November-22-1963-Death-of-the-President.a...
http://history 1900x.about.com/od/1960s/a/Roberty-Kennedy-Assassination.htm
http://history 1900s.about.com/cs/martinlutherking/a/mlkassass.htm

Berlin Airlift and Wall
http://history1900s.about.com/od/coldwar/a/berlinwall.htm
http://www.spiritoffreedom.org/airlift.html

China
www.travelchinaguide.com/attraction/beijing/tiananmen/faqs.htm
http://enwikipedia.org/wiki/Forbidden_City
www.pbs.org/wgbh/amex/china/sfeature/nixon.html
www2.gwu.edu/-nsarchiv/NSAEBB/NSAEBB106/
www.history.com/this-day-in-history/tiananmen-square-massacre-takes-place
http://asianhistory.about.com/od/modernchina/f/What-Was-The-Cultural-Revolution.htm
www.rediff.com/business/slide-show/slide-show-1-special-most-polluting-countries-i...
www.britannica.com/EBchecked/topic/656977/Zhou-Enlai

Computer Technology
www.scaruffi.com/politics/silicon.html
www.thocp.net/hardware/univac.htm
www.computerhope.com/issues/ch000984.htm

Culture, Prices, and Events
www.ehow.com/about_5212740_average-middle-class-salary-range_.html
www.thepeoplehistory.com/foods.html
www.thepeoplehistory.com/1932.html
www.thepeoplehistory.com/30scars.html
www.thepeoplehistory.com/30sfood.html
www.michigan.gov/dnr/0,4570,7-153-54463_19268_20778_52530--,00.html

Farming and Agriculture

www.agclassroom.org/gan/timeline/1930.htm

www.configurator.deere.com/servlet/com.deere.u90947.eproducts.view.servlets.
EquipmentSummaryServlet?

www.configurator.deere.com/servlet/com.deere.u90947.eproducts.view.servlets.
NavigationActionServlet?

www.configurator.deere.com/servlet/com.deere.u90947.eproducts.view.servlets.
ProductSelectionServlet?

www.configurator.deere.com/servlet/com.deere.u90947.eproducts.view.servlets.
QuoteServlet?

www.gardenguides.com/81070-herbicide-history

www.ideals.illinois.edu/bitstream/hndle/2142/8775/index.htm

www.inventors.about.com

www.livinghistoryfarm.org/farminginthe20s/machines

www.livinghistoryfarm.org/farminginthe30s/machines

www.livinghistoryfarm.org/farminginthe30s

www.livinghistoryfarm.org/farminginthe40s/machines

www.tractordata.com/farm-tractors/000/0/1/9-allis-chalmers-wd.html

www.tractordata.com/farm-tractors/000/0/1/10-allis-chalmers-wd.html

Financial Divide: 1% vs. 99%

www.forbes.com/sites/moneywisewomen/2012/03/21/average-
america-vs-the-one-p...

www.washingtonpostcom/blogs/wonkblog/post/who-are-the-99-
percent/2011/08/25/...

http://wearethe99percent.tumblr.com/

www2.ucsc.edu/whorulesamerica/power/wealth.html

Global Warming

http://environment.about.com/od/globalwarming/u/globalwarming.htm

www.nrdc.org/health/extremeweather/

http://environment.about.com/od/globalwarming/a/ipcc_reports.htm

Hippie Movement

www.ehow.com/about_5375320_history-hippie-movement

Iron Curtain

http://history1900s.about.com/od/churchillwinston;a;Iron-Curtain.htm

Korean War

http://www.huffingtonpost.com/2013/04/15/kim-jong-un-north-
korea_n_3061636.html

http://www.history.com/topics/korean-war

Medicine

Bill Bryson, *At Home: A Short History of Private Life*, pp. 165-168, Doubleday,
New York, 2010

http://www.accessexcellence.org/AE/AEPC/WWC/1994/geneticstln.php

http://www.history.com/this-day-in-history/first-human-heart-transplant

Nine-Eleven
http://www.history.com/topics/9-11-attacks

Population Explosion
www.theguardian.com/world/2011/jan/14/population-explosion-seven-billion

Race Relations and Civil Rights
www.blackpast.org/?q=aah/detroit-race-riot-1967
www.cnn.com/2013/12/10/world/africa/nelson-mandela-memorial/
www.nelsonmandela.org/content/page/biography
www.nelsonmandelas.com/nelson-mandela-achievements.php
www.nobelprize.org/nobel prizes/peace/laureates/1964/king-bio.html
libcom.org/history/1992-the-la-riots
www.67riots.rutgers.edu/d_index.htm

Relationships with Arab-Muslim World
http://www.britannica.com/EBchecked/topic/973560/Barack-Obama/296550/
    Wars in Iraq...
http://www.foreignaffairs.com/articles/67693/lisa-anderson/
    demystifying-the-arab-spring
http://en.wikipedia.org/wiki/Execution_of_Saddam_Hussein
http://terrorism.about.com/od/warianafghanistan/ss/AfghanistanWar_2.htm
http://en.wikipedia.org/wiki/Iraq_War
http://en.wikipedia.org/wiki/War_in_Afghanistan_(2001%E2%/80%93present)

Religion/Prayer in Public Schools
www.adl.org/religion_ps_204/pryer.asp
http://voices.yahoo.com/lee-v-weisman-issue-school-prayer-
    establishment-41307.html

Space
www.homeofheroes.com/presidents/speeches/kennedy_space.html
www.ucsusa.org/nuclear_weapons_and_global_security/space_weapons/
    technical_is...
http://space.about.com/cs/iss/a/iss.htm
http://my.execpc.com/-culp/space/timeline.html

United Nations
http://www.un.org/en/aboutun/history/
http://www.un.org/en/aboutun/history/charter_history.shtml
http://en.wikipedia.org/wiki/United_Nations

Vietnam
www.archives.gov/research/military/vietnam-war/casualty-statistics.html
www.pbs.org/battlefieldvietnam/history/index.html
http://dept.kent.edu/sociology/lewis/lewihen.htm
http://history1900s.about.com/od/vietnamwar/a/vietnamwar

Watergate
https://en.wikipedia.org/wiki/Watergate_scandal

World War II
http://en.wikipedia.org/wiki/Attack_on_Pearl_Harbor
http://www.usswestvirginia.org/fdr_pearl_speech.htm
http://en.wikipedia.org/wiki/Hiroshima_Peace_Memorial_Park
http://en.wikipedia.org/wiki/Japanese_American_Internment
http://en.wikipedia.org/wiki/Nazi_concentration_camps
http://www.history.navy.mil/Photos/sh-usn/usnsh-a/bb39-v.htm
http://www.loc.gov/rr/print/swann/mauldin/maudlin-atwar.htlm
http://www.pbs.org/weta/reportingamericaatwar/reporters/rooney
http://en.wikipedia.org/wiki/Service_flag
http://www.world-war-2.info/summary/